810 U St.

3/29/68
LOUISE HAS AN EXTRA COPY.

teaching
the
disadvantaged

NEW CURRICULUM APPROACHES

JOSEPH O. LORETAN

Deputy Superintendent of Schools
Instruction and Curriculum
Board of Education of the City of New York

SHELLEY UMANS

Administrative Director
Instruction and Curriculum
Board of Education of the City of New York

TEACHERS COLLEGE PRESS · TEACHERS COLLEGE · COLUMBIA UNIVERSITY

TO THE READER

This book was written *by* school people, *for* school people. Today's schoolman—whether superintendent, principal, teacher, curriculum specialist, or guidance specialist—finds himself confronted with much philosophy, theory, and sermon, but very little substance with which to put these fine sentiments into practice. He is in the middle—caught between the theorists and the child. He is called upon to *act*. If he moves too slowly, he may be called traditional, conservative, and rigid; if he moves too rapidly, he is called radical and irresponsible.

But, today, we school people can no longer indulge ourselves in the almost philosophical argument of how quickly or slowly we should move; we cannot stop to worry about being labeled radical or conservative. There is a sense of urgency—almost despair—in education. That large segment of our population known as the "disadvantaged"—tired of promises—shows signs of turning its attention to the demagogues and the charlatans, of moving outside society as we know it. As school people, we have the opportunity to prevent this ever-enlarging group from moving beyond the pale by creating educational programs to meet the demands of modern society.

The rationale of this book is based on the theory that children from disadvantaged homes have intellectual capacities far greater than they are commonly believed to have. It is our conviction that with the new developments in the behavioral sciences the school can, to a great extent, counteract the effects of cultural deprivation. The approaches suggested in this book are guidelines to the formulation of a program. The programs described

were selected as samples of the types of approaches important
to the intellectual development of the disadvantaged child. We
do not propose to review all current curricula, nor do we attempt
to suggest what a program for the disadvantaged "should look
like." Our purpose is to present to those responsible for schooling
a new way of thinking, a new set of approaches. If we are to
reverse the effects of deprivation on our youth, then we must
reverse the concepts traditional to educational programs for the
disadvantaged.

JOSEPH O. LORETAN
SHELLEY UMANS

CONTENTS

A NOTE ABOUT THE PROGRAMS

It should be noted that many of the programs mentioned in this book—some of which have been reproduced in part as Exhibits—are in initial, and therefore
transitory, stages. Thus, it has frequently been necessary to base discussions upon material so new that it
may not be in final form. Every effort has been made
to insure that the documentation involved is up-to-
date; where publication is known to be imminent, this
fact and the publisher's name are given. Failure to
indicate forthcoming publication indicates that the
fact of such publication had not been made known to
the authors by the time this book went to press.

LIST OF EXHIBITS

TEACHING
THE DISADVANTAGED

PART ONE

CHANGING CONCEPTS

To many a youth from a disadvantaged environment, schooling is one long obstacle course; all along the way are signs with
arrows pointing to the nearest exit. To resist these directional
signs requires almost superhuman will power; the obstacles are
too massive. Life at school, for this youngster, is uncomfortable;
life for his group is always uncomfortable. Unlike his counter-
parts in other communities, he has been observed and analyzed
by psychologists, psychiatrists, sociologists, and anthropologists
almost since birth. He has become aware, in his own strange way,
of what Thomas Pettigrew calls "the subtle cultural cues which
tell you that you don't count and that good school grades and high
IQ scores are middle class roads to success, not yours."[1] He is of
the class that Patricia Sexton calls "the have-nots, the outcasts."
He will be either aggressive and hostile toward his environment
or apathetic and numbed as a result of repeated failure. He will
become the chief ingredient in the growing stockpile of what
James Bryant Conant calls "social dynamite." He is more danger-
ous than the atomic bomb—because his capacity to destroy is life-
long. His crime is that he was born poor, of parents who are, more
often than not, unemployable and who are, for certain, uneducated. He lives either in the inner city (the hard-core group) or in
the vast, poor, underdeveloped, rural areas of this country. He is
separated from the middle class, our dominant culture, by a mas-

[1]Letter from Thomas Pettigrew, Lecturer in Social Psychology at Harvard
University, to Franklin Patterson, Director of the Lincoln Filene Center for
Citizenship and Public Affairs at Tufts University, January 30, 1964.

sive, almost impenetrable, wall. The odds on his escaping are one in one thousand (not quite as high as the odds on escaping from East to West Berlin). His nemesis is Check Point Charlie. To help him pass through the Check Point Charlies of his environment is the concern of this book.

What is the role of the educator in this process? Is it to understand the plight of these children and evolve programs that will help them "adjust" to their environment? Or can we make it possible for these youngsters, through schooling, to escape their environment—to move through the wall—and join the educated, the well-fed, the employable? Check Point Charlie is two-sided: On one side is resignation and conformity (adjustment); on the other is initiative and individuality (academic achievement). Educators can no longer equivocate or compromise; we must choose sides.

These are strong words; they will be challenged by those who say that nothing can be done unless the home life of the disadvantaged is stabilized and the aid of community groups is engaged. There is some validity, of course, to this theory, since social facilities are crucial to the developing organism. Deutsch says of this, however, that

. . . such a view often leads to negation not only of the essential responsibility of the school but also of the actual and potential strengths of the children. Most important, it induces an elaborate rationale for the further alienation of teachers from their primary function, teaching. The essential element, which is both professionally and psychologically threatening, is simply that, for the child inadequately equipped to handle what the school has to offer, it is up to the school to develop compensatory strategies through a program of stimulation appropriate to his capabilities. Essentially, the disadvantaged child is still further disadvantaged when the school, as the primary socializing and teaching agent, refuses to accept its own failures whenever such a child fails.[2]

Perhaps it is time for educators to shed their "social work approach" and function in the technology of pedagogy, always aware, however, of the child's cultural handicaps.

[2]Martin Deutsch, "Some Psychological Aspects of Learning in the Disadvantaged." Revised version of a paper presented at the Boston University Developmental Conference on the Teaching of Disadvantaged Youth, 1964 (mimeographed), p. 5.

THE DISADVANTAGED—
ONE-THIRD OF A NATION

The youngster from the disadvantaged home is half a reality, half a myth. The reality of him startles us because it is unpleasant and with us all the time—in the subways, on the streets, on the unemployment lines, in the newspapers, and in the so-called difficult schools. This reality affects our emotions, our physical safety, and our taxes.

The myth, on the other hand, does not startle us. It is something we unthinkingly accept. We speak of this mythical youngster as being of a "different breed"; we say that his intellectual capacity is below par, and, therefore, his school experience should be curtailed; we term his educational needs "basic" and so decide that his curriculum must be simplified and repetitive; we call him "culturally different" and spend our time (and his) teaching him to conform.

Let us, however, look at this child, not through our reaction to him, but through a study of his intellectual and emotional anatomy. When we speak of the deprived child, we speak of all nationalities and races—Puerto Ricans, Mexicans, Negroes, and whites—whether born in rural areas, small towns, or cities. The designation of "deprived" should not be equated with membership in any ethnic group, but should be defined in terms of characteristics of the individual and/or his environment. Furthermore, not all such youngsters will exhibit all the symptoms of the "deprivation syndrome"; in some such children, all these may be absent.

What will be described here are those characteristics that are found with sufficient frequency in this population to be given primary consideration.

WHO IS THE DISADVANTAGED CHILD?

The child whom we designate as "deprived" or "disadvantaged" differs from the "undeprived" or "advantaged" in language development, self-concept, and social skills, as well as in attitude toward schooling and society. He has fewer interests than the middle-class child. His form of communication, unlike that of other children entering school, tends to consist mostly of gestures, sounds (nonwords), and local words. Just as he has inadequate linguistic skills of expression, so has he inadequate receptive skills. He does not hear sounds as we pronounce them. He tends to "close out" many noises around him (including the teacher's voice). When he does hear us, our words do not necessarily mean to him what they mean to us. He does not feel the need to communicate through language. In fact, language—like schooling—is for others, not him. Perhaps the most serious characteristic of the deprived child is his feeling of inadequacy. He devalues himself. He comes into school feeling that accomplishment and success are impossible for him. This suspicion, of course, is quickly confirmed, not only by academic failure, which he experiences almost from the day he enters school, but also by his recognition that he lacks the social skills demanded by the middle-class teacher: manner of dress, mode of response, respect for authority. If, in class, he finds himself among children from the dominant culture, his feeling of being different is reinforced—their ways are "acceptable"; his are not.

The disadvantaged youngster has experienced no logical pattern in life; things just happen. He lives *now*, not in the future. He has had little or no experience in setting and proceeding toward goals and in evaluating or reviewing past actions as to whether or not they were "worth it." When the disadvantaged youngster acts, it is usually in response to an immediate stimulus; there is little room in his scheme for second thoughts, meditation, or planning.

Sidney Kingsley's play, *Dead End,* produced in 1936, described what we now refer to as the disadvantaged, although he viewed them as a geographical phenomenon—"have-nots" who were living in a district surrounded by "haves." Today we view these children in another dimension. The "dead end" applies, not only to their physical environment, but to their intellectual environment as well. Because enlarging experiences are missing from their lives, their intellectual world is restricted to the apparent; their experiences are action experiences; a task accomplished is self-fulfilling and seldom opens up other fields of investigation. These youngsters may realistically be referred to as "limited," but limited in scope, not in intellect. The world is not open to them.

Children from disadvantaged homes are not motivated to learn. Schooling has not "paid off" for their kind. They see little value in spending time in school. Perhaps their most perplexing problem in this completely alien world of education is finding their role: Who am I? Am I really different? Will I always be like this? Is it wrong to be like this? Am I guilty? This searching for self is subconscious, rarely verbalized. On the contrary, the disadvantaged child often gives the impression of not caring. All his behavior, however, points to the conclusion that he is searching for an answer, for an identity.

The problems of this youngster become aggravated as he proceeds through school. Although the "deprivation syndrome" is generally recognized by teachers and school people, little has been done to accommodate school experience to the needs of this child. As early as the first grade, he is grouped homogeneously because he is lowest on the scale of readiness to learn. By the time he enters second grade, he has fallen behind the rest of the class— he has become a misfit. At this point, it is justifiable to ask whether the objective of education is to fit the youngster into the school at any cost, or to bring the school into harmony with the child. (Does "child-centered" school really mean "conforming-child-centered" school?) The cycle of defeat starts almost immediately. Instead of overcoming, or at least compensating for, cultural limitations, the school reinforces negative feelings and now adds educational deprivation to cultural deprivation.

The problem of the disadvantaged child is not new to educators. However, in considering children with cultural and educational problems, we appear to have spent most of our time and energy classifying them, describing their characteristics, seeking to isolate the causes of deprivation, and warning society of the consequences if nothing is done. Yet, in terms of actually improving the curriculum for these children, we have done little except to intellectualize the problem. A recent cartoon in a New York newspaper depicts an impoverished sage who aptly expresses this point of view:

> I used to think I was poor.
> Then they told me I wasn't poor, I was NEEDY.
> Then they told me it was self-defeating to think of myself as needy, I was DEPRIVED.
> Then they told me deprived was a bad image, I was UNDERPRIVILEGED.
> Then they told me underprivileged was overused, I was DISADVANTAGED.
> I still don't have a dime.
> But I have a GREAT vocabulary.[1]

Is this what we have been doing—creating a vocabulary, a jargon, a cult, but producing disadvantaged adults to replace disadvantaged children?

The authors of this book predicate their thesis upon two basic assumptions: (1) Despite the negative approach to school and school learnings, children from disadvantaged homes have intellectual capacities far greater than is commonly believed. (2) The school, operating on the assumption stated above, and constructing curricula based upon the new developments in the behavioral sciences, can—to a great extent—counteract the effects of cultural deprivation.

THE INTELLECTUAL CAPACITIES OF CHILDREN FROM DISADVANTAGED HOMES

So long as it was assumed that intelligence was fixed, and was a consequence of the genes, we wrongly accepted the intellectual inferiority of children who tested below normal. We found, by apparent coincidence, that these same youngsters came from backgrounds of economic and educational deprivation. Again we were misled; since a disproportionate number of the children in economically and educationally deprived areas were Negro, it was assumed, at least by some, that there were inherent racial differences accounting for differences in the capacity to learn. However, this theory has been refuted by almost all scientific opinion.

[1]Jules Feiffer, *The New York Post* (February 17, 1965), p. 41.

The UNESCO international committee of sociologists, anthropologists, psychologists, and geneticists said in its report:

It is now generally recognized that intelligence tests do not themselves enable us to differentiate safely between what is due to innate capacity and what is the result of environmental influences, training and education. . . . In short, given similar degrees of cultural opportunity to realize their potentialities, the average achievement of the members of each ethnic group is about the same.[2]

A similar conclusion was reached by the American Association for the Advancement of Science Committee on Science in the Promotion of Human Welfare.[3]

What is now being seriously questioned is the use of our basic intelligence indicators, the IQ test. There is sufficient cumulative research to prove that there are significant differences in intelligence score distribution between children who live in depressed areas and those who do not, and that cultural differences *do* affect IQ scores to the extent that such scores have low predictive validity when used for cross-cultural comparisons.

The Journal of Social Issues (April 1964) offers one of the most direct presentations of current evidences of the effects of culture on the educational aspirations and achievements of U. S. Negroes. As a Supplement, the *Journal* reports the findings of the Work Group for the Psychological Study of Social Issues (Division 9 of the American Psychological Association). The committee concludes flatly that social deprivation challenges the validity of tests. In part, it explains that national norms do not allow for adequate differentiation at the lower end of aptitude or ability scales.[4] In discussing predictive validity, the committee states:

For example, no inequity is necessarily involved if a culturally disadvantaged child is simply reported to have an IQ of 84 and a percentile rank of 16 on national norms for a certain intelligence test. However, if this is interpreted as meaning that a child ranks as well as or will rank no higher in learning ability than does a middle-class, native born child of the same IQ, the interpretation might well be erroneous.[5]

[2]UNESCO, *The Rau Concept: Results of an Inquiry.* (Paris: UNESCO, 1952), p. 100.

[3]Editorial, *Science*, 142, No. 3592 (November 1, 1963), pp. 558–561.

[4]Work Group for the Psychological Study of Social Issues, "Guidelines for Testing Minority Group Children," *The Journal of Social Issues* (Supplement), 20, No. 2 (April 1964), p. 133.

[5]*Ibid.*, p. 134.

Deutsch and Brown conclude on the basis of their studies:

The present data on family cohesion and pre-school experience represent two possible environmental modifiers of intelligence test performance that would seem to account for a portion of differences found between ethnic, class or experiential groups.[6]

Interpretation of test scores is perhaps the greatest danger in testing. If an individual's score is to be used to describe his standing among a *specified norm group,* the fact that a child has had a minority group background is not important. It is when *prediction* enters the picture that background becomes important.

Back in 1900, before he had turned most of his attention to psychometrics, Binet concerned himself with the educability of intelligence, taking five or six aspects of intelligence that he thought could be trained. He organized classes to prove that "mental orthopedics" could be used to improve the ability to memorize, reason, and perceive. Working among the poor in Paris, he suggested that learning and environment interacted and that with a richer environment one's mental abilities could be improved. He wrote:

A child's mind is like a field for which an expert farmer has advised a change in the method of cultivation, with the result that in place of desert we now have a harvest. It is in this particular sense, the one which is significant, that we say that the intelligence of children may be increased. One increases that which constitutes the intelligence of a school child, namely, the capacity to learn to improve with instruction.[7]

Yet, in the years to come, Binet's hypothesis was largely neglected. Training of mental abilities was not considered possible. Some of the experimental work of Thorndike and others was used as proof that attempts to "improve the mind" in a general way through a study of specific discipline was useless. The presumption that genetic factors weighed heavily in intelligence also discouraged attempts at intellectual training. Now these concepts are being modified through the research of Bruner, Piaget, Guilford, and others. IQ is no longer considered "constant," nor is it deemed to

[6]Martin Deutsch and Bert Brown, "Social Influences in Negro-White Intelligence Differences," *The Journal of Social Issues,* 20, No. 2 (April 1964), p. 34.

[7]Alfred Binet, *Les Idées Modernes sur les Enfants* (Paris: Ernest Flamarion, 199), pp. 54–55, cited in G. D. Stoddard, "The IQ, Its Ups and Downs," *Educational Record,* 20 (1939), pp. 44–57.

measure all aspects of intelligence. We now realize the enormous effect of deprivation on learning. More and more the evidence is piling up that grinding poverty, because of its detrimental physical effect on the mother and its concomitant stunting of stimulation in the growing child, is a powerful factor in causing the educational retardation of the children of the poor.

A large number of empirical studies support the assumption that certain environmental conditions may retard intellectual development. We also find that, with the proper environmental conditions, disadvantaged children do learn, and IQ's do increase by forty points or more. In 1951, Lee investigated the relationship between intelligence test scores of Negro children and the length of time spent in northern schools. He retested the children after varying periods of time in the North and found that:

. . . the group which had attended kindergarten averaged consistently higher than the group which entered the first grade with no pre-school experience. Within each of the Philadelphia-born groups there was no consistent tendency for scores to rise upon retesting, but in each of the groups that had migrated to the city, there was a significant tendency for mean scores to improve with increasing length of northern residence. The earlier the entry, the higher the IQs in any one grade.[8]

Brazziel and Terrell, in 1962, conducted an experiment in the development of readiness in a culturally disadvantaged group of first graders. They reported on a six-week readiness program for twenty-six Negro first-grade children. The program included parent meetings once a week, thirty minutes of educational TV watched in the home, and a readiness program to develop vocabulary, perception, word reasoning, and ability to follow directions. At the end of six weeks, the experimental class had reached the fiftieth percentile on readiness, as measured by the Metropolitan Readiness Test, while the three nonexperimental classes in the same school were at the fifteenth percentile. This difference is significant. The average IQ after seven months, for the experimental class, was 106.5; the general expectation for the group was 90.[9]

[8]E. S. Lee, "Negro Intelligence and Selective Migration: A Philadelphia Test of the Klineberg Hypothesis," *American Sociological Review*, 16 (1951), pp. 227–233.

[9]W. F. Brazziel and Mary Terrell, "An Experiment in the Development of Readiness in a Culturally Disadvantaged Group of First-Grade Children," *Journal of Negro Education*, 31 (1962), pp. 4–7.

More recently, Gray and Klaus reported on the Early Training Project in the Murfreesboro, Tennessee, City Schools.[10] The Early Training Project involved two experimental groups, each consisting of approximately twenty culturally deprived Negro children. The two groups were T1, which offered school programs for two successive summers and home contact for the intervening year, and in which the children started at approximately 3½ years of age; and T2, which offered one summer school program for children of approximately age 5. There were two matched control groups. The program was aimed at improving attitudes toward achievement and aptitudes and abilities (language, perception, concept formation) considered necessary for successful school learning. Results of pre- and post-testing over a fifteen-month period showed significantly greater improvement on Binet and Peabody Picture Vocabulary Test for experimental groups than for control groups. Average IQ gains were: for experimental group T1, 10.1 points (from 85.6 to 95.7); for experimental group T2, 5.1 points (from 91.2 to 96.3).

New York City's Demonstration Guidance Project yielded, perhaps, the most dramatic results. Students in a selected junior high school were given remedial work in reading, mathematics, and speech, along with cultural enrichment and group and individual guidance with stress on college and career planning. The project also tried to improve the self-images of the participating students and to help them develop pride in their cultural background. According to the current report, issued in 1961,[11] students who were in the project from 1956 to 1959 gained an average of eight points in IQ. Those in the project from 1957 to 1960 gained an average of fifteen points in IQ, the range of gain being five to forty points. If, as the research indicates, an educational program can "reverse deprivation effects," should we not address our investigations and our energies to discovering what *type* of educational program can do this?

[10]Susan W. Gray and R. A. Klaus, "Interim Report: Early Training Project." Unpublished report, George Peabody College and Murfreesboro, Tennessee, City Schools, 1963 (mimeographed).

[11]Board of Education of the City of New York, "Demonstration Guidance Project Research Report #43. A Comparison of 1958 and 1961 Results on Verbal Ability Tests of General Ability" (November 1961, mimeographed), p. 6.

A CURRICULUM TO COUNTERACT CULTURAL DEPRIVATION

In looking at the curricula developed in the universities and school systems over the last ten years, several factors become evident: (1) They are generally based on the newer findings of the behavioral scientists regarding how children learn; (2) they are developmental; and (3) their content is current, sophisticated, and challenging.

However, almost all curriculum innovations developed in the 1950's and early 1960's were directed toward the gifted youngster. From Harvard to Berkeley, the bright child was the chief object of experimentation. On the basis of his reactions, curriculum experiences were planned and tried. At about the same time, however, scientific inquisitiveness led the developers of these new programs to take their curricula into the inner city and to the Appalachia-like rural districts. They knew their new curricula could be successful with the "haves"; they wanted to know the effect on the "have-nots." What they found was what they had suspected. These youngsters did not, of course, move as fast or as far as the gifted children for whom the curricula were developed, but they did become interested, stimulated, and intellectually restless. In most cases, attendance improved and teachers became more interested in teaching.

What are the elements in the newer curricula that "stir" the disadvantaged youngster? The literature and courses of study concerning disadvantaged children are filled with such statements as: "He needs less," "The curriculum must be simplified," and "We must stress the basic skills." These sentiments are usually reflected in the curriculum. The programs are bland, watered down, and lacking in content. Yet the disadvantaged youngster needs just the opposite of a bland, dull curriculum. He is the one who lives for today, who settles his problems as they come, who seldom plans. He is the one who needs stimulation, motivation, challenging content. He needs exposure, not enclosure.

The new curriculum approaches in the social sciences, economics, anthropology, sociology, psychology, the physical sciences, the English language arts, and mathematics offer content that is both important and interesting. It is current, imaginative, and content-packed. The methodology, in contrast to rote learning of rules and "facts" in tight little compartments, encourages the student, through experiences, to develop his own conclusions or generalizations. Instead of passively listening to what the teacher tells him, he becomes a partner in the learning act.

Piaget designates the years from seven to eleven as the concrete operational stage of children. The entire system evolves during this period to provide a mental structure increasingly capable of developing concepts from representative thought. Youngsters from disadvantaged homes come to school with a high degree of familiarity with the concrete. They believe what they see. Deutsch[12] says that there is a lack of expectation of reward for performance and most tasks are "motoric," have a short time span, and are more likely to be related to concrete objects. Difficulty arises when they must move into conceptualization and abstract thinking. On the basis of Piaget's theory of the fixed nature of stages and on the premise that the initial schooling stage is the concrete stage, a curriculum should act upon this and offer many such concrete experiences.

In the newer curricula, concrete experiences encourage students to form generalizations and concepts that, in turn, become the tools of learning. Children work with such realia as Cuisenaire rods, rocks, minerals, and artifacts. They feel and count and group and experience real things, and learn about other things from the teacher or a textbook; they work with authentic materials. From their many experiences with actual materials and processes, they draw generalizations which we refer to as abstractions. The abstractions are now understood because they are internalized. The children are then presented with new experiences which encourage them to apply their generalizations to new situations. The use of concrete experiences at this level makes it possible for them to evolve basic concepts that can be reconstructed and used to meet other problems.

This methodology may, at first, seem to repeat Dewey's thesis of learning by doing. However, Dewey's philosophy was that concrete experiences were offered for the sole purpose of meeting the child's needs or aims: "The child learns in the light of his *own* aims, the aim of the teacher represents the remote limit. Between

[12]Martin Deutsch, "The Disadvantaged Child and the Learning Process," in A. Harry Passow (Ed.), *Education in Depressed Areas* (New York: Teachers College Press, Teachers College, Columbia University, 1963), pp. 163–180.

the two lie the means . . . acts to be performed. . . ."[13] We accept Dewey's theory of the need for concrete experiences, but we now question the necessity for the child coming to school with his own needs or aims.

Bruner, for one, believes in intervention. To him, readiness is practically an unnecessary concept; children are always ready. When we present experiences to the child, we create aims for him. "The foundation of any subject may be taught to anybody at any age in some form."[14] Bruner emphasizes the importance of teaching structure or the basic concepts in a field of study. Once the structure is learned, individual facts may be forgotten, since they are easily reconstructed into the system. This is particularly important for the disadvantaged youngster because he, more than any other child, needs the basic tools, the basic concepts of the physical and social world—those that can be transferred from one subject to another, one idea to another. He needs a way of thinking and solving problems that is flexible. He needs "short cuts," and the mastery of structure is such a short cut.

The new curricula avoid dead ends. Activities are planned so that one leads into others; each solution raises more questions that require further probing. This is quite different from the approach that has been flourishing for a number of years—the activity-for-the-sake-of-activity school, in which each activity was self-contained and any motivation toward further probing was purely accidental. Knowledge should not be accumulated as in a stockpile, but should be a catalyst at times and a trigger at other times. Knowledge should direct the "knower" into other spheres of knowledge—as in a rocket blast-off where step 1 sets off step 2, which, in turn, sets off the next step. Each group of learnings should open doors to other groups rather than be a self-contained chamber. Because of environmental limitations, children from disadvantaged homes, particularly, need the stimulus of this kind of probing into new worlds and new fields of thought.

In addition, learning tasks in many of the new curricula emphasize logic and sequence. The student is taken, step-by-step, from one experience to another. If the steps are explicit and small

[13]John Dewey, *Democracy and Education* (New York: Macmillan, 1961), p. 127.

[14]Jerome S. Bruner, *The Process of Education* (Cambridge, Mass.: Harvard University Press, 1960), p. 12.

enough, the learner rarely has an opportunity to fail. Whether the curriculum be in programed form or simply ordered sequentially, the student is given the opportunity of mastering one task before moving to the next. For the disadvantaged child, this method is extremely important. His previous experience has been one of disorder, of lack of sequential planning. He needs the discipline and the knowledge that can be achieved only through a scientifically planned program.

This sequentially ordered, step-by-step treatment of material to be learned has other benefits for the disadvantaged child. Given the opportunity to understand one step before he moves to the next, he will meet success far more often than failure. These are children to whom school usually represents failure (reinforced by failure); successful experiences may completely reverse the failure cycle.

The newer curricula put much emphasis on self-instructional learning devices such as computer-based programs and teaching machines. Programed learning, or automated teaching of one sort or another, has merit for all children, but it has particular merit for the disadvantaged youngster. For reasons listed earlier, they do not function well in a school environment which emphasizes verbalization. Almost all the tasks in kindergarten and first grade point to getting the child to speak and read. The problem is more pronounced, of course, when he is in a class of children from mixed backgrounds; there his disability is more obvious. But, regardless of his classroom milieu, he will have difficulty in answering the teacher's questions, and he cannot easily enter into cross-discussion with classmates, if such discussion occurs. Frequently he becomes the quiet child in the class, being more fearful of giving a wrong answer than of not answering at all. The threat of failure now triples into failure in the eyes of the teacher, of his classmates, and of himself.

Deutsch et al., in discussing the disadvantaged child and the unfamiliar school environment, support the use of self-instructional devices:

. . . they could reduce his passivity by giving him greater control over the timing of the stimuli, thus minimizing cultural differences in time orientation. Further, in the self-corrective feedback of programed materials, the teacher's role of giving reward and disapproval would be shared; for a child unaccustomed to these as a means of motivation for intellectual performance, it might help decrease his alienation for school.[15]

In addition, it is extremely difficult for a teacher to pace her lesson so as to hold the interest of both the slowest and the fastest pupils. The teacher's tendency, with disadvantaged classes, is to assume that all are slow, and to pace her lesson to the slowest group. Therefore, one of the most important gains from self-instructional devices, programed and computer-based systems, is the ability to accommodate to individual differences. Dr. Robert Glaser, Director of Research at the University of Pittsburgh, has stated:

. . . in the populations which require special instruction, like the culturally disadvantaged and pre-literate groups, is the need for adjusting the curriculum to the individual. . . . A computerized system which permits the student to learn at his own speed, which gives him instantaneous knowledge of his incorrect patterns, and which guides him toward mastery, can be a tremendous aid to instruction if appropriately employed toward this end.[16]

Given the minimal language facility of disadvantaged children versus the heavy emphasis, in the first few grades, on verbalization, how can they avoid frustration and failure? Piaget has demonstrated that children can handle problems intuitively. He calls for teaching techniques in which children can work on problems without giving verbal explanations. Bruner says that children, during this operational stage from seven to eleven, are capable of grasping many of the basic ideas of mathematics, science, humanities, and social science. Bruner defines this capability as "a means of getting data about the real world into the mind and then transferring them so that they can be organized and used selectively in the solution of a problem."[17] Gallagher says:

The apparent mistake of past generations of teachers was to assume that the child had to be able to present a formal structure of thought (for example, the formulation of a proof for a geometric theorem) in order to demonstrate his grasp of the concept. The child in the stage

[15]Martin Deutsch, A. McIver, B. Brown, and E. Cherry, *Communication of Information in the Elementary School Classroom*, Cooperative Research Project No. 900 (Washington, D.C.: Office of Education, United States Department of Health, Education and Welfare, 1964), p. 4.

[16]Letter from Dr. Glaser to Dr. Louis Bright of the Westinghouse Research Laboratory, December 31, 1964.

[17]Bruner, *op. cit.*, p. 35.

of concrete operations cannot give a formal organization of complex theoretical ideas, but he *can* solve many problems depending upon such ideas.[18]

We make the error of assuming that the child must *verbalize* the answer in order to show he has learned it. At this stage the youngster cannot formulate theoretical ideas, but he can *solve* problems that depend on these ideas.

Many of the programs described in this book do not demand verbal responses; neither do they reject them, if the child wishes to state the concept. The youngster has the learning experience as often as is necessary and may solve the problem in his own mind. The theory, or generalization, can take its time. It may not be until the second grade, or even later, in the elementary school that he formulates the theory. Not requiring verbal responses, however, does not mean that these children do not need help in language development. It merely means that formal verbalizing is not necessary to prove that learning has taken place and that children should not be "pressed" into formulating answers.

It is important, of course, that children from disadvantaged homes be given language experiences as early as they are psychologically ready for them. Deutsch[19] indicates that class differences in perceptual abilities and general environmental orientation decrease with age, while language differences tend to increase. Compensatory programs in language, offering these students experiences in syntactical forms in written and oral language, rather than emphasis on grammatical forms, are not only advisable for language development but important in minimizing language differences as children get older.

In the general area of language development, one might also question the place of reading in the hierarchy of communication. Times have changed, and the media of communication have multiplied. Since the advent of the printing press, books have been the principal repository of man's heritage—intellectual, cultural, and social. "Book learning" was synonymous with education. Today there are other media and repositories of communication,

[18]James J. Gallagher, "Productive Thinking," in Martin L. Hoffman and Lois Wladis Hoffman (Eds.), *Review of Child Development Research*, Vol. 1 (New York: Russell Sage Foundation, 1964), p. 356.

[19]Martin Deutsch, "The Disadvantaged Child and the Learning Process," in A. Harry Passow (Ed.), *Education in Depressed Areas* (New York: Teachers College Press, Teachers College, Columbia University, 1963), pp. 163–179.

such as radio, films, television, and teaching machines. The average man can function in society as a social being, a wage earner, and a citizen with far less reading ability than in the past.

We do not suggest that man could not improve himself if he had more competency in reading, but nevertheless he can still function adequately on a less verbal level. Marshall McLuhan says:

> In the electronic age which succeeds the typographic and mechanical era of the past five hundred years, we encounter new shapes and structures of human interdependence and of expression which are "oral" in form even when the components of the situation may be non-verbal.[20]

Should we not then re-examine the value of giving priority to reading instruction and consider, instead, rearranging the order of communication skills and reading's primary position? This proposal might be considered for all children, but it should be given special consideration for the disadvantaged youngster in whom prereading skills are almost completely lacking upon entrance into school. This child does have other communication skills. For example, the slum child has a highly selective hearing instrument by the time he enters school. He is able to close out sound at will, and he can select, therefore, what he wishes to hear and what he does not. He will usually make his choice, not on an intellectual basis, but on subjective bases, depending upon who is talking or whether he feels like listening at all. When he enters school, he often closes out the teacher and other sounds relating to schooling, electing to listen to sounds that do little for his education. Deutsch, in his experiments with slum children in New York City, bases part of his program on "selected listening." Once the youngster learns to tune in, instead of close out, the school sounds, he has a communication skill that is invaluable for learning.

Another communication skill seen in children from disadvantaged neighborhoods is the use of gesture to convey meaning. They have always used their bodies and their hands to express themselves, probably more so than verbally communicative children. The linguists tell us that bodily movements, as well as the stressing of words and syllables, give meaning. Why not encour-

[20]Marshall McLuhan, *The Gutenberg Galaxy: The Making of Typographic Man* (Toronto: University of Toronto Press, 1962), p. 3.

age this skill and combine it with listening and speaking, so that communication becomes easier and more interesting?

We see, then, that programs emphasizing a variety of concrete experiences, coupled with the communication skills of listening, speaking, and gesture, can provide what Bruner refers to as the "intervening opportunities" that provide children with the cognitive and perceptual abilities needed for reading. They will help compensate for what he refers to as "impairment under a deprived regimen."[21]

Although Bruner's studies do not refer specifically to children from a disadvantaged environment, his remarks seem especially relevant in this context. One must not assume that these children, simply because they have not had the opportunity to develop cognitive skills, are unprepared to cope with the cognitive demands of learning.

A strong argument can be made for giving the disadvantaged child an earlier start. John Fischer compares present-day schooling to a race in which the disadvantaged start twenty feet behind the others. Perhaps an earlier start can help compensate for the experiences denied this child in his home environment and help diminish the twenty-foot "handicap."

Until the middle 1950's, the theory persisted that children should not have their infancy spoiled by having to start school too early. The theories of Washburn and his contemporaries persisted: The very young child was just not ready for school. In the face of later research, however, a new attitude began to emerge. Bloom,[22] in describing general intelligence and using the absolute scales of intellectual development formulated by Thorndike, Thuston, and Heines, suggests that 50 per cent of development takes place between conception and age four, 30 per cent between ages four and eight, and 20 per cent between eight and seventeen. Bloom does not subscribe to the thesis that intelligence is a physical or neurological growth function analogous to height growth and that it must have a definite terminal growth point; however, he maintains that intelligence, as presently measured, does reach a plateau in the period ages of ten to seventeen, after which further growth and development are likely only if encouraged by powerful forces in the environment.

[21]Bruner, *op. cit.*, pp. 203–204.

[22]Benjamin S. Bloom, *Stability and Change in Human Characteristics* (New York: Wiley, 1964), p. 68.

If, as according to the above view, as much development takes place in the first four years of life as in the next thirteen, then any years lost in a poor environment are almost irretrievable. It is impossible to emphasize too heavily the importance of the first few years of elementary school, as well as of the preschool period, in the development of learning patterns and general achievement. Failure to develop learning patterns in these years may lead to failure throughout the student's school career. Bloom, in another study,[23] further breaks down the figures and estimates that 17 per cent of intellectual growth takes place between the ages of four and six. If this is the case, then it is reasonable to assume that schooling during these years can have far-reaching effects in a child's learning patterns.

These studies also raise questions as to the value of remedial programs. If 80 per cent of one's intellectual development takes place before the age of eight, how much can be accomplished by remediation, or unlearning and relearning, after that age? The country is spending millions of dollars on dropout and "last-chance" programs; however, what little evaluation we have done on these programs tells us that few are "saved," and even those who do stay on in school have marginal existences there—the slightest upset drives them out of school. The implications of early intellectual development, coupled with the apparent lack of success of salvage programs, support the basic hypothesis that a curriculum based on learning theory appropriate to the disadvantaged child, and starting at least two years before the traditional schooling, can compensate for much of the deprivation experienced by these youngsters.

A word of caution should be expressed, however, as to the evaluation of preschool programs. Just as the dropout programs have not been adequately scrutinized, so is there a danger that preschool programs will be adopted emotionally, without proper field testing. Although we have theoretical bases for establishing preschool education, we have very few longitudinal studies of present projects to show the results of preschool education. This lack of research may be due to the newness of the programs. It is hoped, however, that educators will not forget to build such evaluation studies into the programs at their onset.

[23]*Ibid.*, p. 110.

VALUE CONFLICTS BETWEEN THE HAVES AND THE HAVE-NOTS

Changing concepts of "moral conduct," "sets of values," or "good behavior"—whatever term one uses—have given rise to many questions regarding social relationships. Morality has generally been regarded as conscience, as a set of culture rules of social action which have been internalized by the individuals. Moral development has been conceived of as the increase of such internalization of basic cultural rules.[24]

When communities were separate and remote, they were entities unto themselves. A value system evolved, and all those who lived in the community were expected to adhere to it. But, as the members of communities increased, people spilled over the boundaries, and the law of one community sometimes clashed with the law of the neighboring community. The United States is moving increasingly toward the establishment of common values. However, when we examine these common values, we find they do not apply to disadvantaged groups. These people have not become acculturated; they guard their identity and live in a culture as different from the standard culture as their speech is from standard speech.

To begin with, children from disadvantaged cultures usually have different codes of behavior. Their values are weighted differently because of their experiences. It is at school that the first confrontation with another culture takes place. Havighurst and Taba describe the basic character traits of our cultural ideal as honesty, loyalty, responsibility, moral courage, and friendliness. With the exception of friendliness, all these traits require adhering to cultural norms of action. The problem for the school, therefore, is to build a bridge to help these children understand the cultural norms of the school.

There are those who argue for *adherence* to the prevailing cultural norms, while others maintain that the school should adapt the culture norms to the community culture. Whichever view one takes, the norms, or standards, should be those that provide for mutual respect among all people.

There are also those who argue that values can only be taught by the home and the church. This is questionable since no

[24]Lawrence Kohlberg, "Development of Moral Character and Moral ideal," in Harold W. Stevenson (Ed.), *Child Psychology*, Sixty-second Yearbook of the National Society for the Study of Education, Vol. I (Chicago: University of Chicago Press, 1963), p. 384.

institution has been found to be the infallible impregnator of values. Perhaps each can attempt inculcation in its own way, but the role of the school cannot be underestimated.

Piaget believes that the cognitive limitation in the child from age three to eight leads him to confuse moral rules with physical laws and to view laws as fixed external things, rather than as the instruments of human purposes and values.[25] Sears, Maccoby, and Levin place the age in which conscience is determined as approximately in the first six to ten years.[26]

If as according to Piaget, the preschool years have little effect in shaping moral values, and if the six-to-ten period is as important as Sears and others claim, then it is incumbent upon the custodians of the child during those years to help him develop an inner moral structure. This is particularly important to the disadvantaged child who may not live by the normal code of the school society.

The problem arises as to how this is done. How does one instill a code of ethics? Can it be achieved through a direct method of moral persuasion, of setting down rules to live by and taboos to avoid? To what extent can one's behavior be shaped by dogma? The research of Hartsharne and May, for example, found no relationship between behavioral tests of honesty or service, and exposure to Sunday school or to the Boy Scout code. In fact, Rau,[27] as recently as 1964, found no positive or consistent relationship between training in good habits and the measure of a child's obedience.

Without completely rejecting the fact that rules or laws may in and of themselves have value to some children, how can one provide other avenues for formulating values? The curriculum thus far has been untapped in this area. Although we have always declared that the purpose of education is to create the better man, there are two questions we have not been able to answer specifically: (1) What do we mean by a better man—(is he rigidly "moral," or is he flexible and adaptable? (2) How do go about creating this man? Values and moral judgments can be

[25]Jean Piaget, *The Moral Judgment of the Child* (Glencoe, Ill.: The Free Press, 1948).

[26]R. R. Sears, E. E. Maccoby, and H. Levin, *Patterns of Child Rearing* (Evanston, Ill.: Row, Peterson, 1957), p. 367.

[27]L. Rau, "Conscience and Identification," in R. R. Sears, L. Rau, and R. Alpert (Eds.), *Identification and Child Rearing* (Stanford, Calif.: Stanford University Press, in press).

taught as part of the curriculum, not in the sense of the "model" or the reprimand, but by introducing through the disciplines the content from which one can evolve values. By introducing into the elementary school and secondary school curricula the study of such areas as political science, sociology, history, psychology, anthropology, the law, economics, government, the family, the work order, the human mechanism, and the interrelationships of man, one can present situations that cause children to make value judgments.

For example, in anthropology, the study of other cultures can lead a student to understand that there are ways other than his own which are compatible with human needs and dignity. He might then be able to re-examine his own culture with a certain objectivity and with a view toward considering his own conduct and the institutions of his own society. If he could understand that each culture has its values and that such values make sense, the youngster from the disadvantaged area might not be as hostile to the values of the school culture. The study of civil rights and civil responsibilities, of the making of revolutions, and of political upheaval and its causes can all lead children to discuss reasons for actions and outcomes. Perhaps he can then see the need for certain values and internalize these values so that he controls and applies them, not because they are "right," but because he understands and accepts them.

At no time should one underestimate the contribution of the teacher. A thoroughgoing "moralist" may antagonize the child by building up an unwholesome sense of guilt, but a teacher with a concientious interest in stimulating moral development may, through subject matter, provide a valuable supplement to concrete experience.

A NEW LOOK AT GUIDANCE

Instilling in youngsters an understanding of values and moral conduct is, or should be, closely allied to that part of the school program known as "guidance." In reviewing school budgets in areas where large numbers of children come from disadvantaged homes, we find that one of the largest allocations of funds is for "guidance." It is interesting to note that children who come into school with what the school terms academic ability are given a rich program of academic subjects. On the other hand, children who come into school with less academic ability are given fewer academic experiences and more "guidance."

In a study published by the Russell Sage Foundation,[28] involving four hundred post-delinquent fourteen-year-old girls who had entered a central Manhattan vocational high school six years earlier, it was found that individual counseling by itself was ineffective in improving their school behavior or in reducing the number of dropouts.

Again we must question the method. Can we change school behavior of a child from a disadvantaged environment by motivating him to learn through an understanding of his problems, which is the general goal of guidance programs? Or, are there other methods of creating motivation and change in school behavior? Ausubel, in discussing intrinsic motivation, suggests that, although culturally deprived children typically manifest little motivation to learn, we may discover a more effective method of developing intrinsic motivation by focusing on the cognitive rather than the motivational aspects of learning, the idea being, that successful educational achievement may develop "retroactively" motivation that was not previously in evidence. Ausubel continues: "Frequently, the best way of motivating an unmotivated pupil is to ignore his motivationless state and to concentrate on teaching him as effectively as possible."[29] Furthermore, success through achievment is perhaps the longest but most effective way of fostering an improved self-concept, of helping children overcome their tendency to devalue themselves as scholars or students.

It is suggested by the authors, therefore, that the cycle be reversed and that more time be given to academic endeavors and less time to guidance, that children be given the opportunity to learn and achieve through learning, and in that way become motivated toward schooling. In addition to improving his self-image by proving that he *can* achieve, the child also learns to understand himself and his problems through a study of the

[28]Russell Sage Foundation, *Girls and Vocational High* (New York, Author, 1965).

[29]David P. Ausubel, "How Reversible Are the Cognitive and Motivational Effects of Cultural Deprivation?", paper read at the Conference on Teaching the Culturally Deprived Child, Buffalo, N.Y., March 28-30, 1963 (mimeographed).

subject disciplines. The English language, the social sciences, and the physical sciences help children, through the study of man, his origin, his psyche, his social environments, his means of communicating, and his physical and social abilities and limitations, to gain a better understanding of themselves. Through an understanding of one's self and one's place in society and school, it is possible to develop a "built-in" self-guidance.

CHANGING VIEWS OF VOCATIONAL TRAINING

An article in the *New York Times* stated:

Unemployment among teenagers declined to 15.2 per cent in January; it was 15.7 per cent in December. Given the high degree of possible error in this volatile figure, department experts did not consider the decline significant.

A comparison with the rates of October, 1957, indicates the extent to which unemployment among teenagers has represented a growing problem. That month the unemployment rate among adult men was 4 per cent, among women, 4.2 per cent, and among teenagers, 10.2 per cent.[30]

Despite the fact that this quotation refers to the total teenage population, we may safely assume that a high proportion of them are the uneducated and poorly adjusted teenagers from disadvantaged homes, bearing handicaps that have been further aggravated by the conventional educational approach. Whereas most middle-class children are not encouraged to think of vocations until they reach high school, these disadvantaged children, even in their elementary grades, have been given curricula which emphasize job descriptions, how to apply for jobs, how to be a *worker*. Even the new urban readers, published with the best of intentions and used in many elementary schools, emphasize, not the man on the streets or in the fields or in the school, but the man at *work*. Yet Super and Overstreet, in their study of *The Vocational Maturity of Ninth Grade Boys*, found that "a substantial number of boys are not yet ready, in the ninth grade, to decide on direction of endeavor, or specifically, on a future occupation."[31] They see this stage not as one of "making and implementing a vocational choice, but rather of developing

[30]"Steady Increase in Jobless Continues," *The New York Times* (February 4, 1964).

[31]Donald E. Super and Phoebe L. Overstreet, *The Vocational Maturity of Ninth-Grade Boys* (New York: Teachers College Press, Teachers College, Columbia University, 1960), p. 152.

planfulness, of preparing to make a series of educational and occupational decisions. . . ."[32] They suggest then that the educational program ready the pupil for making these decisions. Therefore, it would be well to reconsider the "age of decision" and not predestine disadvantaged youngsters to vocational training so early in their school careers.

We must also look at the whole spectrum of vocational education. We must ask ourselves whether we may not be mistaken in assuming that children from disadvantaged homes, in order to be successful, must be relegated to vocational education. Indeed, if this is the case, how are we to account for the high rate of unemployment among the disdavantaged? A more important and basic question must be raised: What are the elements of learning that are vital to becoming a successful worker in the working society?

To begin with, children need a knowledge of the work process: What does it mean? What is its structure? Students can be introduced into the work process through the social sciences— anthropology, sociology, and psychology. They can learn how people have used work as a means of bettering themselves through the centuries and discover how to achieve personal satisfaction from doing a job well. Technology must not be regarded as something divorced from the essence of humanity. Technology is inseparable from men and communities. When the Peace Corps builds a road in tropical Africa, that road is more than an exercise in civil engineering. It is a major experiment in social anthropology, for it affects the primitive, up-country villages and acts as a communication link which will stimulate the acculturation of these people to modern Western society. Nearly every technical activity has social consequences; technology is of humanistic interest, not only because it is a product of the human mind, but also because it affects the course of human and social development.[33]

As noted by President Johnson's recent Panel of Consultants on Vocational Education, the worker of tomorrow will need a *sound general education* which will give him the knowledge, the skill and flexibility he needs to learn new techniques and adapt himself to new jobs. He will need even more mathematics and

[32]*Ibid.*

[33]Melvin Kranzberg, "Technology and Culture: Dimensions for Exploration," *The Journal of Industrial Arts Education,* 23, No. 5 (May–June 1964), p. 25.

science than he has now. Should we not, then, plan a curriculum that offers mathematics and the physical and social sciences, rather than vocational subjects that often are obsolete by the time the student finishes the semester? With this general education as a foundation, a child can move on *with understanding* to the more complicated studies of the sciences and mathematics and, hopefully, receive a better training for future vocations.

Therefore, although not rejecting completely the need for some specifics in vocational preparation, the present authors propose that emphasis be placed on academic subjects as preparation for work experiences.

THE SCOPE OF THIS BOOK

A book, like a curriculum, must set limits. It cannot do all things. Therefore, there will be certain obvious omissions. We do not mean to imply that aspects omitted are of no importance or that they do not deserve investigation and discussion. It merely means that we have given *priority* to guidelines for *curriculum, its content,* and *its methodology.*

Teacher education is important to all programs; without it, the best approach—the best curriculum—is poorly implemented. However, we do not present teacher education programs in this book because of the limitations of space and of the fact that teacher education will vary with the preparation of the teachers and the facilities of the school or school system. Before leaving the subject of teacher preparation entirely, however, we would like to issue a word of caution, as far as *selection* of teachers is concerned. Teachers of the disadvantaged must have a feeling of confidence in their students. Teachers who have made up their minds that these children cannot learn, do not care to learn, and have parents who are not concerned are poor risks as teachers for the disadvantaged. Deutsch calls this negativeness a projective device to relieve the professional of responsibilities.

. . . often older siblings and neighbors of the lower-class child have experienced so much failure and so much class and cultural arrogance as to generate a great apathy out of which none of them expects positive consequences from the school experience. This very apathy is sometimes reflected in the attitudes of the educational apparatus toward the lower-class community.[34]

[34]Martin Deutsch, "Some Psychological Aspects of Learning in the Disadvantaged." Revised version of a paper presented at the Boston University Developmental Conference on the Teaching of Disadvantaged Youth, 1964 (mimeographed), p. 5.

Johnson[35] reported on a study of how a teacher's behavior toward a child is influenced by his perceptions of what guides, directs, or causes the child's behavior. The findings indicate that if a pupil does poorly on a task, the teacher will tend to perceive the cause of this performance as internal to the student and attribute negative characteristics to him (low IQ, low social class, troublesomeness). If the student does well, the teacher usually attributes the positive characteristics to himself ("I did a good job; my lesson was well prepared.").

Both Deutsch and Johnson agree that teachers often attribute "poor behavior" and negative characteristics to *internal* causes. (There's nothing I can do for him; it is within him.") Such an attitude can be completely destructive to the education of the disadvantaged.

We are not suggesting "special training" for the teachers of the disadvantaged, but we are trying to make a case for selecting teachers who believe that the disadvantaged *can* learn and succeed in school. Perhaps the better approach is to help teachers become so knowledgeable in curriculum content and in helping children learn how to learn that they can look at children as Binet did, as "fields for cultivation."

Another area not treated in this book is school organization. All too often, those planning programs for the disadvantaged try to solve matters with organization—vary the size of the classes, change the bell schedule, put in an assistant teacher, give a bonus to teachers who elect to work with the "difficult" child. These suggestions may have merit, but they should not be given priority. Organization and staffing are byproducts of what we teach. Organization is no panacea; it does not "teach"; it merely facilitates teaching.

At no time in this book do we treat the process of integrating schools racially and its related problems. Again, both the process and the problems differ from region to region, from school system to school system, from school to school; and the authors do not feel that any master plan can be superimposed. However, the problems of integration are treated in the chapter on history and the social sciences, since understanding the problems of political, economic, and social power redistribution should be part of understanding the world today. Kvaraceus has observed that the conventional high school curriculum. . .

[35]Thomas Johnson. Untitled paper delivered at the Association for Supervision and Curriculum Development Conference on Research, Miami, Florida, November 1964.

. . . is careful to skirt and detour around real-life problems and controversial issues involving race relations, alcoholism, materialism, religion, politics, collectivism, consumer competency, marriage, and family life . . . involves the learner in a type of artificially contrived busy work and shadow boxing that either lulls the adolescent into a stupor or drives him in his resentment out of school to overt aggression. In protecting youth from real-life problems, the school enters into a tragic conspiracy of irresponsible retreat from reality. The perversion of the high school curriculum to neutral and petty purposes emasculates the school program and disintegrates the ego.[36]

The authors of this book propose that we not only look again into the "shadow-boxing" that characterizes the high school curriculum but also address ourselves to these studies in the elementary grades. Real-life problems are with children all the time; they are especially with the disadvantaged. Perhaps, with an understanding of these problems at an earlier and more impressionable age and on an intellectual basis, they can dissipate much of the emotion and achieve a more satisfactory solution.

The purpose of this book is to reject the traditional tranquilizer, the "modified curriculum," and to present instead a curriculum that will treat the disadvantaged child as one who has a tremendous potential for participation and leadership. We fully realize that there is no single curriculum that will meet the needs of any one group of children. A curriculum must be a blending, a synthesis, a compound that changes its ingredients to suit its functions.

The authors of this book also acknowledge the fact that not *all* children from disadvantaged homes can be expected to succeed any more than can any other group of children. We all know children whose abilities are extremely limited and will remain so no matter what type of program we present. These are children for whom a simple, bland curriculum is the only one with which they can cope, children whose only future is the world of work in its most menial sense, and children who need the help of guidance personnel almost to the exclusion of teachers and classroom experiences. Our problem as educators is to distinguish and sift out those who fall into this category—the hard core, the *few* intellectually limited (statistically, only 5 per cent of our popu-

[36]William Kvaraceus, "Negro Youth and Social Adaptation: The Role of the School as an Agent of Change." Unpublished paper, Lincoln Filene Center for Citizenship and Public Affairs, Tufts University, Medford, Mass., 1963 (unpublished paper), p. 63.

lation). For the others, the great bulk of the disadvantaged population, a far richer, more motivating, more interesting curriculum must be presented if we are to save what is gradually becoming a third of our nation. Passow calls for:

. . . an educational program which will insure meaningful growth, provide a sense of attainment and accomplishment, help youngsters understand and face their limitations as well as their strengths, provide for healthy attitudes toward school and society, and generally turn the indifference or antagonism of the disadvantaged child into acceptance and understanding. This represents *content*. . . .[37]

Many of the programs suggested in this book are not in use long enough to be supported by extensive evaluation, others are based on approaches that have not yet been accepted; yet they all have something in common that makes them important to the child from a disadvantaged background and that is a basic respect for the intellect and for the power of education.

[37]A. Harry Passow, "Instructional Content for Depressed Urban Centers: Problems and Approaches," paper presented at the Post-Doctoral Seminar of the College of Education, The Ohio State University, October 23, 1964 (mimeographed), pp. 23–24.

SELECTED READINGS
ON CHANGING CONCEPTS

Books on the Subject

Bloom, Benjamin S., Davis, Allison, and Hess, Robert, *Compensatory Education for Cultural Deprivation* (New York: Holt, Rinehart and Winston, 1965).

Working papers contributed by participants in the Research Conference on Education and Cultural Deprivation, University of Chicago, June, 1962, are reported and edited by the authors. The report talks about the early needs of culturally deprived youngsters and about curriculum implications for elementary school and adolescent education levels. The most valuable part of this collection of papers is the "recommendation" section for each level (elementary-secondary) and the annotated bibliography which comprises three quarters of the book.

Bruner, Jerome S., *The Process of Education* (Cambridge, Mass.: Harvard University Press, 1960).

What shall we teach and to what end? The author concludes that the basic concepts of science and the humanities can be grasped by children far earlier than has ever been thought possible. The task is to present the fundamental structure of the material to be learned. The important ideas of structure and interaction so basic to the new curriculum programs are set forth in this book.

Cervantes, Lucius F., *The Dropout: Causes and Cures* (Ann Arbor: University of Michigan Press, 1965).

This research was "designed to examine," in an explorative fashion, both the sociocultural and psychodynamic factors involved in withdrawal from the academic milieu," or, more simply, dropping out of high school. The areas of investigation included "the structure, dynamics, and emotional climate of the family"; the influences of family friends and of the teenager's teenage friends; the school experiences; and pyschic characteristics as evaluated by means of the Thematic Apperception Test.
Sociologists should read this book for the light that it sheds on, and the myths that it dispels regarding, family structure and youth culture.

It should also be read by those who can bring action to bear on the dropout problem. Most particularly, it should be read by social workers, high school principals, teachers, and counselors who may be able to compensate, in some measure, for the inadequate families of the dropouts or potential dropouts. They may, on occasion, be able to transmit the message to the parents.

Flavell, J. H., *Developmental Psychology of Jean Piaget* (Princeton: Van Nostrand, 1963).

A detailed and integrated summary of the work of Jean Piaget is offered in this book. It includes a description of Piaget's theoretical systems and their various roles within his scheme of developmental stages. This volume has the advantage of offering a critical evaluation both methodologically and in light of related research by others of Piaget's systems at work.

Heath, Robert W. (Ed.), *New Curricula* (New York: Harper and Row, 1964).

This book discusses curriculum reforms in education that began soon after the Second World War and that are still in progress today, and reports on the methods and programs for teaching science and the humanities which promise to revolutionize American education. The pioneer work, such as that of Zacharias, Beberman, the American Council of Learned Societies, and the Biology, Chemistry, and Mathematics Projects, and the more recent developments in English and the social sciences are not only described but also placed in historical perspective.

Hunt, J. McV., *Intelligence and Experience* (New York: Ronald Press, 1961).

As stated by the author, "this book is a kind of case history in behavioral science, presented before all of the cases have become history." Evidence from various sources has been forcing a recognition of central processes in intelligence and of the crucial role of life experiences in the development of the central processes.

The theme deals with the transformation between the traditional concept of a fixed intelligence and its relationship to experience.

Inhelder, B., and Piaget, J., *The Growth of Logical Thinking from Childhood to Adolescence* (New York: Basic Books, 1958).

This comparatively new book treats children in the more advanced stage of mental development, from age eleven to fifteen. First-hand observational and experimental studies with fifteen hundred boys and girls document this investigation of the formal psychological structures that, in the author's words, "mark the completion of the operational development of intelligence." This book is one of the few in the area of the "older learner" and has much bearing on curriculum building and teaching.

Kerber, Angus, and Bammarito, Barbara, *The Schools and the Urban Crisis* (New York: Holt, Rinehart and Winston, 1965).

This is a collection of readings reprinted from various journals. Descriptions of ongoing experiments, action projects and vital speeches concerning the disadvantaged are featured.

Passow, A. Harry (Ed.), *Education in Depressed Areas* (New York: Teachers College Press, Teachers College, Columbia University, 1963).

Educators from twenty-four cities were invited to Teachers College to explore the problems of educating culturally disadvantaged children. Thirteen specialists in various fields prepared working papers. This book offers the thirteen papers plus two additional papers and some of the highlights from the discussions. The papers are divided into five subtopics: "Schools in Depressed Areas"; "Psychological Aspects of Education in Depressed Areas"; "Sociological Aspects of Education in Depressed Areas"; "Teachers for Depressed Areas" and "School Programs in Depressed Areas." The section of the bibliography on "Selected School Reports and Bulletins" is helpful for those who want to know about programs in operation in some of the school systems.

Phenix, Philip H., *Education and the Common Good* (New York: Harper and Brothers, 1961).

The author argues that the major issues of contemporary civilization must furnish the basis of what we should teach our children. "The clue to choice in the curriculum lies in the demands that are imposed by the development of modern civilization." Race and social class problems because values are at stake, because people care about the outcomes. The use of such topics means that purposeful conduct in relation to genuine issues is involved.

Democracy, the author states, presupposes a single standard of worth and equality of all persons with respect to truth. Democracy is the social expression of belief in objective qualities of goodness and a common loyalty to them.

Phenix, Philip H., *Realms of Meaning* (New York: McGraw-Hill, 1964).

This is a philosophy of a curriculum for general education. The author analyzes the fundamental disciplines in a way that helps curriculum builders decide on priorities. The emphasis on inquiry and logic makes it particularly useful for teachers of the disadvantaged.

Piaget, Jean, *The Psychology of Intelligence* (New York: Harcourt, Brace and World, 1950).

Piaget's theory of showing that the act of intelligence consists essentially in a "grouping" operation according to certain definite structures is the basic premise of this book. It discusses the relationship of intelligence to perception and to habit, as well as the quest for its development and for its socialization. This is an excellent "basic book" on Piaget's philosophy.

Rosenberg, Morris, *Society and the Adolescent Self-image* (Princeton: Princeton University Press, 1965).

An individual's self-image "largely determines his thoughts, feelings and behavior." According to the teachings of any school of psychology, the interaction between the way we behave and the way we perceive and judge our behavior is inordinately complex. When qualities admired in one group are rejected in another group, the author writes, the resultant "sense of difference may lead the individual to question himself, doubt himself, wonder whether he is unworthy," and this "negative self-picture may generate anxiety," which is defined as evil. This book was a co-winner of the annual sociopsychological prize of the American Association for the Advancement of Science. It has four technical appendices and an index.

Schramm, Wilbur (Ed.), *The Science of Human Communication* (New York: Basic Books, 1963).

A series of articles by scholars in which problems and research findings on human communication are discussed. The "new" rhetoric, semantics, and the social effects of mass media and their impact on personality are some of the featured topics.

ARTICLES FROM PROFESSIONAL PUBLICATIONS

Brookover, Wilbur B., Thomas, Shailer, and Paterson, Ann, "Self-concept of Ability and School Achievment," *Sociology of Education,* 37 (Spring, 1964), pp. 271–278.

Bruck, Max, and Bodwin, Raymond F., "The Relationship Between Self-concept and the Presence and Absence of Scholastic Underachievement," *Journal of Clinical Psychology,* 18 (April 1962), pp. 181–182.

Bruner, Jerome S., "The Course of Cognitive Growth," *American Psychologist,* 19 (January 1964), pp. 1–15.

Deutsch, Martin, and Brown, Bert, "Social Influences in Negro-White Intelligence Differences," *Journal of Social Issues,* 20 (April 1964) pp. 24–35.

Erlenmeyer-Kimling, L., and Jarvik, Lissy F., "Genetics and Intelligence: A Review," *Science,* 142 (December 13, 1963), pp. 1477–1479.

Gill, Lois J., and Spilka, Bernard, "Some Non-Intellectual Correlates of Academic Achievement Among Mexican-American Secondary School Students," *Journal of Educational Psychology,* 53 (June 1962), pp. 144–149.

Glaser, Robert, "Instructional Technology and the Measurement of Learning Outcomes," *American Psychologist,* 18 (August 1963, pp. 519–521.

Inhelder, Barbel, *Some Aspects of Piaget's Genetic Approach to Cognition,* Monographs of the Society for Research in Child Development, 27, No. 2 (1962), pp. 19–34.

Katz, Irwin, and Greenbaum, Charles, "The Effects of Anxiety, Threat, and Racial Environment on Task Performance of Negro College Students," *Journal of Abnormal and Social Psychology,* 66 (June 1963), pp. 56–57.

Kennedy, Wallace A., Van De Reit, Vernon, and White, James C., Jr., *A Normative Sample of Intelligence and Achievement of Negro Elementary School Children in the Southeastern United States,* Monographs of the Society for Research in Child Development, 28, No. 90 (1963), pp. 1–112.

Klineberg, Otto, "Negro-White Differences in Intelligence Test Performance: A New Look at an Old Problem," *American Psychologist,* 18 (April 1963), pp. 198–203.

Loretan, Joseph O., "The Decline and Fall of Group Intelligence Testing," *Teachers College Record,* 67, No. 1 (October 1965), pp. 10–17.

Loretan, Joseph O., "A Curriculum for Integration." Paper delivered at the Sixteenth Annual Curriculum Conference of the Board of Education of the City of New York, January 1964.

Lorge, I., "Schooling Makes a Difference," *Teachers College Record,* 46 (1945), pp. 483–492.

Piaget, Jean, "The Genetic Approach to the Psychology of Thought," *Journal of Educational Psychology,* 52 (December 1961), pp. 275–281.

Semler, Ira J., and Iscoe, Ira, "Comparative and Developmental Study of the Learning Abilities of Negro and White Children Under Four Conditions," *Journal of Educational Psychology,* 54 (February 1963), pp. 38–44.

Sexton, Patricia, "Negro Career Expectations," *Merrill-Palmer Quarterly,* 9 (October 1963), pp. 303–316.

Williams, J. R., and Knecht, Walter W., "Teachers' Ratings of High School Students on 'Likability' and Their Relation to Measures of Ability and Achievement," *Journal of Educational Research,* 56 (November 1962), pp. 152–155.

So much of what we today consider innovation is built upon certain classical studies in education and philosophy. The following books are recommended as "basic reading" for those who are interested in the roots of contemporary thinking in education.

Dewey, John, *The School and Society* (Chicago: Chicago University Press, 1899).

Dewey, John, *Democracy and Education* (New York: Macmillan, 1916).

Hall, G. Stanley, *Aspects of Child Life and Education* (New York: Appleton, 1921).

James, William, *The Principles of Psychology* (New York: Holt, 1890).

Kofka, K., *The Growth of the Mind—An Introduction to Child Psychology* (New York: Harcourt, Brace, 1920).

Krusi, Hermann, *Pestalozzi: His Life, Work and Influence* (Cincinnati: Wilson, Hinkle, 1875).

Parker, Francis W., *Talks on Pedagogics* (New York: Kellogg, 1894).

Reid, Thomas, *Enquiry into the Human Mind on the Principles of Common Sense* (London: Edited and abridged by A. D. Woozley, Macmillan, New York, 1941; London, 1764).

Spencer, Herbert, *What Knowledge is of Most Worth in Education?* (New York: Appleton, 1926, reprinted from 1860 edition).

Thorndike, E. L., *The Fundamentals of Learning* (New York: Bureau of Publications, Teachers College, Columbia University, 1932).

Whitehead, Alfred North, *The Aims of Education and other essays* (New York: Macmillan, 1929).

PART TWO

THE
ENGLISH LANGUAGE

A language program begins in the home. The moment the mother speaks or sings to her baby and elicits a gurgle, a smile, a cry, or even a swing of the baby's fist, communication has started. Every child except in the most extraordinary circumstances, is exposed to this early communication, at least for the first few months of their lives. It is during this period that the child starts to develop his motor and language skills, along with concepts of objects and time.

The child from the disadvantaged home very often has more contact with his mother in the first few months of life than a child from a more advantaged home. In homes of the poor, there are no "mothers' helpers," nurses, or sitters to relieve the mother of the care of the baby. Grandmothers and older sisters and brothers will care for the child when he grows older. Therefore, the child from the disadvantaged culture starts life with the advantage of close contact with the mother. However, this contact is soon severed. Either the mother must go out to work or she has a younger child to care for, and the older child (very often not quite a year old) is placed with a grandmother, an aunt (not always a bonafide relative), or a neighbor, or to a combination of all three.

Whether with his mother or with someone else, the child is usually one of several children who must be cared for. In addition, there are many other household chores; there is simply no time for the verbal give-and-take between adult and child that is common in more favored home environments. "It takes too long to say it." As the child grows older, younger children come along, and, of necessity, the attention of the available adults is shifted to the infants. The result is that, by the time the child reaches three or four, he is spending most of his time in the company of other children, his age or a little older, who have had the same experiences or lack of experiences. This environment can be restrictive and arid for the child at a stage in which he needs a richness of language experience.

However, if the child is given to the care of a group of people, the result might well be different. Margaret Mead suggests that children who grow up in a culture where there are several good mother figures learn to trust more people and therefore are better able to tolerate separation. It is her impression that such children tend to develop more subtle and more complex personality characteristics, presumably because of more varied identification figures.[1] This is an interesting point of view, since, in our culture, we assume that human infants are basically mono-tropic, and that multiple mothering is harmful to the child.

Underdeveloped language, or verbal inadequacy, may take several forms. It may take an abbreviated and less communi-cative form—what Bernstein, speaking of lower-class children, describes as a convergent or restrictive language rather than a divergent or elaborate language.[2] An exclamation or an impera-tive or a partial sentence frequently replaces a complete sentence or an explanation. If a child asks for something, the response is too frequently "yes," "no," "go away," "later," or simply a nod.

Templin conducted a study[3] in which 480 children, from ages three to eight, were compared on articulation, sound discrimi-nation, vocabulary, language complexity, and sentence length. In 230 possible comparisons, the lower socioeconomic group was found to be higher in only thirteen instances. Such retardation

[1]Margaret Mead, "A Cultural Anthropological Approach to Maternal Dep-rivation," *Deprivation of Maternal Care*, Public Health Paper No. 14 (Gene-va: World Health Organization, 1962), pp. 45–62.

[2]B. Bernstein, "Language and Social Class," *British Journal of Sociology,* 11 (1960), pp. 271–276.

[3]Mildred C. Templin, "Relations of Speech and Language Development to Intelligence and Socio-Economic Status," *Volta Review,* 60 (September 1958), pp. 331–334.

was particularly notable, among school children, in articulation, grammatical complexity, and vocabulary and, among preschool children, in sentence length. The differences in terms of socio-economic class were greater than those found on the basis of sex or intelligence. Templin suggests the need for "more specific dimensions of environmental stimulation. . . ."

ᷜᷜ2ᷜᷜ

SCHOOL LANGUAGE
AS A SECOND LANGUAGE

A youngster coming to school with a highly developed language of a kind that is not acceptable in the school culture suffers from another form of verbal inadequacy. Many situations arise where the teacher and the student *never* make contact. The situation is similar to that of a Spaniard and a Portuguese talking to each other, with neither one quite knowing the other's language. There is, of course, a certain similarity between the languages, and now and then meaning does come through, but comprehension is not frequent or precise enough to lead to fruitful communication.

In looking at language deprivation, we must also think of the union of concepts and languages. As O'Shea pointed out more than fifty years ago, "a man is effective linguistically in those situations, and those only, in which he has often been placed, and in reaction upon which he has been constantly urged, by force of circumstances, to express himself readily and to the point."[1] Children from deprived homes may not have the experiences that give meaning to "school vocabulary." This does not necessarily mean that they may not have achieved a highly developed vocabulary from their own experiences; but this vocabulary is simply not the same as the school's. As one youngster said, with tears in his eyes, to a teacher who repeatedly asked him to talk

[1]M. V. O'Shea, *Linguistic Development and Education* (New York: Macmillan, 1907), pp. 234–235.

about a subject completely foreign to him, "Ask me to talk about what I talk about."

Some of the newer approaches to language study take into consideration the factors of lack of opportunity to use language, the use of a different kind of language, and the lack of experiences in the school language. One might classify these approaches or curricula under the heading of compensatory education, since their purpose is to offer the disadvantaged youngster a counterbalance to the language facility of his advantaged peers.

The traditional method for establishing communication with a verbally limited child is to teach the child to imitate the teacher's speech. In effect, her speech becomes the model. This could be described as "direct transfer" from dialect to standard speech.

A second approach, suggested by modern linguists, is that, instead of making the child parrot the teacher's speech, the teacher might try to become facile in using the child's language, thus creating a bridge for communication with the child. The teacher, by communicating on the child's own terms, can gradually lead him into the more acceptable regional speech pattern.

There are two sound reasons for accepting the child's speech "as is" during his early language education. First, it gives the youngster the advantage of bringing something of his home and neighborhood environment into the school. If we begin setting up models of behavior—in speech or in any other activity—on the very first day the child enters school, we are, in effect, saying to him: "Reject the things you bring with you from your home; they are not desirable. Learn to do things our way." This, of course, is never verbalized, either by teachers or by curriculum guides, but the rejection is implicit in much that is done.

The second reason is that a child does not *need* to change his speech pattern in order to learn how to read. Standard, printed English is the same, whether one speaks the dialect of the North, of the South, of New England, or of the West. People speaking all the dialects of the immigrants to the cities learn to read the same printed words. Therefore, the argument that retraining of speech patterns is needed in order to teach reading is not based upon fact. Donald Lloyd, in studying subcultural patterns affecting language, asks that we let these children "in on literacy," that a successful language arts program should, for these children, begin

. . . where they are in language, wherever they are. It rests on the rich and viable culture that almost any child carries within him to school, and it respects that culture. It relates the children's actual language to the printed page, and it lets the reading child talk the way his parents talk instead of "sounding out words" painfully, one by one, tonelessly, with strange and difficult sounds.[2]

A third approach is that of Raven I. McDavid, Jr., of the University of Chicago, who is also associate director of the Dialect Atlas of the United States. He suggests that inner city children, who come to school with a dialect of the language, be taught standard English as a *second language,* side by side with the dialect.[3]

The one objective, however, agreed upon by all—the proponents of standard models, the defenders of regional or local patterns, and the advocates of letting the child become bilingual within his own language—is that the youngster, in time, should be able to use the standard speech pattern. The difference lies in how this objective is to be reached. Those who believe in "emulating a model" introduce the model concurrently with the school experience. Those who believe in the teacher's adopting local speech patterns to bridge the gap, introduce acceptable speech patterns after the relationship has been established and the youngster feels secure in the school surroundings.

Whatever the approach—the standard English model, the acceptance of the dialect, or English as a second language—it is hoped that eventually the youngster will take on the acceptable speech pattern and, in McDavid's words, "the child is thus introduced to the values of the dominant culture."[4] If the school is to be effective, and if these youngsters are not to be discharged into the ever-larger group of unskilled unemployables, then meaningful, expressive, and receptive language training must become a conscious part of curriculum organization. Inability to speak and understand standard English can make social mobility in our society almost impossible.

[2]Donald J. Lloyd, "Sub-Cultural Patterns Which Affect Language and Reading Development," in *Language, Linguistics, and School Programs* (Champaign, Ill.: National Council of Teachers of English, 1963), p. 54.

[3]Raven I. McDavid, Jr., "Dialectology and the Teaching of Reading," *The Reading Teacher,* 18, No. 9 (December 1964), p. 206.

[4]*Ibid.,* p. 206.

3

PRE-KINDERGARTEN
LANGUAGE TRAINING

Most of the language programs for children from disadvantaged homes are started as early as it is possible to reach both child and parent. Israel, facing a similar problem in acculturation of the oriental Jews, established pre-kindergarten schools several years ago. The Israeli program is more far-reaching than most, as it begins on the prenatal level; social workers visit *future* parents to discuss with them the importance of playing with, talking to, and singing to the newborn baby. The social workers supply records, books to read, and songs to sing; toys are loaned to the family by the government until the youngster is ready to enter nursery school. The Israelis are convinced that anyone, given the proper preparatory background and subsequent appropriate instruction, can be taught to function in an educated society.

Pre-kindergarten programs are emerging in the United States: Pennsylvania's Environment Enrichment Program; programs in Racine, Wisconsin, Dayton, Ohio, and White Plains, New York, the Texas program for Mexican-American children; and several programs in New York City. These, among others, have all been pioneers in establishing programs for pre-kindergarteners.

Most of the new preschool and primary-school language programs are based upon structural linguistics. The young child learns his language through imitation. By presenting common language patterns and having the child repeat and manipulate them, the teacher instills in him the concept of the sentences. No matter how depressed the background of children, they can all learn to speak *simple* sentences. These sentences fall into four common language patterns:

1. noun + verb   The man came.
2. noun + verb + noun   The man bought a book.
3. noun + linking verb + adjective   The man is good.
4. noun + linking verb + noun   The man is my friend.

The important column is the one on the right. These basic sentences can be manipulated and repeated with other words. The idea is to help the youngster, by practicing, to see similarities and differences in the sentences and eventually to adopt these into his own language pattern.

In such presentations as the one described above, timing is an important factor. If the child is introduced too early to the accepted language pattern, the student-school relationship may be destroyed. Gradual presentation of the desired language patterns can be far more effective than if such presentation is made at the outset of the school experience.

The Philadelphia Public Schools' language program urges children to "play" with words in patterns. Jingles, simple poems, and nonsense poems are used. Gradually, the youngster achieves an awareness, not only of sentence forms and manipulability, but of sounds and of the fact that letters represent sounds. Most linguists suggest teaching, first, words of "orthodox" spellings, such as: hat, fat, cat; cat, cap, cab; cat, cot, cut. After listening to the teacher and saying the words themselves, children should be encouraged to discuss the words and to find additional words they can bring into the pattern by substituting either individual vowels or consonants. In this way children begin to realize that every word is not completely different from every other word, but, rather, that there *is* order and system to English. This is where the "old grammar" and the "new grammar" (linguistics) differ. The old grammar emphasized words in a linear sequence; the new grammar emphasizes relationship. Words are related to each other by common sounds and by their effect upon each other. Sentences form a hierarchy of construction within construction on different levels.

Linguistics, however, sheds light on only one facet of instruction: that of a relationship of sounds and structure. The fact that the child learns most readily those words relating to concrete experiences makes it important that he be given more than just oral practice with words and sentence combinations. As a starting point, children from disadvantaged homes should work within content that is familiar to them, content that is real, observable, and interesting. Illustrations in books should be realistic. A mother should look like *their* mothers, a home like *their* homes, a neighborhood like *their* neighborhood. The disadvantaged child often comes from an integrated community, even if his immediate neighborhood is not integrated. Therefore, pictures of people in books and magazines and charts should show a *pluralistic society* in which the child can picture himself. Children in this group should have as many sensory experiences with letters and words as possible: alphabet letters that have texture, words in color, and opportunity to see words, feel words, hear words, and build words.

One current effort is the **Enrichment Program of the Institute for Developmental Studies.** In his work with young children from disadvantaged homes, Deutsch[1] stresses the verbal and perceptual skills needed for all types of communication. Many of these children come from homes where things are seldom referred to by name; a chair, a table, or a lamp is pointed at, but not identified. Deutsch stresses labeling in his approach, getting across the idea that everything has a name, a name to be seen and a name to be used. In training the child to offer oral responses, the teacher first discourages pointing and "partial" language. Once the oral response is given, the teacher encourages the child to play with the word, or with a word like it, in a phrase, a sentence, or a jingle. Deutsch combines the learning of concepts with perception and linguistics.

Another aspect of this program is combating the disadvantaged child's habit of closing out school sounds (see Chapter 1). Deutsch has developed a series of tapes in which background noise is used to mask an important sound; the volume of the background noise is gradually stepped up to sharpen the youngster's sense of discrimination. With practice, the child learns to identify the important sound and trains himself to listen to it regardless of the volume of external noises.

[1]Martin Deutsch, "The Role of Social Class in Language Development and Cognition," *American Journal of Orthopsychiatry* (January 1965), pp. 78–88.

In the Wilmington, Delaware, Three-Year Experimental Project on Schools in Changing Neighborhoods, the focus is on developing language skills through planned experience units which will help children grow in human relations sensitivities, skills, knowledge, and information. One of the media through which these units are taught is that of role playing, aloud or in pantomime. The purpose of this is to give children the opportunity to express themselves as *other* people do, through gestures, words, or a combination of both. Any child will often find the role of another person easier and more fun to deal with than his own role in life. This is especially true for children from disadvantaged backgrounds, who are sensitive as to the color of their skin, their clothes, their lack of identity. Role playing gives them a ready-made, "safe" identity, one they may choose for themselves, and yet it also opens doors into other people's lives and into their own. Role playing has many variations; "foreign characters," "real people," or even inanimate objects such as trees, clouds, and mountains. Classroom situations are rich in real character possibilities. Some of the scenes suggested by the Wilmington Project appear in Exhibit 1.

The value of this type of experience depends very much on the questions proposed by the teacher. Some questions suggested in the Wilmington Project are:

What motives did each person have for acting as he did?
How does each of the characters feel about the others?
What attitudes or actions of either of the characters would make you want him for a friend?
Do you think either of the characters would want the other for a friend? What actions caused this to be true?
Do you think other children would like the attitude of either of the characters? What made them feel this way?
How could each of the characters have acted differently?
If either of the characters had acted differently, in what way do you think the other character would have acted?[2]

Role-playing experiences of the Wilmington type not only allow for discussion and oral exchange, but make it possible for children to express themselves physically while acting out the problem; the children can build on what might be, for them, a successful means of expression (physical), at the same that language is subtly introduced through the dialogue.

[2]Questions adapted from the unpublished edition of the Wilmington, Delaware, Three-Year Experimental Project on Schools in Changing Neighborhoods, "An Adventure in Human Relations."

Exhibit 1

ROLE-PLAYING SCENES FROM THE WILMINGTON PROJECT

Walter is writing at his desk. Albert is writing, also, Albert needs an eraser. He reaches over and takes one from Walter's desk. Walter says, "Leave my eraser alone," and then slaps Albert. When Albert is hit, he hits back. A fight ensues.

A group of girls is standing near the schoolhouse. Jane arrives on the playground. She calls to the girls. The older girl, Dorothy says something to the group of girls. Then the girls run to the other end of the playground. Jane calls again, realizes she is not wanted, and walks over toward the teacher and some other girls.

Several girls and boys are playing around the tether ball. Two girls are playing against each other and several children are standing in line awaiting their turn. Alice and Janet are the first two in line, and should follow the two now playing.

Grace arrives on the playground. She runs up to her friend, Janet, and says, "Let me play against you."

Janet replies, "Sure."

Alice is annoyed and says, "Oh, no, you don't. I was here first and you are not going to get head of me."

"Shut up or I'll beat you to a pulp! I can easily beat you at this game. Grace is more my style," says Janet.

Kenny, who has been standing listening, says, "If you want to play against Janet, then why don't you both go to the end of the line?"

Janet's reply is: "Give up my place? I will not. I'm staying right here, and I'm not going to play with Baby Alice."

As Grace pushes Alice back, Alice breaks into tears and says, "It's not fair. I'm going to tell the teacher."

Source: The Wilmington, Delaware, Three-Year Experimental Project on Schools in Changing Neighborhoods, "An Adventure in Human Relations," unpublished edition. This material has now been published under the title, Adventures in Human Relations (Chicago: Follett, 1965).

One of the characteristics reportedly more common among lower-class children than middle-class children is their tendency toward physical rather than verbal communication. Miller and Swanson[3] describe lower-class children as more likely to attack problems, express feelings, and establish social relationships in physical or motor style.

The **Baltimore, Maryland, Early School Admissions Project** has the same objectives as the Wilmington Project, but it differs a little in the activities and materials. The emphasis is almost entirely on sense acuity and is developed through activities such as those listed in Exhibit 2.

The Baltimore Project utilizes a unique scheme of team teaching in which only one member of the team is a teacher from the Baltimore school system. Each project center is staffed by a teaching team of four adults: the senior teacher, the assistant teacher, the teacher aide, and a volunteer who serves on a once-a-week, rotating basis. At least three members of the team must be present daily.

The senior teacher, selected from the staff of the Baltimore City Public Schools, is a competent teacher of young children, one who is experienced and skillful in working with disadvantaged children and their parents and who enjoys working with them.

The assistant teacher is also a trained person with satisfactory work experience among young children, but she is selected from sources outside the staff of the Baltimore school system to avoid depletion of the existing school staff (private nursery schools, kindergarten, parochial schools, etc.).

The teacher aide is basically responsible for clerical work and maintaining records, but she also assists other staff members with duties that do not require teacher training.

The volunteer may or may not live in the community where the project center is located. During the academic year 1962–1963, volunteers were recruited, not from project center communities, but from the membership of three community agencies: the Baltimore Council of Parent Cooperatives, the Baltimore Section of the National Council of Jewish Women, and the Young Women's Christian Association.

Perhaps the most structured approach to the teaching of language is that of Omar K. Moore. He has reported, in a number of studies, successful experience in teaching children from cultur-

[3]D. R. Miller and G. E. Swanson, *Inner Conflict and Defense* (New York: Henry Holt, 1960).

Exhibit 2

SENSE-DEVELOPING EXPERIENCES FROM THE BALTIMORE EARLY SCHOOL ADMISSIONS PROJECT

Sense: Seeing

Observe traffic near the school to observe kinds of vehicles, size, shape, color of vehicles, and response of vehicles to traffic controls.

Observe demolition of buildings in school neighborhood to note procedures involved, machinery used, necessary personnel, and necessary safety precautions.

Visit a pet store to purchase a pet. Note variety of animals available, and care given pets. Learn about one means by which a pet is acquired.

Identify objects by sight, using size, shape, and color to assist identification.

Note details of an object.

Compare objects (size, shape, color, function).

Note gross differences in similar objects.

Note fine differences in similar objects.

Note gross and fine differences in a series of objects.

Sense: Hearing

Children who live in crowded, noisy quarters often learn to "close out" sound. Learning to listen is important.

Listen to sounds in the environment and identify their source. Describe them.

Listen to sounds made by familiar objects (ball bouncing, scissors, egg beaters, etc.).

Relate source to sound after sound is produced behind a screen.

Identify familiar songs as a result of hearing part of the melody.

With eyes closed, listen to a classmate's voice. Identify the speaker.

Identify differences in rhythm, pitch, and tempo in familiar songs and music.

Listen to tape recordings of familiar voices and identify the speaker.

Sense: Touching

Touch articles; learn to describe "feel" of surface texture.

Compare textures.

Classify objects according to texture.

After many experiences, begin to relate texture characteristics with certain materials (plastic, marble, wood, metal, etc.).

Sense: Smelling

Learn to relate odor to its source (fruits, vegetables, smoke, etc.).

Learn to note similarities and differences in odors.

Sense: Tasting

Learn to relate taste to its source (fruits, vegetables, jelly, etc.).

Source: Baltimore Public Schools, *An Early School Admissions Project* (Baltimore Public Schools, 1962). Suggestions taken from pages 38–44.

ally different and educationally deprived homes. Like Deutsch, Moore believes in starting early, but his approach is different in that he uses reading as a "self contained" method. Whereas Deutsch develops language through concept and perception formation, Moore uses the typewriter to develop language. The "talking typewriter," developed by the Thomas Edison Research Laboratories, teaches reading by programing the machine. After allowing the child to press the keys at random for a while, the program gradually becomes more structured. As the child strikes a key, the letter appears on a sheet of paper in the typewriter and is spoken by a recorded voice. After two or three sessions, the recorded voice assumes more authority; instead of repeating letters as they are struck, the voice starts to dictate them to the pupil. At this point, all keys on the typewriter lock except for the demanded letter, so the child has no choice but to strike the correct letter. In the next step, the recorded voice dictates whole words and, gradually, sentences. The learner is expected to respond by typing the words and the sentences on the machine. Another feature of this approach is that the typewriter keys are coded in eight colors and the child's fingernails are painted in corresponding colors; thus, the child learns touch-typing while he learns to read.

There may be several reasons for the success of this approach with the disadvantaged youngster: first, the tactile or physical attraction to the child of using a machine; second, the opportunity the child has to see, listen, touch, and speak, all at almost the same time; third, the sequential teaching by means of small, discrete steps, in which the child moves on only after he has responded with the correct answer. Moore's program includes another advantage—one found in all self-teaching devices—for children who do not respond well in public: errors and corrections may be made without public censure. (This is what Deutsch means when he suggests automated devices for children from "unacceptable cultures.") Moore's program deserves careful watching, as it seems to contain certain elements that are successful with children from almost all types of backgrounds.

One cannot talk about early childhood language programs without referring to the work done at the turn of the century in a slum area of Rome by Maria Montessori. Every aspect of the individual as a learner was taken into consideration. Actually, the Montessori method was a form of programed instruction in its finest sense. An independent program was established for each youngster in all areas, whether it be language or manipulative skills or social skills; he was taken in small steps from one level to another, always being allowed to rest on a plateau until he was ready to go on. Whereas Maria Montessori called this a "prepared environment," today we talk about a controlled environment. Whatever the difference in terms, it has taken us almost half a century to understand the value of this approach. There are approximately a hundred and fifty schools in this country that are presently using the Montessori method.

4

READING AND LISTENING
SKILLS IN THE EARLY GRADES

The school years begin for some children at a pre-kindergarten level and for others at kindergarten. However, for most children formal schooling begins in first grade (especially those from disadvantaged homes). For these youngsters, school should provide in this grade the many language experiences offered in the pre-kindergarten and kindergarten. They should be introduced to activities in perception, verbalization, and other experiences in the first grade.

On the other hand, the child who has had the advantage of preschool experience should not be required to repeat them but should move on in a developmental language program. The programs described in the next few pages are designed for the child who has had pre-kindergarten and kindergarten experiences.

For these children, the listening skills now take on more importance because there are more things to listen to and for. In addition, listening should be taught in connection with the other language arts—reading, writing, speaking—rather than as an isolated skill, since each is dependent upon the other.

The Department of School Services and Publications of Wesleyan University has classified listening habits into seven categories; they are as follows:

1. Attentive listening—when there is strong interest and great motivation.
2. Accurate listening—when listening is encouraged by clear-cut,

clearly understood, specific items for which to listen.

3. Critical listening—when the pupil thinks as he listens.
4. Selective listening—when a pupil listens for statements that please him or suit his purpose and tends to ignore other statements. This kind of listening can have both good or bad results.
5. Appreciative listening—when an emotional reaction is appropriate.
6. Uncomprehending listening—when a pupil hears but does not comprehend. This type of listening may be traced to a number of causes: poor attention, poor vocabulary, failure to understand concepts, limited experience background, or inadequate listening readiness.
7. Marginal listening—when "half listening," the pupil allows his attention to wander, and the teacher must pull his attention back repeatedly.[1]

These categories can be helpful to the teacher giving instruction in the listening skills. In the early grades children listen more to the teacher than to anyone else. The teacher gives directions, tells them when they are right, when they are wrong, and more important than anything else, the teacher tells them about things they know and things they do not know.

Much of this telling is done through stories that the teacher tells or reads aloud. The stories must be interesting and, for the most part, built around the world the children know. This is the period that Piaget refers to as the concrete stage of development, the time that the child responds to things he can feel, touch, see, and is familiar with. Since many of these children have never been to a zoo or an aquarium and have never had pets at home, a story about a turtle, a minnow, or a bear is meaningless. Stories should be about people who are real to them and about things they see every day—the fire pump, the water sprinkler, the garbage truck, the snowplow, the hole in the ground. Through such stories, the child will begin to develop a meaningful vocabulary, one he will recognize upon hearing it. After this point, when he has begun to feel secure with language, he is ready to move on, to experiment, to use language.

To suggest that stories should tend to involve life as the children know it does not mean they must hear *only* stories about the real and easily "seeable." It merely means that one should build upon the concrete in order to make language relate to the world around them. It is, on the contrary, of great importance that these

[1]Department of School Services and Publications, "The Improvement of Listening Skills," Curriculum Letter No. 41 (Middletown, Conn.: Wesleyan University, October 1959).

children—in view of the bleakness of their lives—hear stories that are completely in contrast to the real, stories that stir their imagination, stories that are sheer fantasy. There is always the man who grew ten feet tall, the princess who let her hair down from a tower so the prince could use it as a ladder, elves who spun yarn and saved a princess' life—these are themes that are so removed from anything possible that they put children into a never-never land of the imagination. Stories such as these free children from "rational thinking" and might open doors to divergent or creative thinking. As Wann and his colleagues point out:

> To assume . . . that those stimuli which arise from immediate phenomena or events are more pressing and challenging than others and thus warrant the elimination of the remote from consideration by children is fallacious. A well-presented television show about prehistoric animals or an overheard adult conversation about the immediacy and dire effects of another world war may present for a time a greater need for understanding by young children than the newly fallen snow or the sprouting bean seeds on the window ledge.[2]

Whatever the stories the children hear, they should be given an opportunity to react, to say what they think, to exchange views and ideas, to learn to think through listening and observing.

As we have said, teaching English to English-speaking children whose language patterns are unacceptable is not very different from teaching English to non-English-speaking children. Both groups of children will necessarily suffer from a paucity of ability to express themselves in acceptable English. At Teachers College, Columbia University, the Materials Development Project for the Teaching of English as a Second Language is being carried on, sponsored jointly by the College and the Council for Public Schools Improvement of Boston, under a grant from the United States Office of Education. The materials being developed in this project are geared to young learners, but the method is one that has tremendous potential for junior and senior high students as well.

The lesson plans are based on the assumption that communication is a twofold process: The speaker must choose expressions adequate to convey his thoughts, and the listener must understand the expressions. A teaching program will not be effective

---

[2]Kenneth D. Wann, Miriam Selchen Dorn, and Elizabeth Ann Liddle, *Fostering Intellectual Development in Young Children* (New York: Teachers College Press, Teachers College, Columbia University, 1962), p. 39.

unless it can deal with both halves of the process. The lessons will be designed for use with small groups of students. Each new expression will be learned, and the learning evaluated, by means of activities and games. For example, after a series of new expressions is meaningfully introduced and drilled by the teacher, one student in the group is shown a picture and is expected to respond by using the appropriate expression. The listening students then perform some physical action to indicate their comprehension of the expression. Thus, both production and comprehension occur in a meaningful situation, and both are evaluated. This process by which nonverbal means of communication are used to stimulate understanding is an excellent motivating factor in leading into reading and writing experiences. For the disadvantaged youngster, it capitalizes on his abilities to perform in areas other than reading and writing, and then builds on these abilities.

Another program based on the philosophy that English is a second language for children from disadvantaged homes is the **Dade County, Florida, Language Program.** When, starting in 1959, thousands of Cuban refugees began settling in Florida, Miami suddenly found itself with the problem of teaching English as a second language. Pauline Rojas, Director of Reading for the Dade County School System, has developed, with the help of a Ford Foundation grant, the *Miami Linguistic Readers,* a modified linguistic approach, wherein reading, speaking, and writing of English are taught almost concurrently.

The Cuban youngsters reacted so well to the material that Dr. Rojas, in order to discover whether the approach could be applied to youngsters with other language problems, applied the series, without adaptation, to a large Negro population. These Negro children are being treated as bilingual speakers, for whom standard English is their second language. The series is based on the following postulates:

1. That the presentation of sound-symbol correspondences in beginning reading materials should be in terms of spelling patterns rather than in terms of individual letter-sound correspondences.
2. That the child must learn to read by structures if he is to master the skills involved in the act of reading.
3. That grammatical structures as well as vocabulary must be controlled.
4. That the materials must reflect the natural language forms of children's speech. [See Figure 1, p. 56.]

```
┌─────────────────────────────────────────────┐
│          Structure                          │
│ Is (this, that) a (cat, dog, etc.)?         │
│ Yes, it is. No, it isn't.                   │
│ (This, That) isn't a (cat).                 │
│ It is a (dog).                              │
│ Is (the pig) (in, on, under) the (chair)?   │
│ Yes, it is. No, it isn't.                   │
│ (The cat) (is, isn't) (on) the (table).     │
└─────────────────────────────────────────────┘
```

Figure 1.

5. That the content of beginning reading materials must deal with those things which time has shown are truly interesting to children. An example of this is that the characters are all animals that behave like human beings. Children are fascinated by this since this is just one level above animism.
6. That the learning load in linguistically oriented materials must be determined in terms of the special nature of the materials.
7. That the child must have aural-oral control of the materials he is expected to read.
8. That writing experiences reinforce listening, speaking, and reading.
9. That the materials must be so selected and organized that they will enable the learner to achieve success as he progresses through the materials.[3]

Around these nine premises is built a body of organized, sequential materials that provide the pupils with systematic practice on the essentials of the language. The pupils practice listening to and speaking the content to be read before they read it. They later reinforce the oral and reading practices by writing. However, the language learning experiences of pupils who use these materials are not limited to this structured program. They also participate in unstructured English-language activities during the larger part of the school day. (See Figure 2.) A large body of "uncontrolled" books (i.e., books on a variety of subjects, with reading material that offers the youngster an opportunity to apply his newly acquired knowledge of spelling and grammatical structure) is made available to them. They read uncontrolled books in the other subject areas as well. In addition, they use English for communication, to the extent that they are able, in a variety of out-of-class situations, clubs, school social functions, and ath-

[3]Adapted from the *Teachers Manual* for the *Miami Linguistic Readers,* experimental edition (Miami: Board of Public Instruction, 1964), pp. i, ii. This material has now been revised for final publication by D. C. Heath.

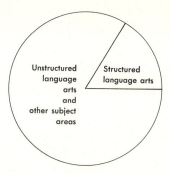

Figure 2.

letics. This unstructured language practice can be expected to give the pupil an understanding of English far beyond his ability to speak, read, and write it.

It is the combination of modern linguistic science, the interesting and almost profound content of the reading materials, and the planned opportunities to extend their use of language through out-of-class experiences that makes this such a promising program. It is really the type of eclectic approach that we have been wrongly crediting to many traditional reading programs.

Another method that might have merit for the child for whom the school language is a "second language" is the **Initial Teaching Alphabet** method. Basically, it is a plan that modifies the phonic system, using forty-six letter-symbols instead of the twenty-six in our alphabet (see Figure 3, p. 58). It stresses each distinct sound by means of only one representative letter; it removes confusion from the already confused listening skills of the child. It is sequential in small step-by-step levels. It leads the youngster into a successful experience before he moves on to the next step or level.

The "Early-to-Read Series" is the official publication of the protagonists of the Initial Teaching Alphabet (i/t/a) method.[4] Since using a forty-six sound alphabet does not preclude recognizing whole words, this program has the advantages of both the phonic and the "look-say" methods.

However, as promising as this method is, there are still many unanswered questions. For example, when the time comes for "transfer back" to the twenty-six letter alphabet, will it be too diffi-

[4]Harold J. Tanyzer and Albert J. Mazurkiewicz, "Early-to-Read Series" (New York: i/t/a Publications, 1963).

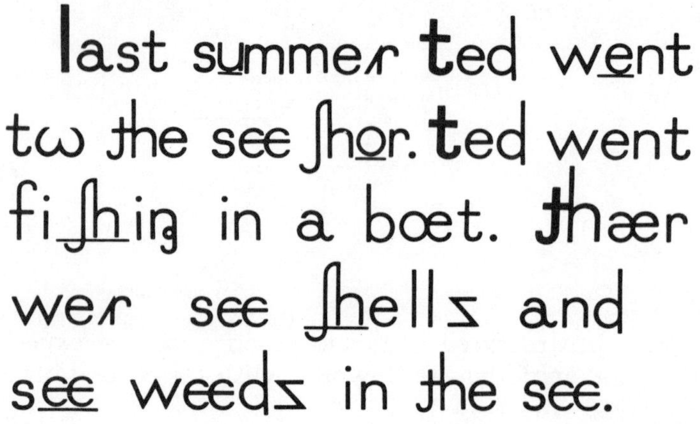

last summer ted went
tω ϳhe see ʃhor. ted went
fiʃhiŋ in a bœt. ϳhær
wer see ʃhellʒ and
see weedʒ in ϳhe see.

Figure 3. A paragraph written in the forty-six letter alphabet. Reproduced from Harold J. Tanyzer and Albert J. Mazurkiewicz, *Teachers Manual and Key for Books 2 and 3,* "Early-to-Read Series" (New York: i/t/a Publications, 1963), p. 13.

cult? Doesn't this program negate almost everything we know in learning theory? Is it not wrong to learn something that we must then unlearn?

Whereas some of the programs described in this section are developing their own texts, others are using the newer commercial texts. As with all "new directions," many publishers have suddenly "jumped on the bandwagon" and are busily changing the color of the faces in the basal reader figures, dressing up a few concepts, and coming out with "integrated" reading series. There is value and merit in and need for such series or individual trade books, but school people should be wary of superficial changes and the inclination to create stereotypes.

The "Detroit Public Schools Reading Series" (Great Cities Program), published by Follett, is a move in the direction of integrated texts. However, they have fallen into the trap of simply changing the pictures from a suburban white family to a suburban Negro family. The vocabulary, the concepts, and the structure have not changed, to any perceptible degree, from the traditional basal readers.

Macmillan has begun publishing a series entitled "Bank Street Readers," which aims at discarding the stereotype. On the drawing board since 1962, the series will be completed in 1966 and will provide a complete set of reading materials for grades 1 through 3. Presently available are two preprimers, *In the City* and *People Read,* a primer, *Around the City,* and a first reader, *Uptown and Downtown.* A second reader, *My City,* is scheduled for publication in February 1966.

Even at first glance, these new books have extraordinary appeal for children. They picture brightly colored metropolitan skylines, riverboats, airplanes, city streets with cars and traffic lights. Laundry is strung out between fire escapes. The books portray city people, not merely as "black and white," but with hints of many different complexions and features.

The "Bank Street Readers" have some disadvantages as well. The vocabulary is still extremely limited (twenty-eight words in the preprimer), causing the phrases to seem repetitious and dull. *In the City* lacks a coherent story and, except for the illustrations, differs little from the traditional reader. However, they must be credited with an improved introduction to language usage. Plurals and punctuation have been added, and there is a slight attempt at introducing pattern structure. John Niemeyer, president of Bank Street College, says that the purpose of the book is to break with books in which the typical American family consisted of "father, mother, dog and two or three exemplary children." He points to the new books as a literary meeting place of children and people "who—whatever their skin color, social status or economic position—think, feel and dream" just as the little boy or girl in school does. At last, "the urban child will meet himself."[5]

As attractive as these books are, and as appealing as they may be to children from different cultures, they may be leading us too far afield. Simply mirroring city life for the child who lives in it every day, can confine his interest to the present and the tangible. These books, have merit only as "springboards." Although we want to build upon the real and the concrete, we also want to open up new worlds, new discoveries, new possibilities. Urban readers can threaten this goal if used too often and for too long a period.

[5]Cited by Fred Hechinger, *The New York Times,* Sunday Education Section (January 24, 1965).

5

MOTIVATING EXPERIENCES
IN THE MIDDLE YEARS

As the student moves further along in his school career, he moves farther away from "the sun." Almost all the energy presently being put into the curriculum is directed toward the lower grades. This would be perfectly understandable if the sole concern were to begin the program at the "best" time, in terms of a child's age and development. However, the child inevitably moves out of the warm, rich environment of the early grades, and he will lose much if the middle and upper grades do not keep pace. Thus, instead of losing these children in first grade, we lose them in fourth, seventh, or tenth grade. It is therefore imperative that programs be developed for the middle and upper grades—not remedial, or "dropout" programs, but developmental program that will continue any excellent work begun in the early grades.

The curriculum for the middle and upper grades must meet still another challenge: the needs of the youngster who has not had the advantages of a rich and full curriculum in the early grades.

Yet, despite the obvious need, the programs developed by universities and school systems for the middle grades seem to offer little that is really new or different. Are we not performing a disservice to the child in giving him a head start at the beginning of his school career and then chaining him to an outmoded curriculum in the middle grades? Children from middle-class home environments are exposed to newspapers, magazines, adventure stories, dinner conversation, television and radio news-casts, and other educational experiences. For these children, such activities help fill the gap faced by the less fortunate students whose parents have not had the time or education to supplement the barren curriculum of the middle grades—sometimes referred to as the "desert years." However, there is much evidence that *all* children—regardless of background—could profit from better stimulation during this period. It is interesting to note, in most of the current studies, that creativity appears to take a dip at about fourth grade. Torrance[1] suggests that children unnecessarily sacrifice their creativity—go into a slump—at about the fourth grade. Because of this, we lose much valuable talent, and many problems (mental apathy, delinquency, etc.) begin to develop.

In another project, Torrance[2] says that this slump is not purely developmental, but is man-made or culturally made. If this be the case, might there not be a high correlation between the lack of interesting, well-structured language programs and a slump in original thinking?

Recently, there have been a number of studies concerning special materials and programs to develop creative learning for the normal and gifted youngsters. Could not some of these approaches be applied to the culturally disadvantaged youngster, since he certainly, as much as if not more than other children, needs stimulation and "awakening"? The **Programmed Experiences in Creative Thinking Study,** at the University of Minnesota, bases its program on extending and refining the listening skills in the middle years. A team of investigators, under a United States Office of Education grant, is preparing *Programmed Experiences in Creative Thinking.*[3] They have developed a set of audio tapes or discs and lessons designed for fourth grade use (basing their grade placement on the studies of fourth grade slump in crea-tivity). An example of how these are used to "stretch the imagina-tion" and to stimulate children to listen to sounds appears in Exhibit 3. (See p. 62.)

[1]E. Paul Torrance, *Education and the Creative Potential* (Minneapolis: University of Minnesota Press, 1963).

[2]E. Paul Torrance, *Guiding Creative Talent* (Englewood Cliffs, N.J., Pren-tice-Hall, 1962).

[3]E. Paul Torrance and Ram Gupta, *Programmed Experiences in Creative Thinking* (Minneapolis: Bureau of Educational Research, College of Educa-tion, University of Minnesota, February 1964).

Exhibit 3
STIMULATING LISTENING SKILLS WITH SOUNDS

SOUNDS AND IMAGES, FORMS I AND II
(Without Word Cues)

Narrator:

Today, you and I are going to do something a little different together, we're going to listen to sounds. At least one of these sounds may be familiar to you, and you'll probably recognize it straight off. The other sounds, though, are going to seem rather strange, and you'll likely scratch your head a bit as you wonder what they might be.

Now, this recording contains four separate sounds. Each sound will be repeated three times. As you listen to these sounds, try to picture them in your mind. Then—write them down. Some of them, however, you won't recognize at all. You'll probably have a little trouble in picturing and describing them. These are the sounds I want you to use your imagination on, and write down the word pictures they make you think of.

Before you now is a sheet of paper [Figure 4] on which has been printed 12 rectangles or squares. Your job is to write down in these spaces the word pictures each sound suggests to you. For example, let's say that the first sound you hear suggests the ringing of an alarm clock. Your job would be to describe the sound that way, in the top row. This row is labeled "A," and that first space is labeled "Sound One." Now, let's say that the second sound you hear might suggest the noise of breaking glass. So, you would describe it that way in the second space, in the Space Number Two. Get it? When you have heard all four sounds . . . and described each one . . . you will have filled in all the spaces in the top row. Then, the four sounds will be repeated again, and you will describe each one by filling in the four spaces across the second row, which is labeled row "B." Finally, the four sounds will be repeated once more, and this time, you will describe them by filling in the four spaces in the bottom row, labeled row "C."

Does it sound complicated? Actually, it will really be quite simple, and fun too, once we get going. Now, let's listen to those four sounds. There will be a brief period of silence between each of them, so that you will have time to describe each one. The first sound will be easy to describe, but the others are a bit mysterious, and are guaranteed to make you stop and wonder. As you listen to them, use your imagination while writing down the word pictures these sounds suggest to you. The chances are, the sounds will also call up many different feelings, and hold onto them long enough to write them down. Remember—write down your impression of each sound, as it occurs in the recording. As you listen, fill in the spaces from left to right across row "A"—the top row. Here we go, then, into the mysterious world of sound!

Sounds (each followed by a brief pause)

I'll bet that first sound was easy to describe, while the others really made you

	Sound 1	Sound 2	Sound 3	Sound 4
Name_____Date_____				
Form: I_____II_____Age_____Educ. Status_____				
A				
B				
C				

Figure 4

do some thinking. Now then, take your paper, and carefully fold it back along the top row, so that you have covered your answers. If you folded it correctly, row "B" should now appear at the top of the page. You see, I am going to play those sounds again, exactly as before. Only this time I want different answers from you . . . and I don't want you to spoil the fun for yourself by peeking at your old answers.

I want you now to let your imagination FLY this time, so that even everyday sounds will take on new meanings for you. Thus, the thunderstorm may now seem to suggest something altogether different to you—something wild and wonderful. And, as for those other sounds—they will suggest other things to you now, too— provided you let your imagination really soar, high as the sky. As you listen, fill in the next set of spaces from left to right across row "B." All set? Here we go again into the world of sound!

Exhibit 3 (Continued)

Sounds repeated

Did you get something new this time by letting your imagination wander further afield? Well, if you did, the chances are you had quite a bit of fun in the process.

Now, take your paper—and, once again, carefully fold it back along the next row, so that you have covered your last answers. If you folded it correctly, row "C" should now appear at the top of the page. We're going to listen to those sounds once more now . . . and this time, the sky's the limit, for I want you to push the walls of your imagination out as far as they'll possibly go. Thus, that thunderstorm may now seem to suggest something totally different to you than it did on either of the other two rounds. And those other sounds will suggest more interesting things—provided, of course, that your imagination is alert and ready. Just remember—the further you let your imagination carry you, the more fun you'll have. And as you listen, fill in the last set of spaces from left to right in row "C." Are you ready? Here we go once more, then, into the wonderful world of sound!

Sounds

I'll bet your answers this time REALLY had a different twist! Now then: Take a look at all 12 of your answers. I want you to choose from them the one answer which you think is the most interesting of all—and put a dark circle around it. Then, draw or paint a picture about that answer. And, if you have time, write a story to go with it. Be very careful to choose the one answer you think is the most unusual, though, because the more unusual the answer, the more unusual will be your picture or your story. And the more fun you'll have in the long run. Have a good time, now—and good luck!

Source: Sounds and Images: Teachers' Guide and Recorded Text, pp. 15–17, by B. F. Cunningham and E. P. Torrance, published and copyrighted by Ginn and Company, 1965.

This type of lesson is not unrelated to the Deutsch approach in the preschool years. It is an extension of auditory discrimination when the sounds are familiar. But it goes farther. It literally "stretches" the abilities, saying to the youngster, "Some sounds you won't recognize at all. These are the sounds I want you to use your imagination on." This approach invites flights of imagination. It sets no standards, no benchmarks. "No matter what your answer is, you are right." The lesson requires not only listening, following directions, and recording, but also art representation and composition; moreover, it provides a delightful experience for the students. Children from disadvantaged homes need such motivating experiences—ones that have no boundaries to start

Exhibit 4

**PUPIL-SUGGESTED PROBLEM SITUATIONS
(THE MILWAUKEE PROGRAM)**

If I could improve enything, I would first improve all the trouble in the South.

I'll get all the teachers of the southern states, both color and white, and try to explain that in order for us to have a free world and have other countries respect us, we must stop fighting among ourselves.

When they understand, they will start to live like brother and sister.

My first wish is that everyone in the world will get their rights.

Source: Milwaukee School System, *The English Language Arts Program in the Junior High School* (Milwaukee, Wis., The School System, 1962).

with and for which they need no special training or skill, yet experiences that slowly lead up to a structured lesson in which skills can be taught.

Very few programs have attempted, in any planned or structured fashion, to discuss with young children the immediate problems of the world around *them*. Integration is an adult war (although it very often employs children as ammunition). The developers of the **Milwaukee, Wisconsin, English Language Arts Program in the Junior High School** are using an interesting approach; they are combining current problems with the understanding of language. Problem situations are either offered by the teacher or, if possible, drawn from the students. All of the English language arts skills are taught *within* this problem situation. This differs from the familiar "problem" approach only in that the problems are real, not superimposed by a course of study. Some examples of the problem situations offered by pupils, as reported in the Milwaukee Program, are illustrated in Exhibit 4.

Similar programs are being developed for older children and will be discussed later in this chapter, but Milwaukee is practically unique in offering this approach to young children.

Two other areas show promise in the middle grades: the use of textbooks and trade books and the introduction of programed instruction. Children from disadvantaged homes need pride in themselves, a feeling of identification with something or someone important. Too many of these children are told that they will grow up "no good, like your father." This becomes the image—almost a self-fulfilling prophecy. They definitely need someone to be proud of. Some of this feeling can be given to children through books, books about their heritage, about their people's contribution to the building of this country. One of the first attempts in this area has been Doubleday's "Zenith Series on Minorities." Seventy-five books, written at the fifth- to sixth-grade levels, are being written by outstanding historians on the history and contributions of minorities in this country. The first four have already been published: *Worth Fighting For, A Glorious Age in Africa, A Guide to African History,* and *Lift Every Voice.* (It will become obvious to the reader, in reading Chapters 7, 8, 9, and 10, that these books have great relevance to history and the social sciences.)

Textbook publishers have been extremely loath to publish books —either fiction or nonfiction—involving minority groups. Social studies textbooks have been notorious in their inaccuracies about the role of the Negro in American life, in both commission and omission. Equally negligent treatment has been given the minority groups in English language arts textbooks and trade books.

Charles E. Merrill has published a programed series, "Building Reading Power," for pupils reading on the fifth grade level. This was developed through working with a population of disadvantaged children in New York City and was specifically designed to improve reading comprehension. It is comprised of three separate sections: Context Clues, Structural Analysis, and Comprehension Skills. The subject matter is sophisticated and current, in contrast to the subject matter of many basic reading textbooks, and, thus, can be used effectively with children who, although disadvantaged in academic areas, are nonetheless mature in real-life situations. The Merrill program has the advantages of all programed material: allowing a student to go at his own pace, recognizing and reinforcing him when he is right, and correcting him immediately when he is wrong. There are also disadvantages: the possibility of boredom, the possibility of standardization by giving all students the same program, and the possibility of the program becoming the sole tutor.

6

ADVANCING

IN COMMUNICATION SKILLS

The titles of books in English language arts are often misleading. "Upper-grade reading material," especially, is a rather nebu-
lous term. A book may be labeled "Grade 7," "Grade 8," or "Grade
9," but it usually turns out to be closer to the fourth- or fifth-grade
level in terms of difficulty and interest. As the child grows older
and moves further along in school, the gap widens between the
advantaged and the disadvantaged; the differences become more
outstanding. Children in the lower grades are more alike than
different; it is the older youngsters who become more different
than alike, as cultural and educational differences become more
pronounced. However, it can be hoped that the new, enriched,
early programs now available in the schools, together with a
movement toward a similar extension in the middle grades, will
lessen these differences in the upper grades.

We do not mean to suggest, of course, that no programs whatever are being developed for the older student. One of the more
important ones is "Gateway English," developed by the **Project
English Curriculum Study Center** at Hunter College, New York
City, under a grant from the United States Office of Education.
The objective of the program is to develop English language arts
materials for seventh through ninth grades for children in disadvantaged urban areas. These materials are for students whose
abilities in English have been diminished because of environmental disadvantages. The program is not geared to the clinical

and remedial aspects of reading. It is aimed at those who have remained in the mainstream, who go through the motions of reading, but whose reading abilities are generally two or three grades below their grade levels.

The materials produced by Hunter College are complete curriculum units. Each unit emphasizes problem solving as a means of learning, and each is organized with a problem situation as its theme. These themes are judged to be of great interest to the underprivileged (largely minority-group) adolescents who are the project's concern. For example, aware of the need of these youngsters to develop a wholesome self-concept, the developers have entitled one unit *Who Am I?* The unit is based on the assumption that the school must play an increasingly important role in helping junior high school pupils meet the unresolved problems of childhood. The concepts emphasized in this unit are variously described by such terms as "self-concept," "self-image," and, frequently, simply as "self." Within the context of this unit the term "self-concept" is intended to mean the sum total of the individual's thoughts, feelings, beliefs, commitments, and values. Through the careful examination of the characters in the fiction included in the unit, the pupils are expected to improve their self-concepts and make progress toward the development of personal integrity, self-respect, and self-confidence.

Developmental reading and work-study skills are presented in the reading materials and learning activities of this project. In most cases, the reading skill is incorporated in the problem for pupil inquiry and in the questions and activities after each story. Word-attack skills are utilized in developing vocabulary for writing and discussion. Drill work in developmental reading skills has been deliberately avoided, and high-level critical reading and thinking skills have been emphasized instead.

Additional stories have been selected in case a particular story proves unsuitable for use with a particular class. These include fictional and factual material dealing with other minority groups, for which they may be substituted. The unit, however, has clearly stated objectives. Again, you will notice the combination of interesting reading material plus understandings, values, and skills. These objectives are stated below:

I. Understandings:
    A. What self-concept is.
    B. How self-concept is developed.

    C. How self-concept influences attitudes, feelings, beliefs, commitments.

    D. How family, friends, and community influence self-concept.

    E. How ethnic background contributes to self-concept.

II. Values:

    A. Appreciates others for qualities of character.

    B. Appreciates dignity of individual.

    C. Appreciates contributions people of all ethnic background make to the nation.

III. Skills

    A. Distinguishes main and minor characters.

    B. Identifies methods used to develop character.

    C. Recognizes sequence of events in story.

    D. Recognizes author's theme or purpose (generalization).

    E. Writes a topic sentence with controlling idea.

    F. Writes brief paragraphs of description and narration.

    G. Writes brief paragraphs of exposition: cause and effect, description.

    H. Prepares and delivers short oral compositions.

    I. Improves skill in oral reading and interpretation.

    J. Improves skill in selecting appropriate words for written and oral activities.[1]

The following materials are suggested for use in the unit, *Who Am I?*

1. "The World of Happy Differences," a filmstrip produced by the Friendship Press, New York City, with script and adequate instructions for teacher. Purpose of the filmstrip is to develop experience background and necessary concepts to understand the unit.

2. "As You See It," by Catherine E. Steltz. Twenty-four pictures of children, young adults, adults to stimulate group discussions and role playing of social and moral problems.

3. Pictures of junior high and senior high school youth, collection of newspaper and magazine pictures for class study and writing.

4. Magazine and newspaper articles about youth, a collection of magazine and newspaper articles featuring both good and bad activities of youth for classroom study, discussion and analysis.

5. "Giovanni and the Narrowback," by Edward Fenton. A short story about a high school boy who struggles for acceptance in a new school and community.

6. "Jam Session at Abby's," by Helen C. Gregutt. A short story about a girl in the Brooklyn tenement, also striving for acceptance.

7. The Trouble with Johnny. A one-act play about a boy who is discriminated against by fellow students because of his nationality and social class.

[1]Project English Curriculum Study Center, *Teachers Manual* for use with *Who Am I?* "Gateway English" (New York: Hunter College, 1965), pp. 2–3.

8. "Horatio," by George Felsen. A short story about a poet.
9. "The Wise And Weak," by Philip Aponte, a New York City high school student. A short story about a lower Manhattan gang initiation.
10. "The Powerless Ones," by Yvette Patterson, a high school student. A short story about a high school girl and her reactions to the news that her father and mother are separating.
11. "All the Years of Her Life," by Morley Callaghan. A short story about a teenage boy who gets caught stealing from his employer and is saved from embarrassment by his father.
12. "Achilles Deatheridge" by Edgar Lee Masters. A poem about a young soldier who almost kills General Grant for failing to identify himself.
13. "Little Brown Boy" by Ralph Melendes, a high school pupil. A courageous poem urging support for civil rights.
14. "Little Brown Boy" by Helen Johnson. A poem expressing the beauty of Negro music.
15. "Mother to Son" by Langston Hughes. A poem expressing a mother's courageous determination to carry on in spite of hardships and her advice to her son to carry on the fight for success.
16. "Benediction" by Georgia Douglas Johnson. A poem urging continuation of fight for dignity and freedom.
17. "To James" by Frank Horne. A poem encouraging Negroes to fight for equality and freedom.[2]

The lessons in Exhibit 5 demonstrate how the teacher uses the story or film or poem as a basis for teaching specific skills, values, and understandings.

Another useful aspect of "Gateway English" is that it helps teachers learn to create their own materials. The paucity of materials for the "older" disadvantaged youngster, along with the slowness of publishers to provide the kind of materials these youngsters need, makes it more and more evident that teachers must learn to produce many of their own materials, especially in the middle and upper grades. "Gateway English" has attempted to create some guidelines for creating materials, emphasizing the need for logical sequence; the necessity of contrasting the real and the fictional, yet including both; and, primarily, the importance of highly interesting, "fast-moving" materials. Also noteworthy is the fact that, in almost every guideline, there is a reference to skills—but skills taught through the content and not in a vacuum. These guidelines are summarized below:

1. The interests and experiences of the learner delimit the possi-

[2]*Ibid.*, pp. 3-4. The sources for reading materials in the above list are given in *Who Am I?* "Gateway English," p. iii.

Exhibit 5

LESSON PLANS FOR *WHO AM I?* ("GATEWAY ENGLISH")

Lessons 1, 2, and 3:

Motivation: Establishing concepts; building experience background; vocabulary preparation.

Writing a topic sentence; forms of support for an idea.

Lessons 4 and 5:

"Giovanni and the Narrowback"

Spelling; word-attack skills; reading to answer specific questions; reading to frame generalizations; characterization; author's purpose; theme; conflict; problem. Definition.

Lesson 6: (Optional lessons are 6a, 6b, 6c, and 6d.)

Picture analysis; observation skill; using the senses; describing a person, place, object, event.

Writing a description.

Lessons 7, 8, and 9:

Reading and analysis of newspaper and magazine articles.

Writing cause and effect paragraphs.

Improving listening and discussion.

Lesson 10:

Speaking; preparing and delivering oral compositions.

Criteria for evaluating oral presentations.

Lesson 11:

Evaluating one's personality and character.

Lesson 12:

Identifying three "selfs."

Lessons 13 and 14:

"Jam Session at Abby's": characterization; author's theme and purpose; identifying main character; identifying character's problem or conflict.

Reading to answer specific questions; vocabulary extension.

Writing descriptions of persons pupils know.

Lesson 15:

The Trouble with Johnny: characteristics of a play; differences between play and prose fiction; problems of staging, directing, and casting for a play.

Interpretive reading.

Lesson 16:

"Horatio": characterization; problem.

Writing character descriptions.

Lesson 17:

"The Wise and the Weak": review of aspects of fiction.

Lesson 18:

"The Powerless Ones": application of principles of interpretation; oral reading; discussion techniques.

Lessons 19, 20, 21, 22, 23, and 24:

Poetry (one day allotted for reading and discussion of each poem): idea in poem; poet's use of words; imagery; figures of speech.

Source: Project English Curriculum Study Center, *Teachers Manual* for use with *Who Am I?* "Gateway English" (New York: Hunter College, 1965), pp. 5–6.

bilities of organization. The writer must know in advance what abilities and expectations his reader will bring to the page.

2. A simple and logical plan of organization should be obvious in the finished material. The bones of structure must show, in the form of sub-heads, topic sentences, etc., if the reader is to relate the parts into a meaningful whole. Particularly if the material is factual, a direct, no-nonsense approach is best. The material should have a single over-all theme and proceed with the clarity of an outline. Excessive motivation, "interesting" asides, and literary devices such as flashbacks are usually to be avoided.

3. Conventional distinctions between fact and fiction tend to blur for the poor reader. The culturally deprived child finds, in fiction a large amount of the general information he lacks. On the other hand, he can often be made interested in factual material by the deliberate use of fictional techniques, such as personification, dramatization, and suspense. One of the abilities this reader often lacks, in fact, is the ability to distinguish between fiction and fact.

4. Whenever possible, the general should be presented in terms of the specific. The policeman's day, for instance, is vastly more interesting than the functions of the police department.

5. Incidental humor should be used with caution. Reading is a serious and often grim business to this student. Much of the humor in conventional materials is lost simply because nothing can be "funny" that requires effort of understanding. This does not mean, however, that the light touch cannot be attained. There is a broad general area between pure pie-in-the-face slapstick (which the student likes), and the subtleties of wit (which his teacher likes). Within this area, amusing incidents can arise out of the characteristics of humorous people, but these incidents should be obvious and extended, not incidental.

6. The beginning must arouse the student's interest or curiosity. It should do this as quickly and as briefly as possible. A good beginning is a necessity. It need not, of course, be written first.

7. As a preliminary check on organization, it is helpful to think through the material from the standpoint of a reluctant reader. This procedure will often disclose poor sequences, rough transitions, and omitted or superfluous material. Time spent here will often preclude extensive revision.

8. The slow reader is used to the narrative pace of television, motion pictures, and speech. One reason for his dissatisfaction with conventional materials is that he cannot read fast enough to maintain the pace he finds emotionally satisfying. For this reason, materials written especially for him must move quickly. The writer must strip his material to its essential features, omitting lengthy descriptions, etc.

9. In his struggle for simplicity, however, the writer must be careful not to omit what is necessary to bring the material within the "life space" of the child. *Time* and *place* should be made explicit, for the culturally deprived child is deficient in temporal and geographical understandings. He often fails to respond to conventional clues within

the context of the material itself. For example, mention of blue and gray uniforms and reference to General Lee will not suffice to signal "Civil War . . . United States . . . 100 years ago." These things must be stated—and often repeated.

10. The style should be vivid, simple, and direct. The reader's "suspension of disbelief" is facilitated by the use of real people in actual situations. Fantasy, if used, should be so fantastic that the reader knows exactly what distortions or reality he is asked to make. Stereotypes must often be used, but even here the writer cannot assume that the reader will be familiar with the stereotype at first meeting.

11. Similarly, the poor reader is not familiar with other "signals" obvious to the average child. The writer must often pause to make emotions and plot questions explicit:

> John opened his eyes wide. His mouth dropped open. *He was very, very surprised.* "What will happen to Dirty Sam now?" he asked himself.

12. Transitions in time, space, and ideational content must be made obvious. They should be anticipated and spanned as smoothly as possible, since the reluctant interest often tends to wane when shifted.

13. Metaphors are useful, but if they are to add to the material the vehicle must be meaningful and not misleading to the child. Even *threadbare* metaphors can throw the inexperienced reader *off stride* and become *bottlenecks.*

14. Every story has an end. If the writer stops as soon as he can after the climax of his story, leaving the reader wanting more, a positive attitude is established toward the next reading experience.[3]

"Gateway English" has much merit because of its focus on important themes and its awareness of the specific needs of these youngsters. However, the developers have a tendency now and then to fall back to a remedial approach. If this comes through as the main purpose of the program, it will soon lose its effectiveness for the disadvantaged.

The University of Florida is developing a program for students whom they refer to as the "linguistically untalented." The objective of this program is to raise the child's threshold of experience by introducing new feelings and new thoughts. The program's thematic units will represent four basic human relationships: man and duty; man and other men; man and nature; and man and himself. Six "thematic categories" have been established:

---

[3]These fourteen objectives were selected from Robert R. Potter, *Developing Original Materials in Reading: A Guide for Teachers* (New York: Hunter College Project English Curriculum Center, 1965), pp. 9–17. Numbers added by the present authors.

"Men in Action"; "The Unknown"; "Decisions"; "Teamwork"; "Frontiers and Horizons"; and "Human Relations." Each year one specific unit relating to each of these general categories will be taught. Under "Man in Action," for example, will be "Man and nature" (seventh grade), "Man among enemies" (eighth grade), and "Man alone" (ninth grade). Literature is more or less the center of focus in this curriculum, but language study is involved, with varying stress, in each unit.

Similar to this series, *The American Challenge* is the **New Rochelle, New York, School System's Program.** It is primarily a social studies program, the theme being American and world history; but the selected materials are appropriate to the English curriculum as well as to social studies. This, like the University of Florida series, is based on values, ideas, and problems. In addition, each unit is followed by "Let's See What You've Learned," a group of questions that combine the social studies and English language arts skills. Exhibit 6 is a short skit aimed at dramatizing the protection of the citizen against excessive bails, excessive fines, and cruel and unusual punishments as stated in the Eighth Amendment to the Constitution (Article VIII of the Bill of Rights). The "Let's See What You've Learned" section that follows the skit can be used to initiate class discussion. The program is less structured than "Gateway English" inasmuch as "skills" are not stressed, but are incidental to the subject matter. However, as interesting as this material may seem, it can easily be overdone. Too great an emphasis on current problems can tip the scales and put things out of perspective. It has the tendency to be "enclosing." What is needed is a combination of this type of material and a study of the courts and the law or a study of the development of group action against government; this will avoid "enclosing" and produce an enlarging and "opening" experience.

The experimenting institutes, publishers, and individuals described in this section could be categorized, in developing programs, as having put their emphasis on what they think will interest children from disadvantaged homes. The materials are problem centered, tend to emphasize the real and the concrete, and, for the most part, are tailored for the disadvantaged. In contrast, the language programs to be discussed in the remainder of this chapter have been developed for the average and the bright youngster. These programs do not take into consideration, for example, the problems of the poor or their language disabilities.

Exhibit 6
UTILIZING A PROBLEM SITUATION
(THE NEW ROCHELLE PROGRAM)

"A Sweet Kind of Justice"

The Scene: A small, dirty cellar jail, dimly lighted and damp, in any town in Mussus-suppu. Two men stand face to face. One is a Negro; the other is a white man with a badge pinned on his shirt. A set of heavy iron bars separate the two men.

Sheriff: Now you listen here, nigger! You ain't got no rights no more. You had your fair trial and you was found guilty!

Thompson: You call that mockery of justice a fair trial? I had a drunk for a lawyer and a jury that publicly stated I was guilty before the trial began.

Sheriff: Well, it's true that the eminent defense lawyer does take a few once a day, but just because he was throwed out of law school doesn't make him a bad lawyer . . . that's all you're worth anyway!

Thompson: That's a laugh and what about that jury?

Sheriff: Nigger—those men are white and they're entitled to their opinion . . . what's the difference if they decided before or after the trial?

Thompson: Is that what you call justice? Is that your idea of innocent until proven guilty?

Sheriff: As far as you're concerned—it sure is!

Thompson: What happened to my rights as a citizen? Have you ever heard of the protection of individual rights?

Sheriff: Boy, your kind ain't got no rights because your kind ain't no good.

Thompson: I was good enough to get wounded in Korea.

Sheriff: Now ain't that too bad.

Thompson: How long am I suppose to rot in this hell hole?

Sheriff: You heard the honorable judge—$5,000 or five years, and we all know that your kind couldn't raise 5¢.

Thompson: How about giving me a chance to use the telephone?

Sheriff: You know something, boy—the phone just went out of order.

Thompson: You're really a pillar of justice, aren't you?

Sheriff: You shut your mouth, black boy, or I'll teach you what my kind of justice really is!

Thompson: The bruises you put all over my body are enough evidence of that already!

Sheriff: Why you dirty no-good-for-nothing nigger, I'll break every bone in . . .

Policeman: *(Running down the steps and breaking into the sheriff's threat.)* Hey sheriff! There's a couple of guys upstairs who want to see you. I think it's important!

Sheriff: Tell them to get lost! I'm busy.

Policeman: I think you better see them, Sheriff, they're flashing federal credentials and they want some action!

Exhibit 6 *(Continued)*

Sheriff: Those damn Feds—they'll never learn to stop meddling in our local affairs. *(The two Justice Department agents enter by walking down the steps.)* Why good morning, gentlemen—welcome to our beloved city!

First Federal Agent: Sheriff, let's kick the formalities. We haven't much time so open the door and let Thompson out!

Sheriff: Now just who the hell do you think you are—coming down here and toying with our local justice?

Second Federal Agent: Well, Sheriff, let's look at your local kind of justice. First: Thompson did not have a proper defense. Second: A predetermined jury passed judgment on him. Third: Excessive bail was set which forced Thompson to sit here for seven months before your so-called trial. Fourth: There's the general question of cruel and unusual punishment—shall I go on?

Sheriff: *(Addressing his remarks to the policeman.)* Open this door and let this nigger out! It's better this way, anyway—look at all the money the fine people of Bigotry, Mussussuppu will save by not havin' to support the likes of this pigsmelling filth.

First Federal Agent: *(Smiling.)* Come on, Bill, let's get out of here. You've got a lot of work ahead of you supplying evidence against this fine system of justice.

Second Federal Agent: By the way, Sheriff, before we go, I want you to meet William H. Thompson, Federal Agent for the Justice Department.

Sheriff: Why you dirty no good, deceiving rats—you tricked me—I got my rights—where's my lawyer?

Second Federal Agent: You'll get your chance—when we *subpoena* you for the investigation!

First Federal Agent: *(As the three men walk up the stairs the following remark is made humorously.)* Tell us something, Bill—we know you were supposed to come down here and get into trouble, but we couldn't get our hands on the statement of charges. How did this mess start in the first place?

Thompson: I committed a serious miscarriage of justice and, for a Negro in the South, it was unforgivable.

First Federal Agent: *(Humorously again.)* Well, what was it—rape, murder, or grand theft?

Thompson: I threw a cigarette butt on the sidewalk!

Let's See What You've Learned

1. Why do you think this story is entitled "A Sweet Kind of Justice?"

2. What are some of the abuses of the law that show Thompson was not treated fairly?

3. Do you like the ending of the story? Why?

4. If Thompson had been white, would you feel as terrible about his treatment? Explain.

Source: Frank Agresta and Alfred Gitlitz, "The Continuing Revolution," *The American Challenge,* Vol. I (New Rochelle, N.Y.: Board of Education, City School District, 1963), Chapter XXVII, pp. 1–4.

They do, of course, stress values, younger people's interests, and literacy, but they do it through different types of subject matter.

The content, although remote, has relevance and application in present-day life. It provides themes that "open worlds" to children and stimulate their imagination. For example, the Dallas, Texas, Independent School District, in their program, Language Arts for Secondary School, has developed a unit for tenth graders called "Mythology and Its Influence upon Modern Times." In their overview they state that, in addition to its influence upon the English language, mythology has its place in the scientific and business world. Its influence upon modern science may be seen in scientific terminology. This is particularly true of astronomy; the student in this field better understands the planets and constellations if he has some knowledge of the divinities for whom they are named. Even the modern businessman turns to mythology to find inspiration for ways of impressing the public with the beauty, endurance, and usefulness of the product he wishes to sell. The authors of the program go on to suggest that a unit in mythology might be introduced by a bulletin board display of mythological symbols in modern use: the "Flying Red Horse" of the Magnolia Company, the caduceus of the medical profession, the winged cap and sandals of Western Union, and Cupid and his arrow for Valentine's Day. One or two stories explaining these symbols will evoke interest.

Moreover, myths appeal strongly to youngsters from disadvantaged environments because they contain many examples of heroism, courage, and a sense of humor. They are colorful, interesting, and inspiring. For the student, myths furnish not only entertainment but also much of the information he needs in order to comprehend and to enjoy more fully the world around him.

Other activities that stimulate interest might include; discussions of a few unusual word origins from mythology and the origins of the names of the days of the week, the months, and the planets; reading of appropriate stories or poems; and presentation of a few of the interesting mythological explanations of natural phenomena, such as the color of brown-skinned peoples, the color of the mulberry, and the changing seasons.

Another program that would be interesting for the disadvantaged youngster is the **Indiana State Department of Public Instruction**—*Wall Street Journal* **Newspaper Fund Program,**[4] which is de-

[4]Indiana State Department of Public Instruction, *Bulletin Number 501,* 1964.

signed to help English teachers give their pupils the background information needed for an understanding of all mass media as well as journalism.

A unit is suggested that starts with the *Acta Diurna* ("Day's Events"), established by Julius Caesar in 60 B.C. The *Acta Diurna* contained official government announcements and distributed the day's news to the citizens. A study of the *Acta Diurna* reveals that readers' tastes have not changed very much in two thousand years; much of the "news" was, as it still is, inconsequential.

The unit goes on to describe the invention of movable type by Gutenberg, four hundred years later. Memorable moments and events in the history of American newspaper publishing are then explained. All of this is preparation for an analysis of the concept of "news" and how one should become "critical in reading the news."

A hard look at the pros and cons of advertising is suggested in this unit:

Long before Madison Avenue, advertisers had their critics. An early critic was Dr. Samuel Johnson, who, in 1758, wrote in *The Idler:*

> Advertisements are now so numerous that they are very negligently perused, and it is therefore become necessary to gain attention by magnificence of promises and by eloquence sometimes sublime and sometimes pathetic. Promise, large promise, is the soul of an advertisement. I remember a washball that had a quality truly wonderful—it gave an *exquisite edge to the razor.* . . . The trade of advertising is now so near to perfection, that it is not easy to propose any improvement.[5]

Today, most adverse criticism of advertising can be grouped under three major allegations:

1. Advertising overemphasizes material values, thus blocking the way to a higher spiritual standard of living.
2. It is often vulgar and in poor taste.
3. It is misleading and dishonest.

The youngster from the disadvantaged home, perhaps more than others, is too often prey to misleading advertisements. The "magnificence of promises," as Dr. Johnson said, has the quality of a rainbow, of achieving what one could never have hoped for. Once again, if we can give children the skill of analyzing *news* and analyzing *advertising,* we can expect that, gradually, their reactions—to news and to life in general—will be the results of

---

[5] A Chalmes, *The British Essayists* (London: A. Strahan, 1817), p. 138.

serious thought, contemplation and planning, rather than of immediate experiences.

Many original source materials are suggested in the unit. For example:

1. The APME Criteria for a Good Newspaper drawn up by the criteria committee of the Associated Press Managing Editors Association.
2. The Canon of Journalism drawn up by the American Society of Newspaper Editors in 1923 as a code of ethics.
3. The Television Code of the National Association of Broadcasters.
4. The Production Code of the Motion Picture Association of America, Inc.

Any of these original sources can be used to teach not only language but the effects of language, both oral and written, on the way we live our lives and the kind of people we become.

Perhaps the medium that shows the most promise and is used the least for the educative purpose is television. Children from disadvantaged homes, like other children, have spent much time with television. They may differ from other children in their choice of programs, but the focus is still on the visual and the aural, and there seems to be little problem with attention span. One cannot underestimate television's influence on language habits, vocabulary, cultural values, and behavior patterns.

For the child who has little motivation to read, and certainly few of the reading skills needed for so-called good literature, television can open many literary doors. The TV presentation of Hemingway's *For Whom the Bell Tolls* (even with its obvious shortcomings) impressed the audience with its feeling of concern for and fascination with ordinary human beings caught up in the maelstrom of war. Edith Wharton's *Ethan Frome* became, via television, an inspiring experience in literature; in fact, it is quite possible that some students might feel that the television production afforded an even more illuminating insight into life than the book. Both of the above are books that are rarely read by disadvantaged children; they are not even suggested in programs like "Gateway English" or the *Miami Linguistic Readers*. Yet, through the medium of television—another form of communication—the beauty and impact of these books were felt by children who normally could not have read them. This does not mean that children from disadvantaged homes should not be expected actually to read books eventually, but, until such time as they wish to and are capable of coping with difficult reading material, television is an excellent vehicle.

There is, among the great works of literature, an almost inexhaustible supply of material with which television can extend the vision of the disadvantaged child—there is the Bible; there is all of Shakespeare. Walt Disney's stories about the American Revolution made it possible for some students to appreciate William Gilmore Simms' poem. "The Swamp Fox," for the first time; they could visualize the Swamp Fox, a legendary figure, as a real person. "Mark Twain's America" was an excellent background program for appreciating the writings of this famous humorist.

There are other valuable programs besides those devoted to interpreting great moments in literature. Such programs as John Gunther's "High Road," Lowell Thomas' adventure travelogues, Walt Disney's features on folklore and folk heroes, "The Twentieth Century" series—all offer much to stimulate the student's imagination as well as to add to his store of knowledge. The telecasting of the Winter Olympics focuses attention on the common points of interest which various cultural heritages have. The special reports on the exploding world population and on the Cuban situation cannot help but provoke thoughtful reflection by youth and adults alike.

Television is a leveler to some extent. However, we each view it and bring to it our own feelings and reactions. James Brunstein says of television:

> It provides a common background of experience which is sufficiently varied and vivid enough so that every student—the slowest as well as the best in ability within a group—could be led to respond in individually desirable and satisfying ways.[6]

It becomes increasingly more obvious that whether the disadvantaged youngster learns and grows intellectually does not depend completely upon how well he reads. By insisting upon reading as the only *acceptable* method of learning we close doors for the person who is not reading oriented. Twenty-five years ago, the consensus was that the reluctant reader could not become an educated man. Perhaps, under the conventional definition of "education," that may still be true. But such a person may certainly

[6]James Brunstein, "Ten Uses of Commercial Television in the English Classroom," *English Journal,* 47 (December 1958), p. 567.

become an informed and knowledgeable person. Today we look upon the electronic age as providing a substitute, somewhat in the McLuhan sense of "expressions which are 'oral' in form."[7]

Children from disadvantaged homes need stimulating, motivating, and constructive English language programs. The native language is the heart of the educational process. No one program described in this chapter will meet the needs of this group of youngsters, but perhaps a combination or adaptation of several will help to break through the language barrier. Much attention has been given in this country to the language problems of the foreign-born immigrant and little to the native-born in-migrant. Both these groups exhibit a class-based language syndrome, one that denies the lower-class person the verbal strategies necessary to obtain vertical social mobility. In our society, if the school is to be effective, students must be trained in how to use the language as a tool with which to improve the mind. As Bruner states, in his introduction to Vygotsky's book, *Thought and Language,*

> For it is the internalization of overt action that makes thought, and particularly the internalization of external dialogue that brings the powerful tool of language to bear on the stream of thought. Man, if you will, is shaped by the tools and instruments he comes to use, and neither the mind nor the hand alone can amount to much . . . .[8]

[7]Marshall McLuhan, *The Gutenberg Galaxy: The Making of Typographical Man* (Toronto: University of Toronto Press, 1962), p. 3.

[8]L. S. Vygotsky, *Thought and Language* (Boston: Massachusetts Institute of Technology Press, 1962), pp. vi–vii.

SELECTED READINGS ON THE ENGLISH LANGUAGE

BOOKS ON THE SUBJECT

Brown, R. W., *Words and Things* (Glencoe, Ill.: Free Press, 1958).

The origin of language and its development into a tool of propaganda is traced in this volume. The chapter "Persuasion, Expression, and Propaganda" is particularly important to those interested in helping children become critical readers.

Bruner, J. S., Goodenow, J. J., and Austin, C. A., *A Study of Thinking* (New York: Wiley, 1956).

This book deals with conceptualization and seeks to describe what happens when an intelligent human being tries to classify the significant events in his environment, in order to be able to treat different things as equivalents. The book has a particularly interesting chapter on "Language and Categories" and can be of great help to a teacher since it deals with speech systems, linguistic meanings and the relation between language and culture.

Carroll, John, *Language and Thought* (Englewood Cliffs, N. J.: Prentice-Hall, 1964).

The treatment in this book is somewhat different from those found in other books on the psychology of languages. One of the major themes of the book is that thought and cognition are presupposed by language—that speech is a consequence of some kind of thought or cognition, even though language structure may channel or influence thought. The author bases his thesis on scientific linguistics and puts forth his belief that psychological study of language and thought requires an accurate knowledge of exactly what language is.

Chukovsky, Kornec, *From Two to Five* (Berkeley: University of California Press, 1963).

Although much has been written by professional educators, anthropologists, and psychologists on the preschool child, this book is the only one by a children's poet dealing with languages, thought processes, and imagination of the very young. Like Bruner, Chukovsky views the child like a tireless explorer. He speaks of the child's mental dexterity in learning to speak, his linguistic creativity, his predilection for poetry, and his loyalty to the fairy tale.

Church, J., *Language and Discovery of Reality* (New York: Random House, 1961).

The first part of this book sets forth some principles of cognitive development. It deals with the way children come to understand and use language. Part II of the book deals with the psychological approach to the problem of meaning and reference. Through its treatment of language, this book gives us much insight into the psychology of human behavior and the kinds of behavior that makes language possible.

Fries, Charles C., *Linguistics: The Study of Language* (New York: Holt, Rinehart and Winston, 1964).

This book is, in fact, just one chapter of a much larger study by the author, *Linguistics and Reading.* The value of this "little" book is its attempt to survey in nontechnical terms the nature and functioning of human language through the problems of language relationships, language history, and descriptive analysis.

Ruesch, Jurgen, and Kees, Weldon, *Nonverbal Communication* (Berkeley: University of California Press, 1956).

The authors attempt to demonstrate how much of communication can be effected and how much can be gained in seeing and in comprehending what is observable. It is easy reading and is appealing to the general reader as well as to the specialist.

Umans, Shelley, *New Trends in Reading Instruction* (New York: Teachers College Press, Teachers College, Columbia University, 1963).

Some of the newer trends and their objectives in reading instruction are described here. Team teaching, programed instruction, television teaching; reading in the subject areas are some of the "newer" approaches discussed. To make explicit the various approaches many sample teaching materials (lesson outlines, semester plans, programed text material) are included.

Umans, Shelley, *Designs for Reading Programs* (New York: Teachers College Press, Teachers College, Columbia University, 1964).

This paperback is really a guide to setting up a developmental and remedial reading program in a school. It includes suggested diagnostic procedures, patterns of organization, and suggestions as to varied types of instructional programs.

Vygotsky, I. L., *Thought and Language* (New York: Wiley, 1962).

This is a study of the interrelation of thought and language. It provides experimental evidence that meanings of words undergo evolution during childhood, and it uncovers the way in which the child's "scientific" concepts develop compared with his spontaneous concepts. It defines the nature and linguistic function of written speech in its relation to thinking and attempts to clarify inner speech and its relation to thought.

ARTICLES FROM PROFESSIONAL PUBLICATIONS

Auer, J. Jeffrey, and Smith, Raymond G., "Speaking," *Review of Educational Research*, 31 (April 1961), pp. 152–160.

Battle, Esther S., and Rotter, Julian B., "Children's Feelings of Personal Control as Related to Social Class and Ethnic Group," *Journal of Personality*, 31 (December 1963), pp. 482–490.

Bernstein, B., "Aspects of Language and Learning in the Genesis of the Social Process," *Journal of Child Psychology and Psychiatry* (Great Britain), 1 (1960), pp. 313–324.

Brazziel, William F., and Terrel, Mary, "An Experiment in the Development of Readiness in Culturally Disadvantaged Group of First Grade Children," *Journal of Negro Education*, 31 (Winter, 1962), pp. 4–7.

Brown, Charles T., and Keller, Paul W., "A Modest Proposal for Listening Training," *Quarterly Journal of Speech*, 48 (December 1962), pp. 395–399.

Carlson, Ruth Kearney, "Recent Research in Originality," *Elementary English*, 40 (October 1963), pp. 583–589.

Carroll, John B., "The Analysis of Reading Instruction: Perspectives from Psychology and Linguistics," in Ernest R. Hilgard (Ed.), *Theories of Learning and Instruction*, Sixty-third Yearbook of the National Society of the Study of Education, Part I (Chicago: University of Chicago Press, 1964), pp. 336–353.

Deutsch, Cynthia P., "Auditory Discrimination and Learning: Social Factors," *Merrill-Palmer Quarterly of Behavior and Development*, 10 (July 1964), pp. 277–295.

Deutsch, Martin, "Facilitating Development in the Pre-School Child: Social and Psychological Perspectives," *Merrill-Palmer Quarterly of Behavior and Development*, 10 (July 1964), pp. 249–263.

Deutsch, Martin, "Early Social Environment: Its Influence on School Adaptation," in Daniel Schreiber (Ed.), *Project: School Dropouts*, Part I (Washington, D.C.: National Education Association, 1964), pp. 89–101.

Downing, John, "Teaching Reading with I.T.A. in Britain," *Phi Delta Kappan*, 45 (April 1964), pp. 322–329.

Duker, Sam, "Basics in Critical Listening," *English Journal,* 51 (November 1962), pp. 565–567.

Erickson, Marilyn T., "Effects of Social Deprivation and Satiation on Verbal Conditioning in Children," *Journal of Comparative and Physiological Psychology,* 55 (December 1962), pp. 953–957.

Foulke, Emerson, et al., "The Comprehension of Rapid Speech by the Blind," *Exceptional Children,* 29 (November 1962), pp. 131–141.

Gelfand, Donna M., "The Influence of Self-Esteem on Rate of Verbal Conditioning and Social Matching Behavior," *Journal of Abnormal and Social Psychology,* 65 (October 1962), pp. 259–265.

Groff, Patrick J., "Children's Attitudes Toward Reading and Their Critical Reading Abilities in Four Content-type Materials," *Journal of Educational Research,* 55 (April 1962), pp. 313–318.

John, Vera P., and Goldstein, Leo S., "The Social Context of Language Acquisition," *Merrill-Palmer Quarterly of Behavior and Development,* 10 (July 1964), pp. 265–275.

Joll, Leonard W., "Development of Taste in Literature, III: Developing Taste in Literature in the Junior High School," *Elementary English,* 40 (February 1963), pp. 183–188; 217.

Katz, P. A., Deutsch, M., *Visual and Auditory Efficiency and Its Relation to Reading in Children, Final Report,* Cooperative Research Project No. 1099, (Washington, D.C.: United States Office of Education, 1963).

Knower, Franklin H., "Speech," in Chester W. Harris (Ed.), *Encyclopedia of Educational Research,* rev. ed. (New York: Macmillan, 1960), pp. 1130–1137.

Lee, E. S., "Negro Intelligence and Selective Migration: A Philadelphia Test of the Klineberg Hypothesis," *American Social Review,* 16 (1951), pp. 227–233.

Lenneberg, Eric H., "The Capacity for Language Acquisition," in Jerry A. Fodor and Jerrold J. Datz (Eds.), *The Structure of Language: Readings in the Philosophy of Language* (Englewood Cliffs, N. J.: Prentice-Hall, 1964), pp. 579–603.

McNeil, John D., and Keislar, Evan R., "Value of the Oral Response in Beginning Reading: An Experimental Study Using Programmed Instruction," *British Journal of Educational Psychology,* 33 (June 1963), pp. 162–168.

Meckel, Henry C., "Research on Teaching Composition and Literature," in N. L. Gage (Ed.), *Handbook of Research on Teaching* (Chicago, Rand McNally, 1963), pp. 966–1006.

Miller, George A., "The Psycholinguists: On the New Scientists of Language," *Encounter,* 23 (July 1964), pp. 29–37.

Moore, Omar K., "Autotelic Responsive Environments and Exceptional Children" (Hamden, Conn.: Responsive Environment Foundation, September 1963).

Parnes, Sidney J., "Effects of Extended Effort in Creative Problem Solving," *Journal of Educational Psychology,* **52** (June 1961), pp. 117–122.

Spaulding, Robert L., "Achievement, Creativity, and Self-Concept Correlates of Teacher-Pupil Transactions in Elementary Schools," in Celia B. Stendler (Ed.), *Readings in Child Behavior and Development,* rev. ed. (New York: Harcourt, Brace and World, 1964), pp. 313–318.

Torrance, E. Paul, and Harmon, Judson A., "Effects of Memory, Evaluative and Creative Reading Sets on Test Performance," *Journal of Educational Psychology,* **52** (August 1961), pp. 207–214.

Tyler, Fred T., "Issues Related to Readiness to Learn," in Ernest R. Hilgard (Ed.), *Theories of Learning and Instruction,* Sixty-third Yearbook of the National Society for the Study of Education (Chicago: Chicago University Press, 1964), pp. 210–239.

Wittrock, M. C., "Verbal Stimuli in Concept Formation: Learning by Discovery," *Journal of Educational Psychology,* **54** (August 1963), pp. 183–190.

PART THREE

HISTORY AND
THE SOCIAL SCIENCES

Barbara Ward, in her discussion of the problems of "have not" nations seeking to join the ranks of the affluent, speaks of the giant thrusts that are needed in order to move from the primitive to the technological form of production.[1] We have, in education, a comparable situation. In order to bring the "have nots," that is, the disadvantaged, to the level of the affluent, we must make great thrusts in the field of education. We must find substitutes for the skimpy, hand tools of a primitive curriculum, the minimum "standards," and the starvation budgets; we need bold goals, a demanding, self-propelling curriculum geared to the most advanced research, a large-scale and imaginative increase in learning equipment, and gigantic budgets. The great foundations and universities, the worlds of business and labor, and the government must join with imaginative educators to plan and program the curriculum for this gigantic forward leap. As a minimum, we should establish for the poor the curriculum that the affluent now take for granted.

THE NATURE OF THE SOCIAL SCIENCES

The social sciences, which study man in terms of his behavior

[1]Barbara Ward, *The Rich Nations and the Poor Nations* (New York: Norton, 1962).

as a political and social animal and of where he lives and how he gets food, shelter, and clothing, are extremely important disciplines for the disadvantaged. These studies are vehicles by which a youngster can gain an understanding of himself, his role as an individual, his relationship with others. The disadvantaged, with their built-in inferiority feelings, need to have their views broadened and their knowledge increased. The culture groups they represent today may have had glorious pasts. Through history and the social sciences these children can learn about the dynamics of their previous cultures—what in these earlier cultures has produced leaders, why one culture has surpassed another, why some have survived and others perished.

The social sciences deal with man as a dynamic, creative person, not as a helpless pawn of blind forces. As an intellectual, social, and ethical being, man exercises initiative and imagination in his relations with other persons. The social sciences help describe man and his relationships to other men and to his environment. They enable us, on the basis of past behavior, to draw inferences as to present and future conduct.

For the disadvantaged child—unaware of the sweep of history—living amid lethargy, hopelessness, and defeat—the knowledge that people like himself have in past centuries broken through barriers of deprivation far worse than his can make a tremendous impression. What are some of the guidelines particularly appropriate for teaching social sciences to deprived children? Studies of slum children indicate that they are weak in communication abilities, in abstract thinking, and in logic. In younger children these weaknesses take the form of a limited vocabulary; in older ones, they are evidenced in a lack of ability to understand general ideas or conclusions. These students are handicapped by an inability to recognize the application of generalizations to new situations.

Skilled instruction and exposure of children to a variety of materials, experiences, and value systems should result in what Bruner refers to as "discovery." The student learns how to ferret things out for himself, how to draw his own generalizations. This is the great highway to learning. On this road teachers talk less and learners achieve more.

The importance of basic social science generalizations, graded on a planned basis, is fundamental. The selection of appropriate experiences and content is crucial if real power to understand

and apply social science generalizations is to be achieved. The knowledge of a scientific principle will leave its impression long after details of the content that led to this knowledge have been forgotten. Learning how to use maps effectively will serve a youngster far longer than memorizing the name of the leading city in a state. Indeed, it would be far better if he learned how that city became the leading city, for, by the time the youngster grows up, the city may have become a third-class town.

The child from the disadvantaged environment needs to learn how to make deductions that he can apply to varied situations. He needs the tools of learning that will make him the technician. Basic concepts in history and the social sciences must be established as reference points. These key ideas, designed sequentially through organized lessons in information gathering and comparing, lead to general ideas that can be applied to new situations without having to extract the rules over again for each application. The methodology by which teachers instill this understanding is vital. The generalizations are not taught directly as rules or laws, but are derived from seeing the connection between understandings and facts.

A sequential, spiral approach over a thirteen- or fourteen-year period (pre-kindergarten through twelfth grade) is more useful for learning generalizations in social science and the structure of the disciplines than the cyclical one used in most school systems in which the same content is repeated several times in the thirteen- or fourteen-year span. As one teacher put it, "Columbus keeps discovering America four to six times in the school life of children." Such repetition of content is plainly wasteful, given the amount of learning there is to be done. In the spiral or sequential approach, basic concepts, expressed in the language of children, are taught in the earliest years and are built onto in increasing depth in later years, using new content, new degrees of abstractness, and more difficult problems in an ascending scale. For the disadvantaged there are real gains in this spiral approach. It helps them develop the ability to make applications of fundamental ideas to new situations. It strengthens associational thinking and aids in memorization. It brings in new and interesting material about the world and its people.

A realistic curriculum in the social sciences for our disadvantaged needs to begin in the pre-kindergarten. On the basis of current research, we know that young children can understand what we have always considered mature generalizations if these ideas are presented in the language and the experience of children. The findings of Easton and Hess of the University of Chicago indicate that the time to teach social science concepts is as soon as the child enters school. They state:

> Every piece of evidence indicates that the child's political world begins to take shape well before he even enters elementary school and it undergoes the most rapid change during these years, . . . The truly formative years of the maturing member of a political system would seem to be those years between the ages of three and thirteen.[2]

This supports Piaget's theory of the early level of conceptualization and Bloom's premise that 50 per cent of development takes place between the time of conception and the age of four (see Chapter 1).

Where, in relation to the politically sophisticated youngster, however, do we find the disadvantaged child? We find him sophisticated, but in a different way from his affluent counterpart. His experiences, if any, with the political world have been negative. The family setup and his role in it are different; his community does not conform to the conventional middle-class model, and his relationship with others is less verbal, less structured, and less planned than is that in the dominant culture. Therefore, the cumulative impact of a middle-class curriculum that assumes a certain positive preschool experience with social sciences, as well as with other subject areas, is unrealistic when applied to the disadvantaged pre-kindergarteners and first graders. For these children, direct instruction must begin on the first day of school. Pictorial material developed in programed fashion may be useful initially. The material created must draw upon the concrete, positive experiences of the youngsters, experiences that frequently involve taking care of younger brothers or sisters, preparing food, going to the store, or the down-to-earth work with plants and animals that is often necessitated by the economic facts of life in an impoverished area. These experiences are significant because of their vividness and personal strength. However, it is equally important to contrast these experiences with those of people in other lands, with primitive man, and with the human being as opposed to the rest of the animal world. A curriculum based solely on the all-too-familiar immediate environment will find it-

[2]David Easton and Robert D. Hess, "The Child's Political World," *Midwest Journal of Political Science*, 6 (August 1962), pp. 235–236.

self restricted, more often than not, to a cultural desert; and this is true whether the child's home is a tenement apartment in the heart of the inner city, a shack in some remote area of Appalachia, or an adobe hut in the isolated deserts of the Southwest.

THE METHODS AND MATERIALS OF THE SOCIAL SCIENCES

As important as exposure, discovery, and the drawing of generalizations are to the disadvantaged youngster, attention must also be given to the methods and skills the social scientist employs to gather his data and establish his concepts. For whether the scientist be physical or social, his method is the same: hypothesizing, gathering data, synthesizing, analyzing, and generalizing.

The social scientist assembles material of every kind about the period he is studying: diaries, letters, speeches, inscriptions on buildings, pictures, newspaper articles, artifacts. If possible, he will visit the area being studied. He will evaluate the truthfulness of various documents by comparing them, by studying their style of writing. He will discard irrelevant trivia. From all these materials he will seek to recreate the spirit of a period as seen through the eyes of its contemporaries. He will study the social institutions, the cultural, economic, geographical, and political factors that are relevant. He will rebuild the period from the point of view of the anthropologist, the economist, the political scientist. Any account of past or present events must make allowance for varied interpretations. In learning to make judgments, to analyze, and to hypothesize, the student needs a wide variety of appropriate instructional materials and procedures far beyond the conventional textbook.

The materials from which children gather data in the social sciences may be pictorial as well as written. The disadvantaged youngster, verbally handicapped, may find pictures just as expressive and just as informative as written textbooks. Students and teachers too often dismiss pictures as a basis for learning, equating them with recreation instead of accepting picture study as a skill. The vastness of the field of the visual arts and its potential has not yet begun to be realized.

Visual aids, in the form of silent or sound films, television, photographs, slides, charts, paintings, or film loops, can become the intermediate step between concrete objects and the more abstract way of learning, the written word. Well-designed charts and graphs can present complex ideas in simplified form. Certainly, the ability of visual presentations to persuade, to explain, and to set an emotional tone is well known to political leaders and advertisers. Pictorial materials should be used to encourage analysis and discussion. Discovering a purpose or an "angle" in a graphic presentation can be more interesting and sometimes more challenging than reading a thousand words. Pictures, for example, can tell a story in sequential degrees of difficulty. Students should be able to point out what is obvious in the picture, to note action, to make inferences, to suggest what will probably occur next, and to generalize from the several pictures. Whatever the value of this approach to students generally, it has particular significance for the disadvantaged. After all, the purpose of the social scientist is not simply to compile an aggregation of facts; it is a method of study, an ordering of the intellectual and affective processes.

The methods and the materials used by the social scientist have tremendous value for all children. But for the disadvantaged child, who needs experience with concrete objects, who needs to be successful on a less verbal level, who needs to learn how to evaluate before making decisions, who needs first to see the value of "next steps" and then to learn how to plan for them, who needs to learn generalizations that can be applied to new situations— for *this* child, learning to imitate the methods and to use the raw materials of the social sciences is more important than learning the content.

THE DIMENSIONS OF THE SOCIAL SCIENCES

In the Greater Cleveland Social Science Program, the student is introduced to a few of the methods of the separate disciplines. They recommend that the student:

. . . learn the geographer's concern for accurate maps and for precision in description of climate, land-forms and ways of life, the historian's devotion to understanding a document and placing himself in the frame of mind of men of other times and places, the economist's use of concepts like division of labor, surplus, capital, means of production and exchange, the sociologist's and anthropologist's concern with accurate description of social structure, and political scientist's interest in government and its functions, techniques, limits and abuses. In general, however, the methodological discipline of social science in elementary grades will be a common-sensible, rational application of the rules of evidence and logic.[3]

For purposes of convenience, the materials in this Part have been organized under the conventional headings of "Political Science," "Anthropology and Sociology," "History and Geography," and "Economics." This is done with the full realization that there is much overlapping and that a good argument can be made for more distinct separation of the disciplines here involved. However, premature integration of the disciplines often leads to unclear thinking and causes confusion, just as *failure to integrate* a specific discipline at the appropriate time leads to an artificial separation of ideas and events.

In studying geography, students need to learn that the place where an event occurred is important. The essence of geography can be found in the answer to the question: "What makes one place on earth different from another and what of it."[4] To seek this answer, students need to learn the methods of the geographer. In connection with a specific problem, the geographer will study the map and interpret the significance of the likenesses and the differences. The maps and charts he creates are important only because of what they explain. Obviously, he will not overlook the nature of the people, their culture, attitudes, goals, and their progress in controlling the place where they live. Students must build up actual case histories about the effects on people of climate, winds, mountains, and oceans and about the inventions created by people to overcome geographic forces. A river can bring wealth or chaos; glaciers have destroyed continents. Students following the method of the geographer will automatically look to maps as an essential part of learning other disciplines. They will form their generalizations initially from many facts and subconcepts before making general applications. By studying the farming methods of mountain people and flatland farmers, they learn that certain machines are not very useful in mountainous terrain but are valuable where the land is level. They will conclude that someday someone will probably invent a farming ma-

[3]Educational Research Council of Greater Cleveland, *Handbook for Social Science Teachers: First Edition—1965* (Cleveland: The Council, 1965), p. 38.

[4]Preston E. James, "New Perspectives on Teaching Geography." Paper presented at the Seventh National Conference on Higher Education, National Education Association, Chicago, March 5, 1962.

chine that will be specifically adapted to mountain use, just as someone has already invented the shaft we thrust into the ocean's bed, seeking oil instead of seafood.

Students can generalize that geographical environment has special meanings for different cultural groups at different stages of their economic development. Students are fascinated by studies of the unique cultures of different people and the methods by which social scientists gain their knowledge. Digging into the vaulted recesses of the pyramids and living with primitive tribes in aboriginal Australia are romantic adventures, and the skillful teacher will build on such adventures to illustrate the nature of the anthropologist's work.

As the student explores the interaction of various groups of people—the roles of leaders and followers, the relation of past and present civilizations—he begins to see meaning and structure in the relationships that compose our society. History, geography, anthropology, and sociology all combine to form the picture that represents organized living.

Methods of causing students to become aware of the nature of politics should include guidelines in the observation and understanding of human behavior. There must be reasons why people act as they do. Why have we had to create laws to protect us against others, against policemen as well as kings, against our next door neighbor as well as against "boundary" neighbors?

The study of political science and jurisprudence—civil rights and liberties—is an element in the study of human behavior. Because of this there must be close collaboration for the student, between the study of political behavior and the fields of sociology, psychology, and anthropology.

Economics is a discipline that affects the child almost from the moment he is born, becoming more "affecting" as he grows older. The disadvantaged youngster becomes a conscious member of the economic world long before his more advantaged peers. He learns only too soon—from taking care of the kitchen and younger children, buying food, holding "odd" jobs, and becoming unemployed—what it means to be a member of the labor force. In fact, he has usually learned this before most of his more advantaged peers have finished high school.

Economics concerns itself with the production, distribution, exchange, and consumption of goods and services. Yet, as with all other social sciences, these concepts cannot be taught in a "social vacuum." They are interrelated with varying aspects of sociology, political science, psychology, anthropology, and history.

History is primarily an inquiry into actual events of the past, so integrated or made whole as to represent as truthfully as possible the facts of what happened. In the present-day curricula, history is more often taught as an abstract chronicle of events with a modicum of personal meaning. For the disadvantaged, this type of history teaching leads to frustration. Unless the past becomes vivid and realistic to him, so that he actively participates in the hopes, fears, elation, and despair of those who lived it, we can expect no interest and no productive response from him.

A central concept in history is time. Understanding time in the abstract is difficult. Accounts of events or happenings, however, are concrete. They can illustrate changes that have taken place. The modern historian studies and interprets the facts, describes events, arranges them in sequence or order, and brings to bear his own interpretations of causality. The problem is to understand that the historian must be selective in what he reports. Economic, political, and social historians must set priorities and select such facts as will be most significant of a period or an incident. History needs to be presented as a well-designed edifice, the columns of which are the separate disciplines, visible, communicative, and integrated.

The Objectives

The first step in building a curriculum is to set forth objectives. This step is influenced by the goals to be sought, and it must be approached warily. Too often a projection of aims tends to be overly restrictive and to make no allowance for the exercise of unconventional or creative talents.

The acquisition of knowledge for its own sake is a sound concept for which a valid brief may well be made. Life is a complex of associations, and knowledge enriches the art of living by adding to the number and value of those associations. However, we are faced here with what might be termed "emergency cases." These children cannot afford the luxury of the incidental acquisition of knowledge. Curriculum building for disadvantaged youngsters should, in the opinion of the present authors, devote itself to goals that have relevance to functioning in society.

In the rapidly growing inner cities of the metropolitan areas and the bleak and desolate rural sections where the poor live, the schools must contribute by accepting certain unique responsibilities. How do we teach poverty-stricken, ghetto-bound pupils to accept and hold as important our national ideals and our society's codes of accepted conduct? How can pupils coming from homes where people feel oppressed learn to accept democracy if their environment teaches them to equate democracy with discrimination? Where does the individual's freedom need to give way to a sense of responsibility to the group? What are the limits of the rights of majorities and minorities in our society? How do we instill patriotism and love of country into frustrated groups? The value system of disadvantaged children is extraordinarily limited. Most often their associations are restricted to their families and those in their immediate area. Their values are shaped by these associations.

A modern program in history and the social sciences must help students to understand why people behave as they do and why a code of social conduct is important. This calls for the development of concepts of behavioral conduct beyond the simple intellectual mastery of the subject disciplines. Cultural anthropology, sociology, social psychology, and political science are the social sciences with great potential for enlarging the child's social spectrum. These disciplines are man centered, rich in human relations concepts; they come to grips with the central issues of our time: values, commitment to societal standards, citizenship, prejudice, social change, and social stratification.

To be sure, all students stand to gain from a better understanding of social problems; however, the disadvantaged have the greatest need and therefore the most to gain. These social sciences present irrefutable evidence that men are basically alike and that history, age after age, is the complex interrelation of the same human ingredients. Projects involving historical happenings can dramatize the struggle of the past and help students understand the attitudes of those who must overcome similar handicaps today. The disadvantaged need heroes to help them in their aspirational goals; institutions are too abstract. Well-chosen biographies, preferably drawn from various ethnic groups, can vitalize the past and bring animation and movement to history.

It is crucial for youngsters to feel that both they and their families are part of the heritage of America. Cultural unity, a sense of oneness with one's neighbors, is essential if the goal of integration in our pluralistic society is to be achieved. Minority group heroes of the past must mingle historically with the greats of all racial and national elements in our society. The social sciences furnish rich opportunities for presenting comparative data about people, places, and things. Where various ethnic groups have helped in the growth of past civilizations, these vicarous experiences can help students identify themselves in a successful role with past or present members of their own ethnic group.

However, the academically oriented curriculum for social science, or any other area of knowledge for that matter, requires much to supplement its approach. Films, tapes, and pictures about other people are all valuable instructional media, but probably most important is the value of *actual confrontation*. Official records of the United States Armed Forces show that prejudices between whites and Negroes diminished as the quality and quantity of the contacts increased. Increased interaction between groups having different value orientations was found to be helpful when these groups were jointly engaged in an action whose result was rewarding. This same diminishing of discriminatory attitudes has been experienced by members of winning interracial teams in sports. Carefully planned programs of intervisitation between schools of different races, or between children who are poor and children who are affluent, can be helpful in changing values through interaction. However, confrontation alone—without skillful organization and guided discussion—is not enough. Unless the activities are planned, persistent, and substantial, little will happen.

Margaret Mead describes her return visit, after twenty-five years, to the people of a Stone Age culture on one of the Admiralty Islands (Manus).[5] The Second World War had happened in the interim, and the Americans had occupied the islands. On meeting men and women whom she had known as children, she discovered that their contact with another culture had led them to establish new, democratically based institutions. They had become a modern people, anxious to progress in education and social living.

Can confrontations between different races and between

[5]Margaret Mead, *New Lives for Old* (New York: William Morrow and Company, 1956), p. 548.

different economic groups in our own country achieve the degree
of change observed by Mead in the Admiralty Islands? How are
values changed by group influences? Students need to learn that
the effect of the interaction of individuals and their environment
varies with time, place, and purpose, and that individuals can
become a prime factor in changing both themselves and their
environment.

If values are to be built, and not just understood academically,
the study of history and the social sciences must go beyond the
simple presentation of historic events. The curriculum must proceed to an inquiry of the moral and ethical issues involved and
help create a climate conducive to a way of life compatible
with our society. What content, what types of action projects
are required for such curriculum building? What methodologies
should guide curriculum builders if we accept the responsibility
for educating the disadvantaged to a real understanding of events
that have led up to our present convictions concerning the place
of the individual, of varied groups and institutions, in our American democracy? If ethical values and moral principles, based on
objective criteria, are to be learned through action aspects of
sociology, social psychology, and anthropology, one needs also to
ask about the place of the study of religious ideals and institutions
and of the concepts of "morality," "loyalty," and "honor." These
are some of the questions to which educators must now address
themselves if they are to help the disadvantaged meet their
problems.

PROGRAMS FOR HISTORY AND THE SOCIAL SCIENCES

Chapters 7, 8, 9, and 10 comprise a survey of curricula in
history and the social sciences, which have been developed within
the past few years and which, the authors feel, have merit for
the disadvantaged youngster. The majority of these programs,
like those described here in other subject disciplines, have been
developed not only for students from the dominant culture, but
also, to a large degree, for that part of the population designated
as "gifted." However, many of these programs have elements
that are desperately needed by the disadvantaged (see Chapter
1). It is true that, as the programs now stand, their subject
matter appears difficult and their reading levels seem high.
However, with adaptation through materials and methodology,

these programs can be used with success among the disadvantaged.

As extensive as the field of history and the social sciences is, it seems to have generated very few programs, in proportion to other subject disciplines. One reason for this might well be that, until 1965, the federal government did not put a great deal of money into the social sciences; another might be the intramural sparring among specialists in the various disciplines, each claiming his area to be the "core" around which the others should be taught. The programs described in the following pages are few in contrast to the extent of interest in the field, and the present collection is by no means all-inclusive. These are merely samples of some types of programs; under each type, there may well be several other programs.

There is much controversy today as to whether or not to teach separately the subject disciplines of the social sciences, whether to fuse them, or whether to forget the classifications altogether. The authors do not wish to contribute to this controversy or to take a position. The purpose of grouping the programs into discrete subject disciplines was one of organization rather than of philosophy.

We might emphasize here that no one discipline can be taught insightfully independently of the others. Yet it is equally true, as explained earlier in this chapter, that each of the social sciences has certain unique structural elements that should be learned. In presenting various social science programs, we have chosen to stress certain disciplines as the best vehicles, in our judgment, for the teaching of selected content and resultant derived generalizations. At times the authors may appear arbitrary in classifying a program under a particular social science discipline, being well aware that a program listed under political science might just as easily have been listed, in the judgment of the reader, under history or economics.

7

POLITICAL SCIENCE

Political science provides insights into political behavior by describing the processes by which political power is attained and distributed, along with the structure and functioning of government. The traditional approach has been to study comparative governments at the national, state, and local levels and to survey the agencies and departments that make up the machinery of government. This approach leaves a great deal to be desired, being external, lacking in opportunities for identification and true understanding, and narrow in scope. Another and more meaningful approach is to view political science as a behavioral science, studying *man* as a political being. The question of authority—the rule of law as opposed to the rule of men—and the concepts of freedom, interdependence, and citizenship fall in this area.

Political science is often difficult to separate from jurisprudence, or "legal science." Jurisprudence aims at analyzing, describing, explaining, and predicting legal behavior. Although jurisprudence overlaps philosophy, sociology, political science, history, economics, anthropology, and psychology, it is most closely related to political behavior, since virtually all rights and responsibilities are set forth by law.

The youngster from the disadvantaged home does not see himself as a political scientist, and certainly not as one who is knowledgeable in the law as an applied science. Yet he has become the "living laboratory" of political change in this country. For a considerable length of time in United States history, the problems of the disadvantaged have had great influence in shaping our laws, in electing our leaders, and even in changing some of the bases upon which our government was formed (witness the Fourteenth and Fifteenth Amendments to the Constitution). In view of such influence, it seems strange that members of this group have played a passive role in these changes. They have been the pawns of politicians, of ideological leaders, and of petty office holders. Their political apathy has been exploited. They are the victims of demagogy, of prejudice, and of vested interests.

In order to activate their role as intelligent political beings, we must help them to understand *applied* political science, or "policy science," that is, practical manipulation and control within the power structure of governmental institutions. Education for political competency has enormous significance for the disadvantaged. The last portion of the twentieth century may be the era when the disadvantaged will have a major role in political functioning.

Political science, as the study of government and the theory and practice of man and his relationships to the state, can contribute concepts relating primarily to the government as an institution of society—to democracy—to citizenship—to the skills of responsible citizenship. One approach to the identification of appropriate content in the political sciences is through an analysis of the large, central ideas around which learning should be organized, the important understandings or abstract principles whose meanings are expanded by the variety and depth of learning experiences occurring throughout the child's school life.

An example of a broad, general theme is: *The purpose of government in a democracy is to serve the people of the community on an equitable basis.* An analysis of this statement would have to include the following concepts: All power comes from the people. Government should be by law, not by the caprice of a man. Public officials are responsible to all the people. The people have the right to influence government by selecting representatives in regular elections, by petitioning the government, by meeting to discuss issues, by running for office themselves. The setting up, by majorities or minorities, of rules that prevent citizens from voting or from seeking office destroys democracy.

The generalizations are the understandings built from observing cepts and sub-generalizations. They are the basis for organizing, relationships between factual data and concepts and between con-

interpreting, and applying known facts in new situations. To facilitate the achievement of these goals, we must reduce the overall generalizations to workable sub-divisions which become reference points for a particular lesson, a learning sequence, or a unit of study. These sub-divisions range from the simple to the complex.[1]

The **Wisconsin Department of Public Instruction Social Science Program** is a plan for teaching social science concepts from kindergarten through the twelfth grade. The approach proposed is one based on simple concepts that lead to more complex ones and then on to generalizations. In the Wisconsin plan, one of the major political science concepts included is "Democracy seeks to protect the rights of individuals and minority groups."[2] The program goes on to list a number of political science concepts that can be presented to kindergarteners and first and second graders through appropriate lessons and experience. Many of the concepts listed here are already in our courses of study. However, some are new—the newness being more in the area of the grade level at which they are taught than in the area of the subject matter. For example, the following concepts are taught in the second grade:

1. A democratically organized society or group reaches its highest peak of efficiency when each member assumes his full share of responsibility.
2. Adults elect men and women from their community to operate the local government including the schools. Most elected officials are paid for their work, but some people serve their community with no pay.
3. The state collects taxes and gives some of its money for schools.[3]

These concepts go well beyond the usual home, family, and community units that are customary in the first three years of elementary school throughout the nation. Exhibit 7 lists the concepts taught in third through twelfth grades in the Wisconsin plan. (See pp. 104–107.)

However, the Wisconsin approach, although basically sound by reason of its direct application to the student as a political

[1]Floyd Marchus, Superintendent of Schools, Pilot Study Project, Contra Costa County Schools, Pleasant Hills, California, 1963.

[2]Wisconsin Department of Public Instruction, *A Conceptual Framework from the Social Studies in Wisconsin Schools*, Social Studies Bulletin No. 4, Curriculum Bulletin No. 14 (Madison: Wisconsin Department of Public Instruction, 1964).

[3]*Ibid.*, p. 2.

being, has—unless class lessons are based upon first-hand experiences—the shortcoming of being too remote. Louis Kottmeyer in St. Louis is producing a curriculum "tailor made" for St. Louis which emphasizes some of the same concepts but applies them to local politics. In Dr. Kottmeyer's words, "this curriculum talks of local politics: its machinery; its personalities; its advantages and its stench."[4] Although his particular material could not be used in other areas of the country, the structure of his program could serve as a model. Local politics, at the precinct level, is rarely studied; it is only hinted at. Yet the disadvantaged youngster is directly influenced by local politics—exorbitant rents, poor health facilities, and inadequate protection, are all elements of local politics. To have the "right man" in office is important to the disadvantaged community; the charlatan will merely perpetuate the state of misery.

The youth growing up in poverty faces special problems as he leaves his neighborhood and learns first hand about the opportunities and the living conditions of his more favored neighbors. He often becomes cynical and bitter when he compares their situations with his own. As a result, he may become inclined to align himself with extremist or nationalist movements such as the Black Muslims and the Ku Klux Klan.

At Tufts University, the **Lincoln Filene Center for Citizenship and Public Affairs** has pioneered in developing materials on emerging nationalism in Asia, Africa, and Latin America. A study of some of the obstacles impeding the growth of democracy in the African, Asian, and Latin American countries—the unsatisfied basic human needs, the nondemocratic aspects of certain cultures, the Western heritage of imperialism, and the superficial attractiveness of totalitarianism—can help children understand their own problems and avoid being lured into emotionally inspired extremist movements. For treating this area in the secondary school, it is hard to find a more informed document than *Ideology and World Affairs: Teacher's Unit Number One*. This document was developed as part of the Northeastern States Youth Citizenship Project on Basic Units in Citizenship. Chapters X, XI, and XII, entitled "Contemporary Right-Wing Totalitarianism," "Authoritarianism in the Contemporary World," and "Democracy and the Afro-Asian-Latin American World," are recommended as partic-

[4]Louis Kottmeyer, from an address given at the Great Cities Meeting in New York City, April 1965.

Exhibit 7. MAJOR CONCEPTS AND SUBCONCEPTS IN

MAJOR CONCEPTS	SUBCONCEPTS	
	Grade 3	Grade 4
I. Every society creates laws. Some laws are designed to promote the common good; other laws protect special interests or groups. Penalties and sanctions are provided for violations of law.	Rules and regulations are a part of community life everywhere. Self-discipline enables people to live and work together in harmony, and it can be more effective than external sanctions.	There are state laws as well as community rules and regulations. People cannot live or work together without laws.
II. Governments are established by men. In some situations people delegate authority to government; in others authority is imposed.	Local forms of government can vary from community to community within the state as well as from country to country.	Wisconsin's government, housed in Madison, evolved under the terms of the Northwest Ordinance until the state was created.
III. Democracy is a form of government in which decision making is in the hands of the people who make their desires known through voting, political parties, and pressure groups. Democracy seeks to protect the rights of the individuals and minority groups.	There are communities outside of the United States that are democratically organized, and the people who live in these communities have some of the same ideas held by people in the United States.	The state government is democratically organized, and its officials are elected by the people.
IV. Citizenship involves active participation in the process of governing.	The residents of many communities around the world are active members of local political organizations seeking to change local conditions.	People from many foreign countries settled in Wisconsin and took an active part in shaping the policies established by the government.
V. All levels of government are interrelated. There is a division of responsibility and an interdependence among all levels of government. At the world level, all nations are interdependent.	Communities in the world tend to become closely related as transportation and communications improve.	There are many examples of how village, town, city, county, and state government work together.

POLITICAL SCIENCE FOR GRADES 3–12 (THE WISCONSIN PLAN)

SUBCONCEPTS

Grade 5	Grade 6	Grade 7
The Constitution is the supreme law of the land—it gives Congress the power to enact national laws.	All cultures have systems of laws to promote order, and as the society becomes more complex it requires and develops more laws.	Laws are made by all levels of government, school districts, municipalities, states, and national. Each governmental unit provides means of sanctions. Respect for law is essential to government.
In the United States the institutions of representative government were extended beyond those ever attempted by man before.	Government is necessary for the survival of all cultures, but its form may vary from culture to culture.	People have established various kinds of government to maintain law and order in their respective countries. A government must be strong, yet remain flexible enough to make changes when the people demand change.
Individualism and equality of opportunity, basic to democracy, are frequently challenged by the racist.	In some cultures all of man's energies are directed at producing enough food to survive. In such cultures the concept of democracy may be poorly developed and seem unimportant to the individual.	In the United States the Bill of Rights is a basic part of the concept of democracy.
People working in groups and through various governmental agencies can assist all levels of government and increase the efficiency of operation.	Cultures are generally more successful when the people of that culture share in the responsibilities.	The organization, regulation, and administration of government are the concerns of active citizens. Engaging in politics by upright and honest citizens is a necessity in a democracy.
There is an interrelationship between local and state government as well as between the state and the national government as it tries to meet the needs of the people.	As cultures become more complex and technology more advanced, there is some need for larger and larger governmental units.	Ideas about government come from many sources and from many people.

Exhibit 7

MAJOR CONCEPTS	SUBCONCEPTS	
	Grade 8	Grade 9
I. Every society creates laws. Some laws are designed to promote the common good; other laws protect special interests or groups. Penalties and sanctions are provided for violations of law.	Laws are an outgrowth of peoples' values and customs. Each nation has its own system of laws.	Non-western nations have systems of law that are the product of their customs and values. Laws and customs serve a purpose in the country in which they evolve regardless of how strange and different they may seem to others.
II. Governments are established by men. In some situations people delegate authority to government; in others authority is imposed.	People frequently rebel against their government when it neglects the welfare of the people and frustrates their desire for a better life.	The form of the government differs from country to country, but its power ultimately rests on the consent of the governed. Governments providing for peaceful change of leadership are usually more prosperous than those resorting to violence.
III. Democracy is a form of government in which decision making is in the hands of the people who make their desires known through voting, political parties, and pressure groups. Democracy seeks to proect the rights of the individuals and minority groups.	The origins of the democratic concept can be found in the history of Western Europe.	The concepts, or ideas of what democracy is will vary from culture to culture.
IV. Citizenship involves active participation in the proess of governing.	Active, alert people working cooperatively through established political parties, pressure groups, or societies have been able to make the government conform to their desires, or have established a new government to meet their needs.	Citizenship has a different connotation in different cultures.
V. All levels of government are interrelated. There is a division of responsibility and an interdependence among all levels of government. At the world level, all nations are interdependent.	Famine, war, and the atomic bomb are problems faced by the nations of the world. The use of the United Nations to settle disputes between nations is one alternative to war.	Nations may need help in order to help themselves.

Source: Wisconsin Department of Public Instruction, A Conceptual Framework for the Social Studies

(Continued)

Grade 10	Grade 11	Grade 12
The continuing conflict between local, state and national law began in the early years of United States History.	The process of judicial review makes the United States Government one of laws and not of men. This has been one way the Constitution has been adapted to social change.	Laws and process of law making differ under various forms of government.
The system of checks and balances can be found at the three major levels of government.	The power of the federal government is increasing relative to that of the state's government.	Government is an institution to serve society and therefore the demands it makes upon its citizens will vary. Few governments provide for control through three major divisions, or levels.
The problems of defining democracy are reflected in the controversial histories of the Jackson period.	The extension of the principles of democracy to all the citizens of the United States has not yet been accomplished.	Liberal, democratic government is not easily or rapidly secured.
The political history of the United States illustrates the role of the individual citizen and the importance of, and the need for political parties.	The extension of the franchise to women and others resulted from the action of a determined group of citizens.	Autocracy, or similar centralization of power in one man, or body, develops when citizens shirk their responsibilities.
During this period the United States attempted to follow a policy of not involving itself with the other nations of the world.	The development of the United States foreign policy is a major factor in world affairs.	All nations in the modern world are part of a global interdependent system of economic sociological, cultural, and political life.

in the Wisconsin Schools (Madison: Wisconsin Department of Public Instruction, 1964), no pp.

ularly useful in this area. A brief sample of some of the developmental activities in the unit follows.

Have selected students assume the role of members of the Peace Corps and of nationals in selected Afro-Asian-Latin American countries. Present scenes which dramatize Americans actually living the basic concepts of our democratic heritage as found in the following: Virginia House of Burgesses, Mayflower Compact, Fundamental Orders of Connecticut, New England Town Meeting, Declaration of Independence, Northwest Ordinance, Constitution of the United States (including the Bill of Rights and other amendments), laws of Congress, interpretation of the Supreme Court, state legislation, and leadership of individuals in the field of human rights.

Activities:

Imagine that you are to go to a country such as Nigeria as a volunteer in the Peace Corps. Prepare a report on the history, culture, and economic problems there, emphasizing those factors on which you can hope to develop an understanding of the meaning of democracy when you work with the people of that country.

Have a superior student write a monograph relating democracy to the present stage of development of a specific country of the Afro-Asian-Latin American world. For example: Ghana, Guinea, or Indonesia.[5]

The Lincoln Filene Center has produced another series, entitled "Basic Issues in Citizenship," in which there is a unit called *Teaching the Declaration of Independence and the Bill of Rights.* This unit is valuable to all schools but has unique application in areas where racial discontent and the passions resulting from deprivation and discrimination threaten to sweep aside the idea of reasoning together. The problem, as aptly described by Gunnar Myrdal in his powerful report on the American dilemma,[6] is that in the social-political field Americans' moral judgments are schizophrenic in nature. Americans believe themselves when they say all men should have equal opportunities. This belief is one they base on eternal general values. But this clashes with other pragmatic values by which particular groups like the disadvantaged are effectively closed out of actual political and social life because of some assumed inherent inferiority.

What makes a unit such as *Teaching the Declaration of Inde-*

[5]Lincoln Filene Center for Citizenship and Public Affairs, *Ideology and World Affairs* (Medford, Mass.: The Center, Tufts University, 1963), p. 25–26.

[6]Gunnar Myrdal, *An American Dilemma* (New York: Harper and Brothers, 1944), pp. 1027–1028.

pendence and the Bill of Rights valuable is its honesty. The material in most textbooks on the development of our Constitution is generally presented without any clear relation to the conditions that produced them or to their modern applicability. There seems to be a notion that preserving these documents under glass in the nation's capital is sufficient to assure their preservation in our consciousness. In teaching the Bill of Rights, the distinctive impress of the law should pervade the entire presentation. The dynamic, evolving nature of the Bill of Rights must be imparted by relating its provisions to contemporary as well as historical situations. It must be made clear that the mere existence of such a document will not alone correct the evils of a social system. The curriculum must highlight the history of the Bill of Rights, the processes by which it operates, however imperfectly, and the forces that shape its operation, so that the student will become aware of his own stake and responsibility in the solution of injustices. The substance of this is understood by the people who wrote *Teaching the Declaration of Independence and the Bill of Rights*. In discussing this unit Franklin Patterson, Director of the Lincoln Filene Center for Citizenship and Public Affairs, says:

> The factors making this unit a unique guide for teachers who want to make history really alive for young adolescents include: (1) A rich background for teachers probing into the fascinating evolution of man's basic drive for freedom; (2) A student text section which unfolds the human struggle accompanying the writing of the Declaration of Independence and the Bill of Rights; (3) A challenge to interpret the meaning and significance of these documents in today's changing world.[7]

Teachers and students are enthusiastic about the "Basic Issues in Citizenship" series because it deals with matters that are *important*. We cannot teach our students everything, but we can teach them *something important*. This implies the responsibility of deciding which topics deserve priority in classroom discussion and which subjects can be left for student inquiry on his own.

Professors Donald W. Oliver and James P. Shaver are developing the **Harvard School of Education Experimental Curriculum in**

---

[7]Franklin Patterson, in the Introduction to *Teaching the Declaration of Independence and the Bill of Rights*, Part II, "Basic Issues in Citizenship," No. 2 (Medford, Mass.: Lincoln Filene Center for Citizenship and Public Affairs, Tufts University, 1960).

Citizenship Education, in which values are the subject of a series of debates, dialogues, and recitations. The content is exceptionally promising for students from disadvantaged areas since their value systems often clash with those of society generally. The bases for the selection of the content for the experimental curriculum are: (1) students should be exposed to public problems within our society—situations over which the individual as well as various groups are in conflict, and (2) students should be taught to analyze societal problems within the framework of western political and social values.[8]

It is interesting to contrast the treatment in this material with "The Living Democracy Series" produced by Holmes and Holmes of the **Tufts University Civic Education Center.**[9] Oliver and Shaver present statements, to be subjected to analysis and debate. The Holmeses, on the other hand, have approached the subject through biographical essays on the lives of people—some real, some fictional—who have shaped history; it is thinly disguised "good citizenship value indoctrination," aimed at children living in slums. "The Living Democracy Series" appeals to the emotions in the Horatio Alger style. The American ideals—equality and justice, personal freedom, peace and order, general welfare, and brotherhood—are all portrayed around actual and fictitious lives in American history. The approach of debate and extensive related discussion used by Oliver and Shaver, as is noted in the points of the following quotation, appeals to logic:

> Right to work legislation would kill the patient (the labor movement) in order to cure a local infection.
> By granting to union officials the entrenched position of a union shop, many employers have withdrawn from ·their union members their most powerful instrument of control over their own officials.[10]

Both methods have merit, but the present authors feel that a combination of both might be the most valuable approach. An ingenious teacher might create a very effective program by presenting the "heroic biographies" of "The Living Democracy Series" to students and encouraging them to subject these essays to critical analysis according to the criteria proposed by Oliver and Shaver.

[8]Donald W. Oliver and James P. Shaver, "The Analysis of Public Controversy" (Cambridge, Mass.: Harvard University Press, 1962, mimeographed).
[9]Olive and Wyman Holmes, "The Living Democracy Series" (Medford, Mass.: Tufts University, Civic Education Center, 1962).
[10]Oliver and Shaver, *op. cit.,* pp. 20–21.

Similar to "The Living Democracy Series" is the **New York City** *Call Them Heroes* **Project.** The series includes four 79-page paperback books and a teacher's manual. Intended to inspire elementary and secondary school youngsters, this series features non-fictional people of humble origin who have improved themselves in the face of great obstacles, using education as their means of ascending in the social order. These "heroes" are unlike those in "The Living Democracy Series" in two ways. They are of every race and ethnic background. In addition, they are still alive; they are still at work performing various unselfish services in their local communities within New York City. As the commentator on a television program featuring the "heroes" remarked, "They have not conquered any dragons, but, through their activities, they are becoming part of the folk-lore of the country."

A few of the biographies in this series include "The Young Man Who Kept Running," a young Negro track star who became a dental surgeon; "The Boy With a Million Dreams," a director of a local Jewish youth center, who works as a typesetter; "She Leads a Back to School Parade," a moving story about a girl of Puerto Rican extraction who in 1960 was signally honored by her compatriots as the woman of the year. A former dropout she now acts as the director of the Eleanor Roosevelt Chapter of JOIN, a counseling service helping youth to return to school via work experience or at least to find rewarding work.[11]

The report of the **Williamstown Workshop,** sponsored by the National Council for Social Studies and the Civil Liberties Educational Foundation, addresses itself to the origins of our constitutional rights and duties. This report can be useful to teachers in both elementary or secondary high schools. It is organized so that there is constant reference to four concepts. (See Exhibit 8, pp. 112–114.)

Major Concept 1:

Respect for the fundamental work, dignity, and privacy of the individual is of the essence in our society and underlies all the specific guarantees of the Bill of Rights.

Major Concept 2:

Ours is a government of laws not of men. No individual or group is above the law. Responsibility means obeying law.

[11]These four short stories appear in Book 1 of *Call Them Heroes* (Morristown, N. J.: Silver-Burdett, 1965).

Exhibit 8

EMPHASIZING THE BILL OF RIGHTS THROUGH MAJOR CONCEPTS WITH ILLUSTRATIVE MATERIAL AND COMMENTARY (THE WILLIAMSTOWN WORKSHOP)

Concept	Illustrative Material	Substance, Commentary on Illustrative Material
Concept #3 Specifically: Right of the accused to refuse to testify against himself.	IN AMERICA Thomas Hobbes' *Leviathan*, 1651, Part II, Chapter xxi	"If a man be interrogated by the sovereign, or his authority, concerning a crime done by himself, he is not bound, without assurance of pardon, to confess it; because no man, as I have shown in the same chapter, can be obliged by covenant to accuse himself."
Right to lawful and orderly procedures in the process of arrest and detention.	Habeas Corpus Act, 1679	The act required that a person arrested must be brought before a judge who "shall certify the true causes of [the accused's] detainer or imprisonment," thereby preventing arbitrary arrest and imprisonment.
Procedural Rights (of all sorts).	Massachusetts Body of Liberties, 1641	See previous reference. This document is interesting, further, because a considerable portion of it deals with procedural rights—uniquely Puritan. It is interesting, too, to note the date for the abolition of Star Chamber with that for this document.
Right of Petition.	IN ENGLAND Petition of Right, 1628 IN AMERICA The Petition of the Inhabitants of Anson County of the Province of North Carolina, 1769, *The People Shall Judge*, Vol. 1.	See previous reference. This presents, as much as an example of the exercise of the right of petition, an intriguing array of "frontier grievances"; indeed it is so titled in *The People Shall Judge*.

Concept #1
Specifically:
The right to freedom from unreasonable search and seizure.

James Otis' Speech Against the Writs of Assistance, 1761, *Documents of American History*, ed. Henry Steele Commager, 5th Edition, Appleton-Century-Crofts, 1949, Document #32

Otis' famous argument against general search warrants whose exercise would rob men of their age-old right to privacy.

Concept #2

Fundamental Law and the British Constitution, Letters of the Massachusetts House to Ministry, Jan. 1768, *Ibid.*, Document #44

Massachusetts Circular Letter, Feb. 1768, *Ibid.*, Document #45

Samuel Adams, "The Rights of the Colonists," 1772, *Select Readings in American Government*, eds. William B. Stubbs and Cullen B. Gosnell, C. S. Scribners Sons, 1948; Reading #11

This series of three letters, as does the Massachusetts Circular Letter immediately following, lays down the principle that a constitution is and must be the highest form of civil law, so high that both king and Parliament are subservient to it.

"'. . . ; but [the Legislative] is bound to see that Justice is dispensed, and that the rights of the subjects be decided, by promulgated, standing and known laws, and authorized independent Judges;' that is, independent as far as possible of Prince or People. 'There shall be one rule of justice for rich and poor; for the favorite in Court, and the Countryman at the Plough.' . . ."

Exhibit 8 (Continued)

Concept	Illustrative Material	Substance, Commentary on Illustrative Material
Concept #2—Cont.	Declaration of Colonial Rights: Resolutions of the First Continental Congress, Oct. 1774, *The People Shall Judge,* Vol. I	Still another example of the growing volume of demands for colonial equality before British law at this period in American history.
	The Virginia Bill of Rights, June 12, 1776, *Liberty Documents,* Chapter XIII	This document anticipates parts of both the Declaration of Independence and the Constitution: "inherent rights"; separation of powers; procedural rights; freedom of worship.
	Declaration of Independence	For Americans this is the classic restatement of Locke's, indeed of all, natural rights theory.
	The Massachusetts Bill of Rights, 1780, *Documents of American History,* Document #70	Gems such as the following are to be found in this document: "The liberty of the press is essential to the security of freedom in a state [;] it ought not, therefore, to be restricted in this commonwealth."
	The Quock Walker Case, Massachusetts, 1783, *Ibid.,* Document #71	Citing the first article of the preceding document, "All men are born free and equal . . . ," Chief Justice Cushing of the Massachusetts Supreme Court declared slavery in Massachusetts to be illegal—the first known case of its kind.

Source: The Williamstown Workshop, *A Program for Improving Bill of Rights Teaching in High Schools* (Washington, D.C.: National Assembly on Teaching the Principles of the Bill of Rights, 1962), pp. 56–57.

Major Concept 3:

The law in the long run reflects the ethics and morality of our society.

Major Concept 4:

Free men are responsible men.[12]

For each of these concepts there is developed a series of related principles, in addition to source materials. Here teachers have an opportunity to study source materials with students. Exhibit 8 shows the subconcepts are listed in the first column, and illustrative and source materials are in the middle. The commentary in the third column contains further valuable clues for the teacher.

Materials such as those produced by the Williamstown Workshop have merit only if the teacher can lead the students, through analysis of the documents, to understand the causes and effects of laws on our way of living. If the student can understand the meanings of major concepts and reasons for their existence, he will then be able to draw generalizations that he can apply to all laws, past and present. These can influence his own code of behavior.

Alan Gartner of the **Harvard University Committee on Programmed Instruction** has prepared, in modern, programed form, the Supreme Court cases and decisions concerning school segregation in this country; the book is entitled *The Supreme Court and School Segregation*.[13] Although it deals chiefly with the law, it also reveals the attitudes of our society toward human rights. It proceeds in the conventional programed fashion. The material is current, substantial, and, as one reads on into the body of the project, exciting. Exhibit 9 (pp. 116–120) includes excerpts of a unit describing the intent of the Fourteenth Amendment. Samples of two cases—*Plessy v. Ferguson* and *Brown v. Board of Education*—are given.

---

[12]The Williamstown Workshop, sponsored by the National Council for the Social Studies and the Civil Liberties Foundation, *A Program for Improving Bill of Rights Teaching in High Schools* (Washington, D.C.: National Assembly on Teaching the Principles of the Bill of Rights, 1962), pp. 20–23.

[13]Alan Gartner, *The Supreme Court and School Segregation* (Cambridge, Mass.: Harvard University Committee on Programmed Instruction, 1964).

Exhibit 9

PROGRAMED FRAMES OF UNITED STATES SUPREME COURT CASES (*PLESSY V. FERGUSON* AND *BROWN V. BOARD OF EDUCATION*)

PLESSY v. FERGUSON
Set 1

Before beginning this set of programmed material, please write the following information in the answer space:

1. Your name
2. The date
3. Set 1
4. The time to the nearest minute

Press Answer Button   All Rights Reserved

Press Advance Button

1-1   Homer Plessy was going by railroad from New Orleans to Covington, Louisiana. The coach in which Plessy sat had a sign, "For Whites Only." Although all but one of Plessy's great-grandparents were white, Louisiana law considered him a Negro; he was ordered out of the "White" car. When he refused, a policeman removed him from the car. The next day, Plessy was tried before Judge Ferguson for breaking the Louisiana law which required special railroad coaches for Negroes and whites.

Plessy was traveling in the state of _____.

Louisiana

1-2   Homer Plessy was going by railroad from New Orleans to Covington, Louisiana. The coach in which Plessy sat had a sign, "For Whites Only." Although all but one of Plessy's great-grandparents were white, Louisiana law considered him a Negro; he was ordered out of the "White" car. When he refused, a policeman removed him from the car. The next day, Plessy was tried before Judge Ferguson for breaking the Louisiana law which required special railroad coaches for Negroes and whites.

According to Louisiana law, Negroes and whites were required to sit in _____ railroad coaches.

separate

116

1-3   Homer Plessy was going by railroad from New Orleans to Covington, Louisiana. The coach in which Plessy sat had a sign, "For Whites Only." Although all but one of Plessy's great-grandparents were white, Louisiana law considered him a Negro; he was ordered out of the "White" car. When he refused, a policeman removed him from the car. The next day, Plessy was tried before Judge Ferguson for breaking the Louisiana law which required special railroad coaches for Negroes and whites.

When Plessy sat in the coach marked, "For Whites Only," he was _____ Louisiana law.

breaking or violating

1-4   Homer Plessy was going by railroad from New Orleans to Covington, Louisiana. The coach in which Plessy sat had a sign, "For Whites Only." Although all but one of Plessy's great-grandparents were white, Louisiana law considered him a Negro; he was ordered out of the "White" car. When he refused, a policeman removed him from the car. The next day, Plessy was tried before Judge Ferguson for breaking the Louisiana law which required special railroad coaches for Negroes and whites.

Plessy was tried before Judge _____.

Ferguson

1-5   The Fourteenth Amendment, passed after the Civil War, guaranteed all citizens equality before the law. Homer Plessy argued that the Louisiana law which required separate railroad coaches for Negroes and whites was unconstitutional because it deprived him of equal treatment granted by the Fourteenth Amendment.

The purpose of the Fourteenth Amendment was to * * *.

guarantee equality before the law

1-6   The Fourteenth Amendment, passed after the Civil War, guaranteed all citizens equality before the law. Homer Plessy argued that the Louisiana law which required separate railroad coaches for Negroes and whites was unconstitutional because it deprived him of equal treatment granted by the Fourteenth Amendment.

Plessy believed that the Louisiana law which required separate railroad coaches was _____.

unconstitutional

Exhibit 9 *(Continued)*

1-7   The Fourteenth Amendment, passed after the Civil War, guaranteed all citizens equality before the law. Homer Plessy argued that the Louisiana law which required separate railroad coaches for Negroes and whites was unconstitutional because it deprived him of equal treatment granted by the Fourteenth Amendment.

Plessy said that the Louisiana law was unconstitutional because it _____ the Fourteenth Amendment.

violated

1-8   The Fourteenth Amendment, passed after the Civil War, guaranteed all citizens equality before the law. Homer Plessy argued that the Louisiana law which required separate railroad coaches for Negroes and whites was unconstitutional because it deprived him of equal treatment granted by the Fourteenth Amendment.

The Fourteenth Amendment required (1) * * *, while the Louisiana law required (2) * * *.

(1) equal treatment before the law
(2) separate coaches for Negroes and whites

1-9   During his trial before Judge Ferguson, Plessy claimed that the Louisiana law which he was charged with breaking was unconstitutional and that the trial should be stopped. When the Louisiana Supreme Court refused to stop the trial, Plessy appealed to the United States Supreme Court. He asked them to order Judge Ferguson to stop the trial.

Plessy asked the United States _____ _____ to stop his trial.

Supreme Court

1-10   During his trial before Judge Ferguson, Plessy claimed that the Louisiana law which he was charged with breaking was unconstitutional and that the trial should be stopped. When the Louisiana Supreme Court refused to stop the trial, Plessy appealed to the United States Supreme Court. He asked them to order Judge Ferguson to stop the trial.

He appealed to the United States Supreme Court because he believed that the Louisiana law was _____.

unconstitutional

1-11 During his trial before Judge Ferguson, Plessy claimed that the Lousiana law which he was charged with breaking was unconstitutional and that the trial should be stopped. When the Louisiana Supreme Court refused to stop the trial, Plessy appealed to the United States Supreme Court. He asked them to order Judge Ferguson to stop the trial.

Because he believed that the Louisiana law requiring separate seating on railroad coaches violated the Fourteenth Amendment, Plessy asked the United States Supreme Court to * * *.

stop the trial, order Judge Ferguson to stop the trial

1-12 Plessy said the Louisiana law was unconstitutional because * * *.

it violated the 14th amendment's guarantee of equal protection

1-13 The case then was between (1) _____, who wanted the trial stopped, and Judge (2) _____, who was conducting the trial.

(1) *Plessy*   (2) *Ferguson*

BROWN v. BOARD OF EDUCATION

64 In looking at the place of public education in America, the Court said that it had to look not to 1868 when the (1) _____ _____ was adopted, not to 1896 when the (2) _____ v. _____ decision set up the (3) "* * *" doctrine, but to the place of public education in America (4) _____.

(1) *Fourteenth Amendment*   (3) *separate but equal*
(2) Plessy v. Ferguson   (4) *now or in 1954*

65 In looking at the place of public education in America at the present (1954), the Court found that it had a(n) _____ place.

central or most important

66 Finally, the Court looked at the effect of segregation upon the _____ children.

Negro

Exhibit 9 (*Continued*)

67   The Court held that segregation _____ Negro-children.

---

harmed

---

68   In answering its own question, "Does segregation of children in public schools solely on the basis of race . . . deprive the children of the minority group of equal educational opportunities?", the Court answered that it* * *.

---

does

---

69   In Brown v. Board of Education the Supreme Court ruled that separate educational facilities were in themselves _____.

---

unequal

---

70   The Court ruled that whether or not separate schools were equal in facilities, such schools (1) _____ the Negro's right to (2) * * * of the law, which was guaranteed by the (3) _____ Amendment.

---

(1) *violated*   (2) *equal protection*   (3) *Fourteenth*

---

71   Thus, the "separate but equal" doctrine, first put forth by the Court in the (1) _____ v. _____ case in (2) _____, was overruled by the Court in the (3) _____ v. _____ case in (4) _____.

---

(1) Plessy v. Ferguson   (2) *1896*
(3) Brown v. Board of Education   (4) *1954*

Source: Alan Gartner, *The Supreme Court and School Segregation* (Cambridge, Mass.: Harvard University Committee on Programmed Instruction, 1964), frames 1-1-1-13 and 66–71.

Many have argued against the use of programed material in a subject as highly personalized as human rights. One might rightfully question the "brain washing" effect of programed instruction in which the learner is led into generalizations with no margin for variance and little room for truly personal involvement. However, if this becomes a matter of concern, a teacher might still use the programed materials as an adjunct to any other program mentioned in this chapter. Programs have the advantage of being logical, sequential, and concise; used in conjunction with discussion, debate, role playing, and a study of documents, this program can act as a unifying and reinforcing approach.

Also valuable in establishing understanding about the development of values in society is a pamphlet written by Rachel Reese Sady called "Teaching About Ethnocentrism."[14] Ethnocentrism has special significance for the disadvantaged, who often have little pride in themselves and little regard for their ethnic or national origin. The negative effects of such thinking lead to apathy, lack of effort, despair, and sometimes fanaticism and violence.

Discussion of ethnocentrism inevitably brings up the question of patriotism. Where does the teaching of patriotism fit into a scheme of teaching history and the social sciences? Muessig and Rogers, two students of education and social science, consider this important aspect, raising the following questions:

1. What *should* the schools do about patriotism?
2. Is there a way of dealing with the love of country that is neither over-saturated with indigestible chauvinism nor totally devoid of intellectual, moral, and emotional sustenance?
3. Is there a respect for one's homeland which transcends frantic shouting on the one hand or apathetic ritualism on the other?
4. Is there a substance in patriotism which can be identified and broken down into components like facts, concepts, generalizations, skills, attitudes, and appreciations?
5. Can dimensions of patriotism be taught and caught, grasped firmly and then transferred to a multitude of situations in these anxious, troubled times?
6. Is there a unique essence to democratic patriotism unlike the love of country conveyed in a fascist or a communist state?
7. If we become more and more like the powers which threaten to engulf us what will we have saved?

[14]Rachel Reese Sady, "Teaching About Ethnocentrism," Occasional Paper No. 3, Anthropology Curriculum Study Project, Chicago, Illinois.

8. Can we afford to ignore the need for an intelligent look at patriotism? [15]

This article goes on to a thoughtful discussion of the importance
of patriotism under such headings as:

A patriotic American should have a balanced love of country.
A patriotic American should understand the underlying meaning of
national ceremonies and symbols.
A patriotic American should realize that democratic means must be
used to achieve democratic ends in this society.
A patriotic American should grasp the import of 'diversity' and
'pluralism' as democratic concepts.
A patriotic American should internalize a deep, abiding and selfless
respect for the rights of others. [16]

On reading the above headings, one might think at first that the
authors have answered the second of the eight original questions
in the negative—that any treatment of love of country must be
either saturated with chauvinism or else devoid of intellectual,
moral, and emotional substance. Yet, for the disadvantaged
youngster who is constantly being tempted to think in terms of
what his country has or has not done for him, a study of the pa-
ternal qualities of nationalism can be effective. However, this
should be used only in conjunction (as with programed instruction) with other inductive approaches. Sometimes we tend to err
on the side of too much intellectualism, neglecting our national
and spiritual traditions.

The present-day revolution in civil rights affords many opportunities for a stimulating, first-hand curriculum. The best possible choice of selections in this area is imperative. Like the children in South Africa, many of the children in our schools may
never have learned about the centuries of "silence" or about the
exploitation of the disadvantaged and the ignorant; nor, indeed,
about the constructive contributions of minority groups. The
modern teacher can render the greatest service to the disadvantaged by helping them plan their next steps forward in knowledge, by encouraging them to dramatize their progress, to obtain
from education the wisdom they need in order to plan more
wisely and perform with greater attention to ideals.

[15]These eight questions were selected from Raymond H. Muessig and
Vincent R. Rogers, "Teaching Patriotism at Higher Conceptual Levels," *Social Education*, 28, No. 5 (May 1964), pp. 266–270. Numbers were added
by the present authors.
[16]*Ibid.*

In a provocative, experimental, spiral approach, New York City's **Development of Concepts in Civil Liberties and Civil Rights** uses key concepts of civil rights and responsibilities as a basis for deriving political science generalizations. This has been tried out in various types of schools, with most interesting reports fed back from schools where community tensions are high. Exhibit 10 (pp. 124–125) shows how one key concept is developed throughout the school career.

This program, although not unique in its selection of general concepts and subconcepts, attempts to do several things that few programs to date have done. Most programs, although admitting the need to teach, as important learnings in their own right, civil rights and responsibilities, usually embody them in larger and more general topics (as does, for example, the Wisconsin Program, described at the beginning of this chapter). Thus, these two important learnings tend to become "incidental" to other learnings. Some of the programs on sociology and anthropology, described in Chapter 8, also seem to teach rights and responsibilities as incidental to the general concepts of group interaction. The New York program, on the other hand, focuses directly on rights and responsibilities.

It is to be hoped that, through a combination of these varied approaches, the subconcepts of rights and responsibilities would eventually become integrated—not incidental—in the larger framework and that the student would see them as parts of a mosaic. To accomplish this, however, we must develop each approach fully and scientifically in its own right; otherwise we will end up where we began, with a blurred, fuzzy conglomeration of facts.

Most programs attempt to teach this material at an early age; yet few, if any, really come to grips with it in the kindergarten or in the first and second grades. The New York program has a definitely laid out plan for the kindergarten and early grades. As so often is the case, however, there is a lack of printed, pictorial, and audio-visual material geared to this age (five through seven). Perhaps now, with funds being made available by the federal government for the development of programs in this field, such materials will be produced.

Political science is a fertile field for curriculum study. Basic concepts about government, law, and the rights of individuals have always been articulated by political scientists and the prac-

Exhibit 10

DEVELOPMENT OF A KEY CONCEPT IN CIVIL LIBERTIES AND CIVIL RIGHTS (THE NEW YORK CITY PROGRAM)

KEY IDEA: MEN LIVE TOGETHER, NOT ALONE

ASPECT 1
Freedom in a group is not absolute.

K - 2
Group living limits freedom and imposes obligations but adds to enjoyment.

Each has a right to his preference as to how but each must contribute to the group.

3 - 4
Men working together succeed better than men working alone.

Interdependence is important for progress.

5 - 6
Increasing interdependence as men progress has reduced the number of political entities.

7 - 8 - 9
Constitutions, bills of rights, statutes fix the limits of power, rights, and responsibilities as between the state and the individual.

10 - 11 - 12
Government, in any society, fixes the rules.

ASPECT 2
Self-reliance—dependence.

K - 2
Each individual must care for his own needs and contribute to the group. He is led to expect like behavior from the rest of his group.

3 - 4
Man's search for a better standard of living and security against his enemies forces him to join with others.

5 - 6
Limited resources lead to conflicts among men and societies.

Colonialism created dependent peoples.

7 - 8 - 9
Men seek to create a relationship between the individual and the state that is clearly defined, understood and accepted by both.

10 - 11 - 12
Historical development reveals the varied relationships created between individuals and different states.

ASPECT 3
Self-willed—obey rules.

K - 2
First contact with school tells the child that group living limits freedom: to make noise, to litter street or hallway, to let water run over, to deface walls of building.

3 - 4
Men organize communities whose rules (rules of law) they agree to obey.

5 - 6
Fear of enemy, real or imaginary or projected, forces individuals to meet the requirement of unquestioning loyalty and thereby limits freedom of expression and action. (Denial of freedom is in response to fear.)

7 - 8 - 9
Meaning of rule of law as opposed to rule of man.

10 - 11 - 12
Individualism, its place in a complex, technological age.

Philosophers search for the ideal relationship of individuals to society and to other individuals; the meaning of leadership, who should exercise it, how much power to assign it, etc.

Meaning of anarchy, oligarchy, aristocracy, etc.

Source: New York City Board of Education, *History and the Social Sciences: A Proposal—K—12* (New York: Board of Education, 1964), pp. 52—54. This material was developed by Dr. Joseph O. Loretan and groups of teachers under his direction.

titioners of legal science. Yet the disadvantaged as well as advantaged child of today emerges from a generation that has managed to produce a Hitler, a Franco, a Mussolini, a Sukarno, a Nasser, and a Mao Tse Tung, among others. Would these people have risen to power if the bulk of their constituents had been alert to the basic principles of law and government? As the disadvantaged and underprivileged in the United States increase in numbers, they become more and more restless. If they do not gain understanding and education, they will be potential pawns for extremists and "happy men with promises." The substance of democracy is rooted in its values. We cannot start too early in a child's school career to begin teaching the basic principles of political science and law.

ANTHROPOLOGY
AND SOCIOLOGY

The youngster from the disadvantaged environment is often bewildered by change. To him change is something that just "happens," something in which he is caught up and over which he has no control. He sees only one dimension, a door with nothing behind it. He does not conceive of himself as part of a continuing culture. His identification with man as history is almost non-existent; he feels little responsibility to continue the chain into the future.

The study of society—its origin, institutions, interaction, social change, social control and its problems, and the law controlling human action—can create for the youngster a feeling of his function in society and his power to change his environment. The study of the people of various cultural areas—their aspirations, problems, values, and differences, together with the various ways in which these problems have been approached—can do much to help the disadvantaged child find his place in the continuum of society.

In a recent proposal, Paul Hanna[1] suggests that the elementary and secondary school social studies program be developed along the lines of anthropology. The bone structure would be "man living in an ever-expanding society." Beginning with the family, the

[1]Paul R. Hanna, "The Social Studies Program in the Elementary Schools in the Twentieth Century," in Cubberly Conference, *The Social Studies Curriculum Proposals for the Future* (Chicago: Scott Foresman, 1963).

school, and the neighborhood, the curriculum would eventually encompass the world as a community. In this approach, the sequence of the community studied should take precedence over grade level placement. The major contribution of this proposal is the identification of certain basic activities as common to all societies.

Not all social scientists, of course, concur as to the importance of teaching anthropological and sociological concepts in the social sciences. However, it would appear that for the disadvantaged child studying such concepts would indeed have merit.

Few curriculum programs in anthropology and sociology have as yet been developed. In separate reports, Dunlap and Sady have described some of the efforts being made.[2] The American Anthropological Association has organized the Anthropology Curriculum Study Project for the purpose of determining ways of introducing anthropological concepts into the high school curriculum. Some materials are now in preparation and a few are presently available. One that deserves consideration for the secondary school student is Robert Hanvey's unit, *The Idea of Liberty in American Culture*.[3]

The programs dealt with in the following pages are currently being developed by school systems and university groups. There is nothing new or startling in the terminology describing the concepts or their objectives; most of it already appears in textbooks and in curriculum guides, to be presented to the pupils as maxims or rules. The difference in the new approaches is that they consistently attempt to elicit discovery; they provide a setting in which student action results in finding out and applying what has been found out. The concepts are taught in a spiral fashion, throughout the period of the child's school experiences. In each successive presentation, however, each concept is treated in greater depth, in connection with new subject matter. This is a new approach in some parts of this country. This method offers the obvious advantage of permitting the learner to absorb the con-

[2]Robert Dunlap, "Teaching Anthropology in the High School," *Education Digest,* 26 (April 1961), pp. 52–53; Rachel Rees Sady, "Introducing Cultural Anthropology into the Curriculum," *The Indiana Social Studies Quarterly,* 16 (1963), pp. 31–34.

[3]Robert Hanvey, *The Idea of Liberty in American Culture*, The Anthropology Curriculum Study Project (Washington, D.C.: American Anthropological Association, 1963).

cepts through a variety of experiences and materials not previously offered.

In its current *Social Studies Curriculum Guide,* the Chicago Public School System suggests that understanding the concept of the role of the individual and the development of that concept can be begun in the kindergarten. These illustrations were selected from one unit dealing with friendship. Among the understandings children are expected to learn are:

> To have friends one must be a friend.
> Being a friend includes caring enough to help others.
> Friends can live close by or far away.
> Being a friend includes sharing and cooperating with others.[4]

The pupil is encouraged to discuss the differences between friends and acquaintances.

In grade one the content of the unit on friendship is extended to include the "friendly arts" of sharing, cooperating, respecting, understanding, helping, accepting. It also includes the following:

> Friendliness among all people is important for the preservation of world understanding and peace.
> A friend is someone who accepts you and respects you.
> Being a friend is sharing oneself and things with someone loved and respected.
> To give friendship contributes to a better understanding of oneself and others.
> Making good friends at home and school promotes responsibility and personal satisfaction.
> Being a friend includes respecting and trying to understand oneself and others.[5]

Study units focused on sharing and cooperation are not new in our public school systems. What is new is the movement away from rules and platitudes, through presentation of personalized experiences invoking the causes and results of the interaction known to children as "friendship." Without identifying the specific disciplines, the Chicago program relies heavily on sociological and anthropological concepts.

An extremely interesting program for teaching of social studies through an emphasis on anthropology and sociology is the **Educational Services Incorporated Social Studies Program.** ESI is a consortium of scholars including historian Elting Morison of Mas-

---

[4]Chicago Public Schools, *Social Studies Curriculum Guide, First and Second Grades,* Unit VII (Chicago: Author, 1964), pp. 94–156.

[5]*Ibid.*

sachusetts Institute of Technology, sociologist George Homans of Harvard, psychologist Jerome Bruner of Harvard, archeologist Robert Adams of the University of Chicago, political scientist Franklin Patterson of Tufts, and anthropologist Douglas Oliver of Harvard. The ESI program places its emphasis on the child's understanding of the "cultural" world. The basic aims for first through sixth grade—which could well be applied to the entire history and social science curriculum—are:

> To give children as deep an understanding as possible of themselves and the cultural world, both past and present, in which they live.
>
> To provide an introduction to some of the basic ideas of social science, such as pattern and function, evolution, etc.
>
> To provide an introduction to the methods of social science, to the rules of evidence and the creation and testing of hypotheses.
>
> To do all of these things by creating educational materials and methods that allow children, in a sense, to be social scientists, to work through real problems, as much as possible on their own, and to arrive at their own conclusion.[6]

At the present stage of development, the work of the ESI Social Studies Program is concentrated primarily on two major areas. The first area, intended mainly for the primary grades, deals with man as a primitive hunter and gatherer and with general concepts regarding human evolution. These primary grade units offer a comparative study of the Eskimos, African Bushmen, and Australian Aborigines as representative of this stage of human evolution. Included in the material being prepared for these units are a film ethnology of a Netsilik Eskimo group in Pelly Bay, Canada, and films on free-ranging primates in Africa.

The second area, intended for the intermediate grades, is concerned with the origins of settled life, the domestication of plants and animals, the beginning of community life and of a tradition that could be called Western in the Bronze Age, or Aegean, pastoral culture. These intermediate units will deal with the human phase of the Neolithic Period and the subsequent rise of urban centers in both the New and Old Worlds, including a more detailed study of the Western tradition as it begins to emerge in Aegean Knossos, Mycenae, and Troy. A film study of the origins of maize agriculture in the New World and a unit on origins of urban life in Mesopotamia are also being prepared.

[6]Summary of aims from Educational Services Incorporated, *A Statement of the Aims of the Courses of Study Being Developed by the Social Studies Program* (Cambridge, Mass.: Author, July 1964), pp. 1–2.

The ESI program uses a fundamental approach, presenting man as the inventor who broke away from his primeval past through the use of his intelligence. The project team selects certain periods to illustrate man's progress in time. Arguing along Brunerian lines, ESI proposes that young children can grasp fundamental ideas if they are involved in the activities, the concrete experiences, and the representational type of teaching found to be successful with young children in math and science.[7]

In developing the idea of evolution from the prehistoric past, the ESI scholars discard the idea that the social science curriculum must begin with the immediate neighborhood. Strict chronology is not adhered to although a rough chronological sequence is employed in the elementary units currently being tried out in Newton, Massachusetts, and in New York City. For the disadvantaged youngster, who rarely thinks about what came "before," this approach has merit. In addition, the materials being developed by ESI rely heavily on artifacts, films, and pictures, giving the nonverbal child a chance to understand the content through his ears, his hands, and his eyes. Reading materials are available but are considered as only one method of communicating ideas.

Another approach to studying of man and society is the **Contra Costa County, California, Social Studies Series.** It too is based on the principle that we can understand ourselves and our institutions by learning how the scientist approaches the study of primitive people and of their institutions. The curriculum starts on the third-grade level with a study of primitives of Africa, the people of the "hot dry lands," the "boat people" of Hong Kong, and the people of Switzerland. The learning experiences are varied, as are those in the ESI Social Studies Program, and are available to the students through many communications media. The children learn to read ideographs as well as original African tales. The program goes a bit farther; the youngsters experience the physical skills used by primitive peoples, such as discus throwing, making fire, and leaping from animals (imaginary in the school, of course). The youngsters are also exposed to primitive music, played on primitive instruments (built by the students, whenever possible). Whereas the ESI Social Studies Program is producing all of its own original materials, the Contra

[7]Jerome S. Bruner, *The Process of Education* (Cambridge, Mass.: Harvard University Press, 1960).

Costa Social Studies Series uses as many existing materials as possible.

The sample of the Contra Costa program in Exhibit 11 (pp. 132–134) is brief and will suffer somewhat from being seen out of context; unfortunately, it does not include all of the experiences involved in this unit. However, it is presented here to illustrate how the program builds understandings by offering experiential relationships between factual data and concepts, past and present.

In the summer of 1964, teachers selected by the State Commissioners of Education of the New England and Middle Atlantic States, working under the direction of William Kvaraceus of the **Lincoln Filene Center of Tufts University**, developed social science teaching materials ("Basic Issues in Citizenship," described in Chapter 7), in which the group process became the basis for the study of the social sciences. Their program had the same general objective as the New York City program—the understanding of the group process—but differed in that the subject matter was more personalized. The concepts are placed in settings easily recognized by the youngster—a club, a team, a student organization, the Supreme Court decision of 1954 and how it affected integration of *their* school from the point of view of *their* relationships.

This approach, although it has particular advantages for the withdrawn, disadvantaged youngster who meets the problem of group membership almost every day, can be equally effective when used with the student who has a dominant role in the group, for only when each youngster understands his own role and the functioning of the entire group will we really achieve the interrelationship so vital to group dynamics.

Exhibit 12 (pp. 135–137) is an excerpt from "Basic Issues in Citizenship." Note that the same concept is being taught in grades five through nine. It differs only in content material and in the depths of understanding called for.

Based on the material in "Basic Issues in Citizenship," a program is presently being developed in New York City, in which emphasis will fall on the concept of group membership as an aspect of the meaning of equality. Although Exhibit 13 (pp. 138–139) is taken from the larger unit, **Development of Concepts in Civil Liberties and Civil Rights** (see Exhibit 10 in Chapter 7), it serves to illustrate how emphasis can be placed on a specific discipline within the context of several other disciplines.

Exhibit 11

COMPARING AFRICAN PRIMITIVE LIFE WITH THE AMERICAN SOCIETY (THE CONTRA COSTA PROGRAM)

Main Idea II: Many activities of Primitive People Are Carried on Through the Family or Tribe; a More Modern Community Provides for These Activities Through Organized Institutions

LEARNING EXPERIENCES

Development (Contd.)

> Note: From these papers the teacher should gain some insight as to how the children feel about such adult expectancies. Their attitudes will guide some of the discussion of this section.

19. Recall the restrictions placed on Nomusa's behavior? What things was she not supposed to do? Where did she learn these things?

20. Ask the children, "Why are girls and boys taught different things?" Follow through in discussion until children conclude that boys and girls do different things in life.

21. Summarize on the chalkboard 1) the things people learn, 2) how they learn it, and 3) what sources they use, e.g.,

Things people learn:	How they learn:	Sources:
to earn a living	watching	books
to read books	reading	libraries
how to behave	doing	churches
games	hearing	schools
etc.	experimenting	people
	etc.	etc.

Discuss the differences in learning in school with teachers, books, and experiments, and learning in families with people and imitating what they do. Bring out such differences as:

    1. where one can check information

    2. where one can learn more new things

    3. etc.

22. Show FS Equatorial Africa (Families Of The World). Recall with the children that the family is very important to primitive man (MP Life Of a Primitive People).
Let the children list some of the family activities that take place at the home of a primitive, such as, caring for children, eating, playing games, etc. Which of these activities are carried on in the children's own homes?

23. Ask, "Which activities of this family were carried on by men and boys?" "Which by women and girls?"

24. Recall the number of wives shown in the above filmstrip (experience No. 22). Do all primitive men have the same number of wives? How many did Nomusa's father have? How do Zulus get their wives? (Thirty-One Brothers And Sisters, pg. 39.)

25. Let each child make a diagram of his immediate family structure, e.g.,

Now with the class plan a diagram of Nomusa's family structure.

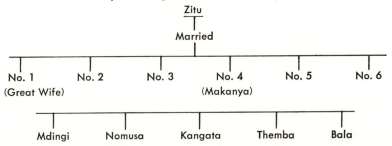

26. Let the children draw pictures of a variety of things a little primitive child might do for recreation.

     Note: Observe whether the children's pictures reflect the learning that there are many children to play with in the primitive family.

     Suggested references:

     Fun Around The World, pp. 54, 70–71

     FS Wambo And Tawa Of The Hot Lands

     Alternate experience:

     Some groups of children planned a tribal party such as the one held by Nomusa's tribe. They planned:

     games   —Thirty-One Brothers And Sisters, pp. 49, 90–94
     dances   —Thirty-One Brothers And Sisters, pp. 89, 91
     contests   —Thirty-One Brothers And Sisters, pp. 79–80
     songs   —Music Near And Far, pp. 86–87

27. Have the children enter these pictures and their family structure diagrams in their notebooks.

28. Let the children write on "How We Settle Disputes."

     Note: The purpose of this activity, which is really an opener, is to assess the range of thinking of the children. Is their functional knowledge limited to "fighting" or do they indicate "talking things over" and "recourse to laws or rules?"

29. Have children list situations which might be taken to court for settlement, e.g., ownership of a bicycle, traffic violations, etc.

30. Recall the hunting episode from Thirty-One Brothers And Sisters. Who settled the ownership of animals killed on the hunt? Who decided on the punishment of a careless hunter?

Exhibit 11 *(Continued)*

31. Let the children discuss what might be good and what might be bad about having an all-powerful chief.

32. Who will be the next chief? (Thirty-One Brothers And Sisters, pg. 72.)
    Note: Do not let the children over-generalize the succession to the role of chief. All tribes do not automatically make the eldest son chief.

33. Let the children write on "How Nomusa's Father Showed He Was A Good Chief."
    Examine these writings and help the children identify qualities, e.g., bravery, fairness, etc. List on chalkboard.

34. Ask the children, "What other rules regulated the lives of the primitive people studied?"
    List these rules on the chalkboard. Ask the children to pick out the ones that
    tell what girls must and must not do
    tell what boys must and must not do
    prevent bad luck
    keep people safe

35. Discuss why rules would be necessary in a large family such as Nomusa's family.

Conclusion

Have the children dramatize situations that show a sharp contrast between primitive and modern activities, such as,

Recreation: A modern family going to a show
            A primitive family telling of a hunt with songs, etc.

Education: Modern children learning to read at school
           Primitive children listening to a story-teller

Law: A father recovering his stolen car in court
     A chief telling his tribe who gets the slain animal

Develop a chart of big ideas that might be asked about people anywhere, but using ideas discovered in studying primitive people as a start, e.g.,

---

BIG IDEAS TO WATCH FOR

1. Is this a primitive culture?
2. What kind of family structure do they have?
3. Is there a reason for the kind of home they have?
4. Do the people have some kind of government?
   Etc.

Note: Such a chart can be a guide in reading and in viewing films through the rest of the unit.

Source: Contra Costa County Schools, *Third Grade Social Studies 1963* (Contra Costa, Calif.: Author, 1963), pp. 21–25.

Exhibit 12

DEVELOPING A SINGLE CONCEPT THROUGH THE GRADES
("BASIC ISSUES IN CITIZENSHIP")

Concept   *Common need or interest determines group membership.*

Grades 5–6

Understanding   Every individual has the responsibility to work for the good of the group.

Motivating Activities

1. Use films or stories which illustrate teams (or groups) at work.

2. Dramatize a team or club working well together and one in which there is no cooperation.
   a. To which would you prefer to belong?
   b. Which is more apt to succeed?
   c. How can group (team) spirit be developed?

3. Are you a member of a team or club? What is your position or role in the group? Could the team or club do without your contribution?

Developing Activities

1. Bulletin board displays a collection of pictures or news items in which individuals are contributing to groups under the heading: We Do Our Share, or The Group Needs Each of Us, or We Are Our Neighbor's Keepers.

2. Children poll members of their family to find out how each thinks he has done some one thing to help the community and why he did it. Children consider whether we have an obligation to be our "neighbor's keeper."

3. Teacher shows class statistics or a film of the conditions in the state of Mississippi or some region in the United States such as Appalachia. The class is asked to decide what is the responsibility of their state, their community, and/or their class to remedy these conditions.
   a. The problems discussed may be poverty, the plight of the disadvantaged, poor educational facilities and standards, primitive conditions in agriculture, soil erosion, etc.
   b. Children are assigned reading about how such conditions were solved in other places by the acceptance of responsibility by the people themselves. The Puerto Rican "Operation Bootstrap," the Israeli story, or that of the TVA may be studied. Class tries to decide whether these methods are applicable to situations in the United States.

4. Make a list of the alliances among nations. Illustrate on a color-keyed map each grouping. The class discusses what keeps these nations grouped together.

135

Exhibit 12 (Continued)

Grades 5–6 (continued)

5. Use a current item in the news referring to U.N. activity in some trouble spot in the world to discuss: Should the American citizen help pay this bill?

Culminating Activities

1. The class may agree to share used books with a class in a developing country.

2. Children prepare an exhibit for Open School Week on the theme: The World Needs Each of Us.

3. The class petitions the student organization of the school to undertake the adoption of another school in an underprivileged area of the United States, and outlines the reasons therefore. They list ways in which the children in this school may help the children in the other.

Grades 7–9

Understanding   Different groups and individuals define equality in terms of their own needs and interests.

1. Role play: A teen-age girl's struggle with her parents for her own room, or the use of cosmetics, or to stay out to an hour of her own choosing. A teen-age son wants his own car.
   a. How reasonable are these requests?
   b. Was the parents' decision just?
   c. How would you feel if that discussion applied to you?

2. Dramatize the campaign of a Parents' Association for a traffic light on a busy through street, as opposed to the interests of a smooth flow of traffic in the morning rush hour as presented by the Traffic Commissioner. (Each community may select a comparable local issue for illustrative purposes.) Or use a cartoon or a selection of headlines chosen from the newspapers of the community indicating opposing views. The class discusses: Who's Right? What should the decision be?

Developmental Activities

1. Children read a summary of the decision of the Supreme Court in the case of *Brown vs. Topeka Board of Education*, 1954. They invite appropriate resource people to class, or read their views on the following issues that have arisen in implementing the Court's decision that separate facilities provided for Negroes could not be equal. Children discuss these and other issues as they arise.
   a. Does integration in schools mean that the neighborhood school cannot remain confined to the children in the community if all are white?
   b. Will the granting of services now supplied to white children in these schools provide Negro children with the equality of opportunity they need?

    c. Can a predominantly white community be expected to pay for special services needed by the Negro children transported into their school district, often contrary to their wishes?

    d. Who should pay the bill for these services?

2. Comparable case studies may be developed with respect to as many of the following situations as a class may need to understand the concept to be taught:

    a. Who should bear the responsibility for retraining those displaced from jobs by technological change?

    b. How can equality in a court of law be guaranteed to minority groups, the poor, the illiterate, the non-English speaking, the new arrival?

    c. What right do property owners have to choose their neighbors?

    d. What is the right of the original settlers to facilities for which they paid as opposed to the demand of newcomers?

    e. Does religious freedom mean the right to persuade others to share your belief or the right of children in the public schools to hear no Bible reading or prayers?

3. Class prepares a series of ideas for cartoons on each of the case studies they have analyzed, and talented students execute these ideas for a school bulletin board entitled: Who Is Equal?

Culminating Activities

1. The class presents a dramatization of episodes in our history that showed how different groups in a conflict each saw their equal rights denied. The students in the assembly are urged to discuss the possible decision appropriate for each case.

2. The class makes a study of student relationships in the school to decide whether there are those who think they are being treated unequally. The facts are presented to the student council for resolution.

Source: Northeastern States Citizenship Project, *Basic Issues in Citizenship No. 3: Equality: A Principle and a Dilemma* (Medford, Mass.: The Lincoln Filene Center for Citizenship and Public Affairs, Tufts University, 1964), Provisional Edition—For Evaluation Only.

Exhibit 13

EXPERIMENTAL MATERIAL ON THE MEANING OF EQUALITY
(THE NEW YORK PROGRAM)

Who Belongs to a Group: The Meaning of Equality

Sub-Concept: People are different, yet alike.

Grades K–2	Men share same needs and hopes no matter how different they look, where they live, how they worship.
3–4	Given the same opportunity, men have an equal potential for adaptation and learning. All men must earn a living. In different places, people earn their living differently depending on the geographical factors and how well informed they are.
5–6	Stages of development from hunting and gathering to complex industrial society are analyzed. Children note that the more complex the society, the more interdependent it is. Men everywhere seek to progress. All do progress but at varying rates of speed.
7–9	Discuss and demonstate the positive duty of the better able to help the less able progress. (a) Illustrate different areas of the world where those with knowledge and skills help the less well developed. (b) UN equality in membership gives meaning to UN effort to help all reach the standard of living of the highest.
10–12	Universality of man and its expression in the Universal Declaration of Human Rights are a modern political phenomenon.

Sub-Concept: All men are equal in rights however different in ability, wealth, interest.

Grades K–2	Rules are the same for all in home, school, neighborhood, highway. Those who disobey the rules expect the same treatment or penalty.
	Public facilities must be open to all who share the same need or interest in them in the same terms: e.g., right to attend an integrated school, play in the park, go to same movie, rent in same house, ride in the bus, sit in the same restaurant.
3–4	Intelligence, creative talent, know no color line. Ability, wealth, and interest depend on factors unrelated to race, religion, ethnic origin.
	Public facilities may be privately or publicly owned. All people, of whatever race, religious preference or ethnic origin, contribute to the well being of all and have the right to share in the wealth created by others on equal terms. All pay taxes, all public services must be equally available.
5–6	Different meanings for ability, wealth and interests in other cultures: e.g., ability for a primitive culture as opposed to an advanced culture (to adapt to one's environment vs. to think abstractly).
	In the U. S. we reject inequality as to rights. In other cultures, there may be acceptance of inequality as to rights based on class or caste (often based on race as in India) or tribal membership (ethnic origin alien to those in power as between Behutu and the Watutsi), or new migrant who is set apart as less worthy (Irish, Jews, Italians, Negroes, Puerto Ricans).

7–9	Application of the same rules for all does not necessarily mean equality: e.g., trial by jury for a narcotics peddler as opposed to a stock swindler. To achieve equality in rights may require methods of compensating for factors that make men unequal in ability and wealth.

7–9   Application of the same rules for all does not necessarily mean equality: e.g., trial by jury for a narcotics peddler as opposed to a stock swindler. To achieve equality in rights may require methods of compensating for factors that make men unequal in ability and wealth.

Meaning of equality: Does it include equal right to hold office, literacy tests for voting, all equally able to run a school or hospital, equal right to sit on a jury, to go to a free college even if less qualified academically, etc.? Must a jury have a cross-section of the population to be fair to the accused?

10–12   What is equality in legislative apportionment in Congress or General Assembly of UN? Should representation be based on numbers or responsibility, rural or urban considerations?

Are differences in ability, wealth and interests compatible with the achievement of equal rights for all?

Extent to which absolute equality is possible among individuals, among nations.

Sub-Concept: Old vs. new members in groups: fear of change.

Grades K–2   Group's members have duty to accept newcomer and integrate him into group: e.g., new baby, new aunt or uncle, new playmate or neighbor, classmate, teacher.

Understand the meaning and dangers of prejudice (prejudging) and stress the contributions which a new member may bring: e.g., newcomer should be given an early opportunity to contribute positively to class.

3–4   New York City's population composed of many different immigrant groups as well as migrants from other parts of the U.S. The variety of their places of origin may be set in juxtaposition to their variety of skills and ideas both within each group and among the groups.

When jobs are scarce, all have equal rights to get jobs, promotion and salary.

5–6   Immigration policy limits number of immigrants but not the number of migrants. An analysis of the causes of migration should show that men share the same reasons for moving.

Problems of a varied population in language, literacy, jobs, health, education.

7–9   Problem of new migrant as "low man on totem pole"—unfamiliar with his environment's expectations, he is less prepared to cope with the problems of living in it.

"Melting pot" vs. pluralistic culture: right to be different vs. national unity and sense of identification with the whole.

10–12   The sociological, economic and political implications of migration and the changing role of government in the resolution of these problems.

Source: New York City Board of Education, *Development of Concepts in Civil Liberties and Civil Rights,* experimental edition (New York: Board of Education, May 1964, mimeographed), p. 6.

The primary value, for the disadvantaged, of an approach such as that of the New York program (Exhibit 13) is that it comes to grips with a basic "fact of life" problem. Until he comes to school, the disadvantaged youngster tends to think that all people are more or less alike, for his experiences are limited and he has seen few outsiders. The situation is reversed when he comes into school and is confronted with many people—fellow classmates, as well as teachers—who speak differently, dress differently, and act differently. Such a confrontation often gives the disadvantaged youngster the feeling that, because he is different, he is inferior. For him, the differences stand out more sharply than do the similarities. However, if he learns at the outset of his school career that people can be both different and alike; that all men are equal in rights, however different they may be in ability, wealth, and interest; that group memberships change and that such changes are difficult to effect, he can attain an understanding of group dynamics and the assurance that one may intervene and cause change rather than simply learning to accept things as they are.

The goals in presenting materials in anthropology and sociology to young people are: to afford them an understanding of human values, human behavior, and resulting problems through a study of the origin and development of these values; to present to them a study of the nature and function of social institutions; to help them comprehend the interdependence of all peoples, especially in our current civilization; and to develop powers of inquisitiveness, of curiosity, and of analytical judgment. Charles Frankel recently wrote that "research into social attitudes, beliefs, and values is naive and incomplete unless the attention that is paid to verbal . . . utterances is supplemented by the investigation of actual institutions and habits of behavior."[8]

[8]Charles Frankel, "Needed Research on Social Attitudes, Beliefs, and Values in the Teaching of Soical Studies," in Roy A. Price (Ed.), *Needed Research in the Teaching of the Social Studies*. Research Bulletin No. 1 (Washington, D.C.: National Council for the Social Studies, 1964), p. 29.

9

HISTORY
AND GEOGRAPHY

Each area of the social sciences provides a rich mine of knowledge for the student to explore. History, as a pioneer social science, instills in man a sense of continuity. History can be defined as a reconstruction of the past with an emphasis on causality and temporal sequence of events. The ability to organize past experiences in sequence enables the individual to grasp his relationship with the past, his "place in the sun," and helps him to anticipate his course in the future.

Until recently, educators have generally agreed that children have little sense of chronology until they reach the sixth grade and that instruction in such concepts should be delayed until children have matured beyond that level. Today, however, this conclusion is being questioned. Lowell and Slater, in studying five- to nine-year-olds in England, found that, although there was a steady increase in "perception of simultaneity with age, the ability can be improved under certain conditions. Overall, the children of this age group were able to appreciate 'order of events'."[1] This concurs with Piaget's findings.[2] John and Elaine Cumming go so far as to define ego identity as, largely, the "idea of continuity and

[1] R. Lowell and A. Slater, "The Growth of the Concept of Time: A Comparative Study," *Journal of Child Psychology and Psychiatry and Allied Disciplines*, 1 (1960), pp. 179–190.

[2] Jean Piaget, *Le développement de la notion de temps chez l'enfant* (Paris: Presses Universitaires de France, 1946).

expectation of sameness, or predictable change."[3] Children from disadvantaged homes, in particular, lack a feeling of being a link in the chain of events that we call history. The present, the immediate, is their way of life. All too soon, however, they learn that the present is only a temporary arrangement and that one must, while in the present, anticipate and plan for the future and not regard each day as a "dead end" and the future as determined by outside forces over which the individual has no control.

Children from disadvantaged environments tend to function on a concrete here-and-now level; remote or abstract ideas are often beyond their comprehension. History, presented through the actual documents of the people and their times, can make the unfamiliar become familiar and the remote concrete. From the study of history one begins to coordinate abstract ideas with concrete practices.

History should be studied selectively, and the periods selected should be studied in depth. Knowledge derived from a concentrated and rich study of a selected period of history will be more interesting to the students and more fruitful in terms of basic generalizations; it will provide the student with the tools of the trade of living. Once he has learned to accumulate data, synthesize, analyze, and draw conclusions about one historical period, he can apply these skills elsewhere. Thus the teaching of history must be thought of as a "method" rather than a course of study.

An increasing number of scholars are committed to the idea that history should be studied with documents and source materials that are varied, accurate, intrinsically interesting, and representative of the period, rather than solely through the use of a textbook. As the student, simulating the ways of the historian, works with these original materials, he will develop a more critical ability to discern fact from fiction and be more willing to suspend judgment in the absence of facts.

Some of the key generalizations that can be drawn from the study of history through the methods of the historian are:

> Growth and development of different civilizations show that each civilization has certain treasured values.
>
> History is a record of events describing changes men have brought

[3]John and Elaine Cumming, *Ego and Milieu: Theory and Practice of Environmental Therapy* (Englewood Cliffs, N.J.: Prentice-Hall, 1962), p. 94.

about or failed to achieve. Adaptability to respond to change is essential if men and institutions wish to develop.

History shows that the actions of men have consequence. Events and institutions are the result of something preceding them.

New generations seek to study the past in the light of their own experience.

Geography may be said to complement history, since it locates the place of action for historical events. Geography deals with the arrangement and association of physical circumstances that make one area of the earth like or unlike another. Although geography has its own set of generalizations, it is, nevertheless, part of history. A full understanding of people and places of the past and present is a basic aim of geographers. An interdisciplinary approach can flourish if the integrity of the individual disciplines is built up by examples that are real and meaningful.

Geography by its very nature lends itself to pictorialization, measurement, and classification. Few inhabited parts of the world have not been mapped, photographed, and talked about. But the full impact of the use of audio-visual facilities on students who are frustrated with the conventional textbooks, has yet to be demonstrated. The documentary films presently in use are, for the most part, too long, too packed with peripheral information, and too impersonal. What are needed are short films, graded in the difficulty of the concepts presented, and so designed as to cause the student to identify with characters in the film.

Observation, discussion, and verification of ideas and skills by means of pictures and maps have more effect on disadvantaged youngsters than does the cold and impersonal textbook. Linear reading can become a phobia to a child for whom reading is difficult. The ancient Greeks, with their amazing record of cultural advance, knew this; they communicated their culture through public debate, dramatics, architecture, and art.

Wendt and Butts used motion pictures, television, filmstrips, and slides to teach world history and geography to average ninth graders.[4] The classes using the films completed the course in one semester while the control group took two semesters. A test primarily of factual information showed no significant difference

[4]Paul R. Wendt and Gordon K. Butts, *A Report of an Experiment in the Acceleration of Teaching 10th Grade World History with the Help of an Integrated Series of Films* (Carbondale: Southern Illinois University Press, 1964).

between the two types of achievers. Cattle used the same design on high and low achievers and found that the materials were equally effective for both groups.[5]

Another interesting aspect of the newer programs in geography is the emphasis on cultural geography rather than physical geography. The essence of this new approach is contained to a good degree in the generalizations stated here:

> Places on the earth (a house, a town, a city, a region) are related in terms of direction, distance, size, time, and culture.
>
> Maps are various types of pictures of earth. They are needed for different purposes by explorers, businessmen, weather experts, statesmen, geographers, and citizens.
>
> People use and are influenced by the resources and to some extent other natural elements of the earth in various ways to fit into or to modify their ways of living and thinking at different times.
>
> Regions are names of political, physical, economic, or cultural areas that have several similar features but are different enough in other ways to make them noticeable.

Although there are many research studies that suggest that geography can be taught in the early grades,[6] few programs for teaching history and geography through generalizations to early childhood classes have been developed.

The **Social Studies Curriculum Project of Educational Services Incorporated,** in its Colonial Unit, is producing a subunit, called "The Emergence of the American," that emphasizes the generalizations of both political history and geography, with the other disciplines playing a minor role.

Encouraging students to acquire the methods of the social scientist in collecting and analyzing data is the basic aim of all the ESI programs. Students need to learn how to make use of original sources, pictures, letters from citizens and government

[5]Eugene Cattle, "An Experiment Using World History Films with Selected 10th Grade Pupils." Unpublished doctoral dissertation, Southern Illinois University, 1964.

[6]*See:* Haig A. Rushdoony, "Achievement in Map-Reading: An Experimental Study," *The Elementary School Journal,* 64 (1963), pp. 70–75; Bernard Spodek, "Developing Social Science Concepts in the Kindergarten," *Social Education,* 27 (May 1963), pp. 153–256; Mary Rusnak, "Introducing Social Studies in the First Grade," *Social Education,* 25 (October 1961), pp. 291–292; and E. L. Greenbladt, "An Analysis of School Subject Preferences of Elementary School Children of the Middle Grades," *Journal of Educational Research,* 55 (August 1962), pp. 554–555.

officials, reprints of news items, historians' accounts of specific periods, and other appropriate materials. These materials are distributed in packets containing, in addition to original documents, cards, maps, games, and cartoons. No "answers" are given to the students; they must study the documents and draw their own conclusions. Teachers with a talent for the dramatic can organize some of this in the form of rallies, town meetings, court scenes, plays, or folk-type chorales.

The disadvantaged youngster, with few experiences outside of his circumscribed environment, finds the conventional study of history unrealistic. For him, history is made up of heroes who lack reality because we learn about them less for their human qualities than for their acts of heroism. In addition, conventional history is made up of a succession of events, which, the textbook says, sprang from the "causes" listed in the first part of a chapter. The effects or conclusions are those of the writer of the textbook; very rarely does the student have the opportunity to draw his own conclusion from a collection of conflicting data. The disadvantaged youngster gains little from this approach. The ESI materials are different. They are built around the everyday people of the period; some became great, but others remained very much the same as the student; they were human beings and acted in a human fashion.

An example of this approach is a section of the Colonial Unit called "The American Revolution Against British Authority," in which there is a booklet called *How Did the American Colonists React to Parliament's Tea Act of 1773?* As shown in Exhibit 14 (pp. 146–147), a crisis situation is set up. Excitement is in the air.

Presenting the very words of "plain people" gives the colonists a reality not usually found in history texts; almost any youngster can identify with a merchant or a government worker. The disadvantaged youngster comes to see that he is not too different from the people who lived before him. Hopefully, he will come to see his place in the continuum of history.

The next step in this subunit is a list of suggestions for a debate. There are two scripts for a role play of debate in the House of Lords. These scripts are based on excerpts from actual debates held in the House of Lords on November 30, 1774, and between October 26 and November 10, 1775. The excerpts themselves are included so that one can read and consider part of the actual Parliamentary Record.

Exhibit 14

SAMPLES OF ORIGINAL SOURCE MATERIAL FROM THE COLONIAL UNIT (ESI)

BOSTON, MASSACHUSETTS
NOVEMBER—DECEMBER 1773

Nov. 4, 1773:   The following notification was issued:

> The freeholders and other inhabitants of the Town of Boston . . . are hereby notified to meet at Faneuil Hall, on Friday, the 5th of November . . . at ten o'clock in the forenoon. . . . They are justly alarmed at the report that the East India Company, in London, is about [to ship] a cargo or cargoes of tea into this and the other Colonies. . . . They have reason to fear, not only the trade upon which they depend . . . is threatened to be totally destroyed, but what is [worse], the [tax] laid on . . . [tea] will be fixed and established, and our liberties, for which we have so long struggled, will be lost.

> A large flag was also hung out on the Pole at Liberty-Tree, and at 11 o'clock all the bells in town were set a ringing . . . .

Nov. 5, 1773:   On Friday . . . there was a very full meeting of the freeholders, and other inhabitants of this town, in Faneuil Hall. . . . After due deliberation [they] came to the following resolutions:

> RESOLVED: That the duty imposed by Parliament upon tea landed in America is a tax upon the Americans . . . without their consent.
> That it is the duty of every American to oppose this attempt [to tax the Americans].
> That whoever shall . . . in any [way] aid or abet in unloading, receiving or vending the tea sent out by the East India Company, while it remains subject to [a tax] here, is an enemy of America.

HOW DID THE AMERICANS REACT TO THE DESTRUCTION OF THE TEA?
Remembering the accounts of the tea parties, the action that was taken, and who took the action, consider the following three comments. With which view do you agree?

1.

After hearing about the Boston Tea Party, John Adams said:
This destruction of the tea is so bold, so daring, so firm, intrepid and

inflexible, and it must have so important consequences . . . that I cannot but consider it as an epoch in history . . . . The question is whether the destruction of this tea was necessary? I apprehend it was absolutely and indispensibly so. They could not send it back . . . . Then there was no other alternative but to destroy it or let it be landed. To let it be landed would be giving [in to] the principle of taxation by Parliamentary authority, against which the continent has struggled for ten years.*

2.

Benjamin Franklin wrote to the Massachusetts Committee of Correspondence:
I am truly concerned, as I believe all considerate men are . . . . that there should seem to any [man] a necessity for carrying matters to such extremity, as . . . to destroy private property . . . . I cannot but wish and hope that . . . our General Court [in Massachusetts] will . . . repair the damage and make compensation to the [East India] Company [for its tea].**

HOW DID THE AMERICAN COLONISTS UNITE TO ANSWER PARLIAMENT'S ACTS OF 1774?

By May of 1774, news had reached the American colonies that Parliament had passed a bill to close the harbor of Boston and that it would take further action to punish the colony of Massachusetts. The colonists reacted quickly to this news.

1.

On May 18, 1774, John Andrews, a Boston merchant, wrote to his brother-in-law in Philadelphia:
Dejection [is] imprinted on every [face] we meet in this once happy, but now totally ruined town. Yes, Bill, nothing will save us but an entire stoppage of trade, both to England and the West Indies, throughout the continent: and that [stoppage] must be determined . . . speedily [and] absolutely. The least hesitancy on your part [to the south] and the matter is over . . . .***

*Works of John Adams, ed. C. F. Adams (Boston, 1850–56), II, 323–324.
**Writings of Benjamin Franklin, ed. A. H. Smyth (New York, 1905–07), VI, 179.
***"Letters of John Andrews, Esq. of Boston," Proceedings of the Massachusetts Historical Society, VIII (1864–65), 327–328.

Source: Social Studies Curriculum Program, How Did the American Colonists React to Parliament's Tea Act of 1773? Packet 1 for "The American Revolution Against British Authority" (Cambridge, Mass.: Educational Services Incorporated, June 1964), pp. 9–10. The above was taken from an experimental edition; the material is presently being revised for final publication by Random House.

Exhibit 15 shows sample role-playing assignments ESI has developed for different groups of students. They will be using as research materials items from newspapers of the period being studied.

Here, again, one sees a direct conflict of ideas, of different points of view. The student is now required to decide which is right—what *his* choice would be. The disadvantaged youngster needs this exercise in selection, in weighing, in decision making. Things don't "just happen." He has a part in their being.

Exhibit 16, showing how people are the substance of history, is drawn from the diary of Noah Blake. This diary does *not* present the traditional, value-laden description of the pioneer teen-ager. The learner must read the day-by-day account of doings and happenings and make his own generalizations. Thus, the student, again, has a chance to discover, to make judgments, to act as a social scientist. Here we have the concrete elements from which comparisons to other colonies, to the Old World, and to the present can be evolved. Relationships between past and present can be inferred. Problems, people, and regions can be classified because of their similarities or differences. Hypotheses as to how people would act at different times and under other circumstances can be formed.

The teachers can help the students derive insights—from documentary sources, pictures, artifacts, recordings, and questions—that will lead students to notice contradictions. The impact of this kind of approach to an understanding of history from source materials will be lost if comparable data and approaches are not used from the events going on in the world today. It will help if the students grasp the point that history, within limits, repeats itself and that from history we learn about ourselves. For the disadvantaged this kind of instruction is imperative. The process of noting differences of opinion, of studying and analyzing judgments, serves to stimulate the child's thinking processes and to extend his horizons. Some examples of the diary, in Exhibit 16 (pp. 150–151), make fascinating reading.

Another part of the Colonial Unit deals with geography. The same method is used as in the history segment. Original documents are reproduced and given to the students. From these they must plant a colony, draw maps, be aware of temperature, rainfall, and nearness to the ocean or river, and read possible relationship into pictures. In Exhibit 17 (pp. 152–154), history and

Exhibit 15

ROLE-PLAYING ASSIGNMENTS IN AMERICAN COLONIAL HISTORY (ESI)

From the Point of View of the British:

THE AMERICAN REVOLUTION AGAINST BRITISH AUTHORITY
LONDON, 1773 to 1776: HOW DOES IT LOOK FROM HERE?

You are in London. During the 1770's, crucial events occur in the colonies of North America, where ever-enlarging groups of colonists are challenging first the authority of the British Parliament and then the authority of the King. Such challenges are met by acts of Parliament and statements of policy by the King.

How is this story told in London?

How do the colonists upset the British?

To answer these questions [and the ones listed below in Part V], you will find in this envelope a set of news stories [on cards] describing the events of the 1770's, as they *might* have appeared in London.

From the Point of View of the Colonists:

THE AMERICAN REVOLUTION AGAINST BRITISH AUTHORITY
AMERICAN COLONIES, 1773 to 1776: HOW DOES IT LOOK FROM HERE?

You are now in the American colonies. The events of the 1770's force groups of British colonists to turn against the British Parliament, then the British King, and finally to separate and withdraw from the British Empire.

How is this story told in the American colonies?

How do the British upset the colonists?

How does the American story compare with the British story?

To answer these questions, you will find in this envelope a set of news stories [on cards] describing the events of the 1770's, as they *might* have appeared in the American colonies.

Source: Social Studies Curriculum Program, *How Does It Look from Here?*, from "The American Revolution Against British Authority" (Cambridge, Mass.: Educational Services Incorporated, 1964). Material taken from experimental edition, presently being revised for final publication by Random House.

Exhibit 16

EXCERPTS FROM NOAH BLAKE'S DIARY (ESI)

NOAH BLAKE, my book
March the twenty-fifth, year of our Lord 1805
Given to me by my Father Izaak Blake and my
Mother Rachel upon the fifteen year of my
Life

Noah Blake's diary follows the events of his life for part of 1805. It should give you some understanding of what life was like in colonial America, even though it was written after the colonial period. This is true because life was very much the same for backwoodsmen and their families throughout the 18th and early 19th centuries. There are some sketches of the things familiar to Noah and some scenes of his daily activities. They will help you to understand his story and to answer some questions about the things he did.

You might like to keep this diary. To help you make it complete, there are three things to do. Read the diary. Answer the guide questions. For each starred (*) question find a picture which best helps you to answer it. Paste the picture on the page opposite Noah's entry in the diary. Then the book will be complete and yours.

1805 March 25th: A cold and windy day. Neighbor Adams with son Robert stopped by. We drank mead and mint tea. No work done this day. Father is going to the woodlot behind the barn tomorrow for floor timbers. I shall assist him.

March 26th: A light snow fell which Father believes will be the last of the winter. We fell'd a fine oak and rolled it upon rail for Spring seasoning. Mother is joyous at the thought of a good wood floor.

March 27th: Father was wrong about the weather, for it snowed again today. We kept within the house, sharpening and making ready tools for the year's farming.

March 29th: Snow stopp'd during the night but it is very cold. My window glass is frosty and my ink froze.

March 29th: I moved bed into the Loft for warmth. It is good to be with Mother and Father but I miss my good window.

March 30th: Worked in the forge barn. The Loft proved too warm so I moved back into my room.

March 31st: A fine Sunday. The roads were bad and we could not get to Meeting. Had Service to our Lord at home.

1805 April 1st: Robert Adams came by in his Father's sleigh to take me to the Adams' place. I shall help them for the week with maple sugaring.

April 2nd: Worked at the Adams place.

April 3rd: Do (ditto)
to
April 6th:

April 7th: Palm Sunday. Went to Meeting with the Adams and returned home with Mother and Father. I earned a tub of sweetening for my week's work. It is good to be home again.

April 8th: The snow has gone and reasonable weather for Spring business has arrived. I finished the Winter's lot of nail-making and put the forge to rights.

April 9th: Flooding all but washed our bridge away. Father says the bridge beams are seasoned and ready. When the waters subside, he shall begin to erect it. We are shaping up the abutments.

April 10th: Worked on the bridge abutments. Daniel helped with the bigger stones.

April 12th: Good Friday. It rained all day. Brook went up.

April 13th: Bluebirds arrived. We finished the abutments with the help of Mr. Adams and his son Robert who came by to assist. River lower.

April 14th: Easter Sunday. A fine Service. Saw Sarah Trowbridge the new girl at the Adams. She is very pretty.

April 15th: Father used Daniel this morning to set the bridge beams in place for homing the joints. I tried my hand at spring plowing in the afternoon, with Daniel.

April 16th: More plowing. Father still setting up the trusses. He says the joints have swollen with the rains and need new chiseling.

Source: Colonial Unit: Life on an American Farm. Material produced cooperatively by Educational Services Incorporated, Watertown, Massachusetts, and the Deputy Superintendent for Curriculum and Research and Districts 21 and 22, New York City. Material presently being revised for final publication by Random House.

Exhibit 17

COMBINING HISTORY AND GEOGRAPHY CONCEPTS (ESI)

The students have three projects to work on:

I. *Being a Colonist Part I:* Why do men plant colonies?

   A. Reading the statements of explorers

   B. Spelling out what other information they need

II. *Being a Colonist Part II: Planting a Colony.* Where do you plant a colony? How do you guarantee its success?

   A. Analyzing pictures of the Virginia and New England areas

   B. Evaluating New England and Virginia and predicting the success of possible colonies in one or the other of these regions

   C. Mapping out the colony you would plant and spelling out how men would live

III. *Being a Colonist Part III:* How did some real live colonies fare?
   Reading the stories

An example of original source material:

John Smith—*The Sixth Voyage, 1606, To Another Part of Virginia*

SECOND BOOK OF TRUE TRAVELS

There is but one entrance by sea into this country, and that is at the mouth of a *very goodly bay,* 18 or 20 miles broad. The cape on the *south* is called *Cape Henry.* The land, white hilly sands, like unto the downs, and all along the shores great plenty of pines and fir trees. The *north* cape is called *Cape Charles,* in honor of the Duke of York. The isles before it are called Smith's Isles, by name of the discoverer.

In the bay and rivers are many isles both great and small, some woody, some plain, most of them low and not inhabited. This *bay* lieth north and south in which the water flows near 200 miles and hath a channel for 140 miles of depth between 6 and 15 fathoms, holding a breadth for the most part 10 or 14 miles. From the head of the bay to the northwest the land is mountainous and so from thence by a southwest line, so that the more southward, the farther off from the bay are those mountains, from which fall certain brooks which after come to fine, principal, navigable rivers.

The mountains are of divers natures, for at the head of the bay the rocks are of a composition like mill stones. Some of marble, etc. And many pieces like christal we found as thrown by the water from those mountains, For in winter they are covered with much snow, and when it dissolves, the waters fall with such violence that it causeth much overflowing in some narrow valleys.

First, therefore, *of the earth of New England.* It is a land of divers and sundry sorts all about Massachusetts Bay, and at the Charles River is as fat, black earth as can be seen anywhere; and in other places you have clay soil, in other gravel, in other sandy as it is all about our Plantation at Salem, for so our Town is now named.

The form of the earth is here neither too flat in the plainness, nor too high in hills, but partakes of both in mediumness, and fit for pasture or for plow or meadow ground, as men please to employ it; though all the country be as it were a thick wood for the general, yet in divers places there is much ground cleared by the Indians, and especially about the Plantation, and I am told that about three miles from us a man may stand on a little hilly place and see thousands of acres of ground as good as need to be, and not a tree in the same.

It is thought here is good clay to make bricks and tiles, and earthen pots as needs be. For stone, there is plenty of slates at the Isle of Slate in Massachusetts Bay, and limestone, freestone, and smoothstone, and iron stone, and marble stone also in such store, that we have great rocks of it (and in the harbor near by). Our plantation is from thence called Marbleharbor.

Of minerals there hath yet been but little trial made, yet we are not without great hope of being furnished in that soil.

The fertility of the soil is to be admired at, as appeareth in the abundance of grass that groweth everywhere both very thick, very long, and very high in divers places; but it groweth very high because it never had been eaten with cattle, nor mowed with scythe, and seldom trampled on by foot. It is scarce to be believed how our kind and goats, horses, and hogs do thrive and prosper here.

Of the Waters of New England

New England hath water enough both salt and fresh, the greatest sea in the world, the Atlantic sea, runs all along the coast. There are abundance of islands along the shore, some full of wood and mast to feed swine, and others clear of wood and fruitful to bear corn. Also we have excellent harbors for ships, as at Cape Anne and at Massachusetts Bay, and at Salem.

The abundance of sea-fish is almost beyond believing, and sure I should scarce have believed it except I had seen it with mine own eyes. I saw great store of whales, and crampusse, and such abundance of makerils that it would astonish one to behold, and likewise cod-fish. There is a fish called basse, a most wholesome and sweet fish as ever I did eat. Of this fish our fishers take many hundred together, which I have seen lying on the shore to my admiration. Yea, their nets ordinarily take more than they are able to haul to land, for want of boats and men they must let many go.

Exhibit 17 (*Continued*)

Samples of Work Sheets for Students:

Planting a Colony: Would a colony thrive and grow in this region?

Directions: Now you will work on the New England area following a pattern which is similar to your work on Virginia. Some tasks are different, therefore you should read all directions carefully.

New England

Location:

Directions: In addition to Smith's description of New England, you have available a map of the Atlantic coastal region. *Locate* on your map the area Smith calls New England. Put in latitude. Locate as many places as you can by carefully underlining them with a pencil and a ruler. Indicate by *symbols* that you make up some features of the coastline, vegetation, forests, islands, good harbors, etc. Michael Spark's writings may also help you in this job.

Climate:

Directions: In writing your description of the climate of New England keep in mind, as you did for Virginia, the things your audience would most want to hear, namely, how they would react to it. Be certain to include as many aspects as you can: temperature, rainfall, nearness to the ocean, etc.

Problems the Colony Might Face:

Directions: State the specific problems the colony might face in its initial stages. Be realistic and honest. Also try to anticipate how they might be effectively overcome.

Looking Into the Future:

Directions: Look into the future and predict what might be happening in the colony fifty years from now. Be specific about how men might earn a living, what patterns of life they might follow, what new industries might develop.

Source: "Being a Colonist," mimeographed materials developed by Educational Services, Incorporated and tried out experimentally in New York City's public schools under the direction of Dr. Joseph O. Loretan.

geography are woven together, while the special concepts of geography are emphasized. Teachers using the geography segment of the Colonial Unit should keep in mind that its basic purpose is to give students an understanding of:

1. Why men became colonists.
2. The kinds of arguments used to further such enterprises.
3. The expectations of those who went and hoped to get others to go.
4. The geographical differences between the two English settlements.

The **Philadelphia Public Schools Geography Curriculum** is a course of study on the eastern hemisphere in which the dominant idea is that studying geography means thinking like a geographer.[7] With this course, Philadelphia becomes one of the first major communities to treat geography as a separate discipline. Its theme is that our shrinking earth requires that each pupil clearly see the significance of building up his country's resources and removing the barriers between nations.

Yet, in reviewing the material, we find that so many of the other disciplines are involved that one can question the claims of the Philadelphia program. The very opening statement, "The teacher should discuss with her class the importance of current affairs," calls upon history. Perhaps it would be more accurate to say that in this program the major emphasis is placed on the geographer as a social scientist. Exhibit 18 (pp. 156–159) is an excerpt from the program.

The child from a disadvantaged environment, lacking, perhaps, in verbal ability, can fit into any of the current affairs committees described in Exhibit 18. The materials in the classroom geography laboratory are imaginative and should be stimulating. The use of varied types of maps, weather maps, political maps, maps of wind belts, vegetation, oceans, railroads, air routes, and so on, should extend the horizons of those youngsters. These are experiences, even though vicarious, that they never dreamed of. But more important are the two words found throughout the program: "Prove It!" It is this challenge to the thought process that the disadvantaged youngster needs to develop his skills. Given the materials, the learner must become a

[7]Philadelphia Public School System, *Geography of the Eastern Hemisphere* (Philadelphia: Public School System, 1964).

Exhibit 18

GUIDING STUDENTS TO THINK LIKE GEOGRAPHERS
(THE PHILADELPHIA PROGRAM)

CHAPTER ONE—METHODS OF TEACHING

Does it show a clear relationship between man's activities and his natural environment?

At the beginning of the school year the teacher should discuss with his class the importance of current affairs in the study of the Eastern Hemisphere. Copies of newspapers can be scanned for inclusion of items relating to the people, countries, or continents to be studied. Pupils may be urged to seek and collect worthwhile articles for use when needed. Perhaps a committee can maintain a bulletin board pocket or a classroom library folder to which all contribute clippings and from which all can borrow.

While an outline of content is provided in Chapters Three to Six of this course of study, flexibility in the order of topics is encouraged in order to take advantage of developing major news stories. In addition, "open-end" lessons are scheduled for each continent so that countries in the news can be studied. Through these provisions, full use can be made of the opportunties offered by the newspaper, radio, or television for making geography a vital learning experience for pupils. Every current event has a specific and significant location. The geographic basis of world affairs should be emphasized, with frequent reference to maps.

The exciting nature of recent developments in the Eastern Hemisphere makes it likely that a current event can be used to motivate interest in an assigned country. During the study, news items can be collected by the entire class if possible, certainly by a committee. Individual pupil notebooks of the loose-leaf type can be used for newspaper items regarding the continent being studied.

There are many sources of information about significant current affairs: daily newspapers, weekly news magazines, current events papers printed exclusively for classroom use, and daily radio and television news reports, supplemented frequently by special programs giving detailed coverage to a major development. The school library will provide such valuable magazines as the NATIONAL GEOGRAPHIC.

Illustrations of the Use of Current Affairs:

a. Current Affairs Committees

The class can be divided into four committees which are assigned to bring to its attention the latest of geographic information.

1) Picture Committee—to collect, mount, and file pictures.

2) Map Committee—to collect, mount, and file maps.

3) Filing Committee—to save clippings from magazines and newspapers.

4) Bulletin Board Committee—to arrange news items, pictures, maps.

b. Notebooks

The class can be directed to leave several pages blank after the regular notes taken for each country. These pages should be filled at any time of the year with news items of that country.

c. Current Affairs Board

The teacher can post a large map of the Eastern Hemisphere. As a pupil reports on a significant current event, he can tack the clipping at the map's edge and connect clipping and location of event with colored yarn.

d. Forum

Periodically the teacher can conduct forums, in which review and analysis of news items about a certain continent are made.

e. Bibliography

Classes can keep class bibliographies of references to the Eastern Hemisphere in current newspapers and magazines. They should arrange the list according to countries and products mentioned. For example, a news item about sheep-raising in Australia would be listed under "Australia" and under "wool."

Guiding Pupils to Make Inferences

A pupil may be interested in geography, read extensively, use maps skillfully and command much information, and still be inadequate in his geographical knowledge. Facts prove themselves in use. Unless cause and effect are understood, and unless transfer of learning to new situations is frequent, the full meaning of geography is lost.

We seek to help the pupil learn not only the "what" and "where" of geography, but the "why" also. The geographer compares and relates his information. It must follow, then, that we want our pupils not only to identify and locate the capital of each country but also to understand why these cities developed where they did. We want them to know the major industries of the Eastern Hemisphere, but in addition, to explain the development of industries even in areas lacking raw materials.

This questioning, defining, comparing, contrasting, guessing, verifying, comprises a process of discovery that impels the pupil to explore geography to the fullest, that makes his study of each new country an adventure, and leaves him with the depth of understanding that marks one who really "knows his subject."

The discovery-process is based on inductive thinking. Inductive thinking involves making inferences or drawing conclusions from a number of facts. Repeatedly in this chapter on teaching method, we have noted the use of the problem approach to lead the pupil to discover basic relationships. By this approach he learns that as every one of man's activities *occurs in a place,* it is often the character of the place that makes the activity possible. When a pupil understands that much of the nature of Egyptian life is related to the nature of the Nile River; that slow-developing Southeast Asia is handicapped by hot, heavily forested, swampy countryside making transportation and communication difficult; that the new governments of Africa are vitally concerned with agriculture, mineral resources, and river systems, then the pupil not only knows geography but thinks like a geographer.

Exhibit 18 (*Continued*)

Throughout Chapters Three to Six are placed "discovery concepts," each numbered and set off in a box. These discovery concepts are basic geographic axioms or generalizations which the teacher will guide the pupil to understand. To illustrate, in the study of India and its Ganges Valley, the Discovery Concept #25 is, "Major centers of population are located in lowland areas" (page 115). When the pupil has completed the course, he should be in possession of a number of basic concepts which will be indispensable in approaching any geographic question, problem, or topic. In short, he will be equipped with the fundamental tools of geographic reasoning.

Illustrations of the Use of the Inferential Method:

a. Prove it!

Pupils can be challenged to think geographically by such approaches as, "Most cities of more than a million people in the Eastern Hemisphere are located on a river, sea, or ocean. If you agree with this statement, give examples to support your answer." Or, "Why is this a true statement?"

b. If—

Hypothetical geographic situations can be brought up to challenge the class to support their guesses.

"If Australia had a Mississippi River, ..."

"If Japan were connected to Manchuria, ..."

"If there were no mountains in North Africa, ..."

"If oil were produced heavily in Algeria, ..." (For advanced pupils.)

c. Charts

Arranging facts in chart order often helps pupils to make generalizations.

Examples of such charts are:

1) Chart of Daylight—This could be a simple column chart, posted on a bulletin board, comparing the average hours of daylight of the regions being studied, in summer and in winter. Its purpose would be to strengthen the concept of the relationship of sunlight to growing seasons.

2) Chart of Major Rivers—showing their length, navigability, major cities—to develop importance of rivers to growth of a region.

3) Chart of Climate. (For advanced pupils.)

Type of Climate	Where Found	Description	Products Grown	Plant Life	Animal Life

Arranging the Classroom as a Geography Laboratory

The influence of classroom environment is direct and all-pervading, no less in the teaching of geography than in other subjects. As the pupil seeks answers to questions, books and maps should be immediately accessible. The very appearance of the room should provide daily stimulation of geographic interest.

Survey your classroom. Note the use of blackboards for new vocabulary listing and topic outlines. Bulletin boards are an excellent medium for the display of current events clippings, drawings, and maps. In a prominent place should be maps and globes. For exhibits, at least one table is required. Facilitate model construction and map-making with a workbench and appropriate tools. A file cabinet, if available, is helpful for the storing of picture collections.

Printed materials deserve special mention because of their variety, number and importance. In addition to the class text, supplementary references such as world almanacs and atlases are necessary. But the best book is poor if it cannot be understood. Check vocabulary levels and mark books with a notation system to indicate reading levels to help pupils find materials they can read.

Most important of all is the teacher. His own enthusiasm for geography, his knowledge of content materials, his pursuit of truth will affect the level of learning in the classroom.

Illustrations of the Use of the Classroom as a Geography Laboratory:

a. Exhibits

A classroom table can be placed under a bulletin board and the two can be used for current geographic displays. A large paper outline of a political map of a continent might be placed on the bulletin board, while sample products of the continent, with appropriate labels, are placed on the table. For each product a ribbon can be stretched to the area on the map where the product is produced. A paper pocket can be stapled to the bottom of the bulletin board, in which the class can place reference notations and clippings of topics under discussion.

b. Bulletin Board Displays

The pupils should be encouraged to contribute interesting and varied maps to a continually changing map display. If at all possible, the center of the board should contain a map of the country being considered. Weather maps, political maps; maps of wind belts, vegetation, oceans, railroads and air routes, ocean currents, population density, crop distribution, products—can be used. Frequent references to these maps should occur, and, where possible, conclusions should be drawn. For example, population, topography, and rainfall maps of the same country can be compared, and the pupils can be stimulated to advance explanations for the present distribution of population.

Source: Philadelphia Public School Systems, *Geography of the Eastern Hemisphere,* Course of Study for Grade 7 (Philadelphia: Public School System, 1964), pp. 23–26.

detective. He must ferret out, select, reject, synthesize, analyze, and *only then* come to a conclusion.

In a study begun in 1961 and still in progress, the **Portland Public Schools Social Studies Project** is trying out new approaches for teaching social studies, taking into consideration methods of teaching the various disciplines. The Portland study merits careful consideration. The following handbooks are complete and are being tried out in the schools of Portland: *American History, International Relations, Economics, American Government and the Political Process,* and *A Guide to High School Social Studies: An Introductory Course.* While all of these are provocative, the last two are most helpful in developing guidelines for teachers and curriculum materials for disadvantaged students.

A Guide to High School Social Studies: An Introductory Course is intended for ninth-grade students, subscribes to the idea that the student should review the basic concepts in geography and history—the generalizations that are unique to each of these two disciplines—before undertaking units on Europe and area studies of Asia, Africa, and Latin America. Readers will be interested in many of the generalizations referred to in the *Guide to High School Social Studies* concerning geography and history, but only a few can be mentioned here. It must be assumed that the generalizations in geography and the themes in history alluded to are review data, since developing each of the generalizations inductively and also completing all of the other prescribed work in this course would lead either to a great superficiality or to the need to omit substantial blocks of content. Exhibit 19 lists some of the geographical generalizations presented in the Portland program that are of particular use for the disadvantaged youngster.

Generalizations from history emphasize that the great problems of mankind are fundamentally the same. The Portland program lists twelve themes, which appear in Exhibit 20 (p. 162).

Again, one notices in the Portland program an emphasis on the personal, on man as an individual who controls, changes, and plans his life. Whereas the ESI Colonial Unit tends to see man as a political, economic, and anthropological being, the Portland program lays stress on the esthetic aspects of man in the development of history.

The question, how to motivate the disadvantaged to learn, has been asked often. One approach is that taken by ten former

Exhibit 19
SOME GEOGRAPHICAL GENERALIZATIONS
(THE PORTLAND PROJECT)

Man, like other animals, may upset the balance of nature but only he, through the practice of conservation, is able to restore the balance.

The sequence of human activities and cultural patterns is related to the geographic accessibility, location, and the time period under consideration inasmuch as people at different cultural levels assess and use a given environment in different ways.

People are unevenly distributed about the world because certain areas present greater opportunities for livelihood than others, a condition due in part to resource distribution and in part to man's activities.

The character of the influence of the natural environment on man and his activities is chiefly a passive one of limitation and hindrance and man provides the stimulus which leads to action to overcome obstacles or to make use of opportunities with which he is faced.

The economic processes of production, exchange, distribution, and consumption of goods have a geographical orientation, and the nature of the spatial relationships involved reflects the kinds, qualities, and quantities of resources, the technological level, and the prevalent sociopolitical attitudes.

Source: Portland Public Schools, A Guide to High School Social Studies: An Introductory Course (Portland: School District No. 1, Multnomah County, Oregon, 1962), pp. 12–14.

Peace Corps volunteers, who set out to change the history curriculum in the Cardozo High School in Washington, D.C. Cardozo is a public high school in a low-income, delinquency-ridden area of Washington, D. C. These former Peace Corps volunteers, aided by two master teachers from the public school staff, the principal, a curriculum coordinator, and a research specialist, served as interns in Cardozo High School. The ten volunteers worked two periods a day, under the direction of the master teachers. The following is a description of the program as told by one of this group:

In history, the rationale was to teach a course as relevant and as interesting as possible to urban youth. The four interns began the arduous job of creating lessons day by day. In effect, the interns began to write their own texts. Mistakes, lapses, and failures resulted, but the raw material of creative teaching—experimentation—fostered an approach to teaching among the interns that will last long after they leave Cardozo. These lessons, called "readings"—duplicated for the students on a ditto machine—offered a variety of materials to the students. Some examples: a lesson on the six-shooter from Walter

Exhibit 20

UNIVERSAL THEMES IN HISTORY
(THE PORTLAND PROJECT)

1. *The Economic Theme.* Man is an economic individual. The most fundamental problem he, his family, his tribe, his society, and his nation must face is how to make a livelihood . . .

2. *The Social Theme.* Man is a social individual. For reasons of reproduction and convenience man likes to live in groups . . .

3. *The Political Theme.* Man is a political individual. Throughout the ages and in all places man has recognized the need for some sort of authority for the governing of individuals . . .

4. *The Religious Theme.* Man is a religious individual. Always and everywhere he has had some kind of religion . . .

5. *The Legal Theme.* Man is a legal individual. At all times and places man has evolved laws to govern his relations with other men . . .

6. *The Philosophical or Intellectual Theme.* Man, generally speaking, is an intellectual individual. This is one of the basic characteristics that separates him from other animals . . .

7. *The Conflict Theme.* Man is a fighting individual. The record of his existence from the earliest time to the present is filled with constant struggle with his fellow man . . .

8. *The Dominant Theme.* Man is a conquering individual. His record from earliest times to the present is one of his dominations of other men . . .

9. *The Freedom Theme.* Man is a freedom-loving individual. This preoccupation is one of the main threads running through the whole fabric of man's history. Man has been trying to free himself from domination by natural forces, by superstition, and above all by his fellow man . . .

10. *The Literary and Musical Theme.* Man is a literary individual. Literature is another major thread running through the whole fabric of the history of civilized man . . .

11. *The Esthetic Theme.* Man is an esthetic individual. Throughout the ages he has shown a constant impulse to see beauty in or to beautify his surroundings . . .

12. *The Great Man Theme.* Man is a great individual. Although history is no longer viewed as "the essence of innumerable biographies," there have been times in the course of history when individual men have exercised powerful influence on the course of events . . .

Source: Portland Public Schools, *A Guide to High School Social Studies: An Introductory Course* (Portland: School District No. 1, Multnomah County, Ore., 1962), pp. 17–21.

Webb's *Great Plains* to illustrate frontier inventiveness; excerpts from Genesis and Babylonian myths to demonstrate cultural diffusion; Thucydides' description of the Plague during the Peloponnesian War to capture the flavor of fifth-century Athens. Or take a lesson on the Boston Massacre. The standard text version is known to most schoolboys. One intern took the diary of a Boston merchant, aggressively anti-British, who described the event. Comparing the account with the facts, the class saw how the merchant had employed emotion-laden words ("Bloody Murder," "Massacre," etc.). The reading became a lesson in word evaluation. Another teacher approached the same lesson from the viewpoint of one of the participants, Crispus Attucks. Few students realized Attucks was a Negro. A discussion developed around the question: How much of a commitment should a Negro have toward a society that degrades him? The use of Attucks was not accidental. The study of the Negro in American history, according to the interns, is one meaningful way of "connecting-up" with their students. Meaningful in that the study of the Negro may generate pride and respect for one's self within Negro youth or, better yet, offer insights into the contemporary Negro's position in America. If so, then the effort is worthwhile.

One intern completed a unit on slavery by asking his class to write an essay on the "Hangovers of Slavery," that is, how did two and a half centuries of oppression mark a people? Though good grammar and spelling were spotty, the essays showed a depth of understanding and an insight into the Negro's present-day status that were profound. Thus the past and present become inextricably intertwined in the teaching of history.[8]

This "homemade" curriculum incorporates many of the aspects of the more expensively developed university curricula. When the interns wrote their own "textbooks," they included, primarily, original source material, if they thought the youngsters could handle it. They used contrast to teach current concepts and emphasized the role of the individual in changing history.

[8]Larry Cuban, "The Cardozo Peace Corps Experiment in Urban Education," *Social Education,* **28** (December 1964), p. 448.

10

ECONOMICS

All children should understand the importance of the concept of useful work, that is, the idea that children, teachers, and parents should perform services or create products that are economically valuable. This concept has a somewhat more practical application for children from disadvantaged homes than for other children, because the disadvantaged are far more tied to the exigencies and frustrations of the workaday world. Youngsters of the inner city and those who live on marginal incomes from small farms and factories are faced with daily economic decisions. Many of them are responsible for doing the marketing, for taking the money to the landlord and to the electric company, and for performing other economic chores. By the time they reach the first year of high school, most of them have held a paying job of some sort. The world of work is very close to them. From their own experiences, as well as those of relatives, they understand what it means to work and what it means to be unemployed.

The current revolution in learning theory, with its emphasis on teaching broad concepts to young children by presenting them in the language of children, has specific application to economics. As a structured body of knowledge economics is in essence the same in primary grades as in graduate schools. The problem of the schools is to develop appropriate methodology to present the economics structure in a manner interesting and understandable to students of all ages.

There is a growing interest in developing the generalizations from economics as a basic part of the school curriculum. This interest is the result, in part, of the finding of the Joint Council on Economic Education and the American Economic Association that there is a critical lack of understanding of our free enterprise system among teachers and students. This problem of economic illiteracy is fraught with serious consequences. Until it is overcome, an underprivileged one-third of our nation is deprived of a basic tool of economic survival. These people must gain an understanding of the principles of supply and demand, of limitations on purchasing power, and of free enterprise if they are to accept and achieve within our economic institutions.

Economics has so far received little emphasis in most social studies curricula throughout the nation. Courses in economics are not required for certification to teach. How can our teachers meet the responsibility of teaching fundamental economic relationships if they are not required to study the subject? Policy groups, curriculum builders, and education departments everywhere need to face up to this question.

The facility with which most entering junior high school students absorb the basic economic concepts is a measure of the extent to which senior high school students can comprehend such ideas as monopoly, foreign trade, and monetary policy. The Elkhart Project, after several years of experimentation, finds that children in the first three years of school grasp economic concepts with ease. Darrin,[1] in a study in the District of Columbia Teachers College Laboratory School, concluded that more economics can and should be taught in the elementary schools and that this could be done through visits to stores, construction sites, and freight yards, through the use of current news events and audio-visual materials, and through the introduction of economics concepts in classes in mathematics, science, and literature.

For the disadvantaged, there are new communication media (radio, television, printed advertisements, etc.) that can facilitate their participation in discussions and other activities relating to the consumer problems of money, rent, installment buying, unemployment, and Social Security. This child is now freed, in

[1]Garney L. Darrin, "Economics in the Elementary School Curriculum: A Study of the District of Columbia Laboratory Schools." Unpublished Doctoral Dissertation, University of Maryland, 1958.

part, from his major academic handicap—limited reading ability, which, before the advent of radio and television (especially the latter), kept him from acquiring specialized knowledge. His parents, usually, are still uneducated, his home is still devoid of books, the local school he attends may still be backward, and problems of time or transportation often make a visit to a public library difficult. But radio and television have opened up magical new vistas of sight and sound, providing an escape from the restricted cultural ghetto.

The **Seattle Public Schools Economics Program** has used many new media to develop a tentative, experimental curriculum in economics for kindergarten children. One interesting and unique aspect of this program is its emphasis on individual values in economics rather than on colorless "economic principles." For example, it presents, as a universal concept, the idea that *all* people are confronted with a conflict between unlimited wants and limited resources. Certainly, this is a concept that is not foreign to most of us, but the disadvantaged child is often preoccupied with this conflict as he faces it personally. Once he realizes that this problem *is* universal, he is more likely to put aside private disappointment and begin to share with everyone else the struggle for economic advancement.

Exhibit 21 is from a program developed by the Seattle Public Schools for kindergarten through sixth grade. Note that a distinction has been made between the economic concept and the children's interpretation of the concept. Since Concepts III and IV really seem to implement Concept II, they are italicized in this illustration.

The **Elkhart Project**, a twelve-year experimental program begun in 1958, had as its purpose the need to develop "an organic curriculum in economics." The study was based on the hypotheses that children at all grade levels "can become excited about the abstract ideas underlying their experiences, and that these ideas can be presented in such a way as to reflect the basic structure of the body of economic knowledge."[2] Lawrence Senesh, the

[2]Lawrence Senesh, "The Organic Curriculum: A New Experiment in Economics Education," Reprint Series #2, Purdue University School of Industrial Management Institute for Quantitative Research in Economics and Management. Reprinted from *The Councilor*, 21 (1960), pp. 43–56.

Exhibit 21

ECONOMIC CONCEPTS IN THE FIRST GRADE
(THE SEATTLE PROGRAM)

ECONOMIC CONCEPT I

The basic economic problem confronting all people is the conflict between unlimited wants and limited resources.

CHILDREN'S INTERPRETATION

Everyone has many wants.

Goods are the things we want.

Service is the work performed for another person.

To *consume* means to use goods or services.

Everyone is a *consumer* of goods and services.

Some goods are consumed quickly, others are consumed slowly.

We cannot have all the things we want therefore we must make choices.

We try to choose the good or service that is most satisfying.

The real cost of the things we choose is the things we must forego.

Each person is free to decide which goods and services he will buy.

Every family must have a home, food, clothing, and pay taxes.

ECONOMIC CONCEPT II

Goods and services are created by the production process. Individuals who contribute to the process receive a share of the goods and services.

CHILDREN'S INTERPRETATION

To *produce* means to make goods or perform services.

Some workers produce goods.

Some workers produce services.

Not everyone is a *producer*.

A producer of goods or services *earns income*.

Property owners receive income in the form of rent.

Families may produce some goods and services for themselves.

Exhibit 21 *(Continued)*

The goods and services we produce for ourselves are not free. To produce them requires time, effort, skills, and usually tools and materials.

ECONOMIC CONCEPT III

The development of specialization has made people more interdependent.

CHILDREN'S INTERPRETATION

A worker who produces just one kind of goods or service is a *specialist.*

A specialist learns to do his job well.

Most neighborhood workers specialize in producing one kind of goods or service.

A worker producing one special kind of goods or service needs other workers to produce the other goods and services he must have.

A specialist must be able to sell his goods or services to others.

ECONOMIC CONCEPT IV

In our private enterprise economy, individuals and businesses are free to seek economic gain. They may determine the price of their product, make contracts, accumulate capital and own property.

CHILDREN'S INTERPRETATION

People are free to choose the kind of work they want to do.

Each person is free to decide how he will spend his money.

Families are relatively free to decide how much of their money they will spend or save.

Source: Seattle Public Schools, Social Studies Department, *Overview of Economic Education: Grades K-6* (Seattle: Public Schools, 1965), Grade One, pp. 1-2.

principal investigator in the Elkhart Project, has produced a curriculum in economics for young children. His rationale for teaching fundamental economic concepts to young children is as follows:

Children's experiences are as wide in scope as life itself. They touch on every one of the social sciences, and are particularly rich in elements of economic importance. The child asks for many things—from lollipops to electric trains. He learns that his family cannot fulfill all his wishes and discovers that he has to make choices. When he receives his first dime, he thinks of it as riches, but quickly discovers that it will buy him little. He and his family face a constant succession of economic problems. What should they buy at the grocery store? Who should get the next pair of shoes? Should the family spend or save?

Discovering fundamental patterns or principles beneath the welter of raw experience is not an easy task. A special kind of thinking is necessary to make the bridge between a person's experiences and his ideas. Up to now, training for this kind of thinking has been entrusted largely to the secondary schools. By the time youth have reached maturity, bad thinking habits have often become ingrained and respect for analytical thinking is frequently lacking. It is during the early formative years of the child, when he has an unlimited curiosity and an earnest desire for answers to his questions, that the preparations for analytical thinking should begin.[3]

The Senesh program, "Our Working World," is available only for first and second grades. It uses a variety of audio-visual materials to accompany both the pupils' materials and the teacher's—recordings of stories, large and colorful illustrations, and related printed materials. There are twenty-seven lessons presented orally on the recording. The "model teacher," in a specially prepared record, uses her voice to lead the class in a discussion of such topics as: "Dividing the work," "Tools and machines," "How choices are made," "Why some incomes are low and others are high," "What does the bank do with our savings?" "What happens when people buy all that is produced?" Each lesson is illustrated with attractive pictures, and each successive page is decorated in a different color. The classroom teacher may choose to listen to the record at home, and then plan a different lesson for the class, or she may play part of the record for the class and continue on with her own lesson.

In the books to be used by the children, these topics are developed pictorially; the books are also accompanied by records that a youngster can play for himself or listen to with the rest of the group. The stories in the books are attractive to children: "Bobby the Builder," "The Sad Cow," "What Shall I Be?" "Danny's Bicycle," "What Do Taxes Do?" and "Our Wishes Change with Our Needs."

[3]Lawrence Senesh, *Our Working World: Families at Work* (Chicago: Science Research Associates, 1964), p. 1.

Exhibit 22 gives an example of one of the Senesh lessons for first graders. Not only is the text part of this lesson available on a record; there are, in addition, other stories illustrating the same concept available on other records.

The appeal to the senses does much to make this material interesting for both teachers and children; the films, the tapes, the records, the illustrations are all important to the youngster with little verbal ability. However, it is interesting to compare the Senesh program to the Seattle program, which, not having the elaborate audio-visual components of the Senesh material, teaches economics by accentuating value judgments rather than economic principles. It is this emphasis that one would like to see more of in the Senesh material.

Just as in the areas of English, mathematics, and science, there is a paucity of programs in ecnomics for the middle years. Both Senesh and the Seattle School System (and others not mentioned) have imaginative early school programs, but time has not yet permitted them to develop programs for the middle grades.

The **Economic Education Project** of the Industrial Relations Center at the University of Chicago, however, is one of the few starting to develop a program for grades 4 and 5. The complete program will include teacher guides, student readings, records, tapes, films, and tests. Some of these materials have already appeared, and the remainder will be on the market soon. The plan calls for teaching the principles of consumption in fourth grade and those of production in fifth grade. They estimate that the time required to teach the program will range from twenty-four to thirty-four hours and strongly recommend that the economic units be taught in conjunction with history and geography.[4]

Exhibit 23 (pp. 174–175) shows the *Teachers Guide for Elementary School Economics II;* the selection is "Topic III: Wholesalers and Retailers."

As indicated in Exhibit 24 (pp. 176–177), the teacher assigns Projects 16 and 17, which are found in the book, *Projects,* used by the students. As Exhibit 24 illustrates, these projects are pic-

[4]Economic Education Project, Industrial Relations Center, University of Chicago, *Elementary School Economics II* (Chicago: Allied Education Council, 1961, 1962, revised 1964).

Exhibit 22

A PICTURE-STORY LESSON IN ECONOMICS FOR FIRST GRADERS
(THE ELKHART PROJECT)

Fair Trade

Lesson 15

Mr. Baker had a bad tooth. It hurt very much. He hoped someone would fix it.

He said, "I will pay ten loaves of bread to get my tooth fixed."

Mr. Fixit came by with a hammer and saw. He was very hungry. He said, "I want a loaf of bread. I shall make you a table. That will pay for the bread."

"I do not need a table," said Mr. Baker. "But I will give you ten loaves of bread if you fix my tooth."

Exhibit 22 (Continued)

"I cannot fix your tooth," said Mr. Fixit. "My hammer and saw cannot fix your tooth."

Mr. Fixit had to go away without any bread. Mr. Baker's tooth still hurt.

Just then Mr. Dentist came running down the street. "My chair is broken," he said to Mr. Fixit. "I will fix your tooth if you will fix my chair."

"My tooth does not hurt," said Mr. Fixit. "I am hungry. I want some bread."

"But I do not have any bread," said Mr. Dentist.

Then Mr. Fixit had an idea.
He fixed Mr. Dentist's chair.
Then he and Mr. Dentist went
to see Mr. Baker.

Mr. Dentist fixed Mr. Baker's
tooth. Mr. Baker gave Mr.
Dentist ten loaves of bread.

Then Mr. Dentist gave Mr.
Fixit five loaves of bread for
fixing his chair.
Then they all were happy.

Source: Lawrence Senesh, *Our Working World: Families at Work* (Chicago: Science Research Associates, 1964), pp. 210–212.

Exhibit 23

GUIDELINES FOR TEACHING ECONOMIC CONCEPTS IN FOURTH AND FIFTH GRADE (THE ECONOMIC EDUCATION PROJECT)

Labor

> Discuss the illustration of "labor" found on Project #10.

A person who is organizing a business must have labor, or workers, who will produce goods or services. The business owner has to use money to pay these workers.

--Can you think of any business that is run without the use of labor?

--Who provides the labor for a self-employed businessman?

--Who are some of these self-employed people?

> Possible Answers: TV repairman, lawyer, doctor, etc.

A business cannot operate without labor, because goods and services cannot be produced without people to produce them.

> Note to the Teacher
>
> The following three-part exercise will help you to determine if students understand what is included in the terms "labor," "materials," and "equipment." The first part of the exercise can be completed now, and the remaining parts after the discussion of materials and equipment.
>
> 1. Ask students to take a sheet of paper and place it length-wise on their desks. Ask them to divide the page into three columns, and to label the first one "labor." The other columns will be labeled later.

Materials

So far, we have found out why a business owner needs money and why he needs labor. Now, let's find out why he needs materials. Since labor cannot produce goods or services without materials, the business owner must use money to pay for the materials that are necessary for production in his business.

--What does the term "materials" mean?

Discuss the illustration of "materials" found on Project #10. The term "materials" includes all things supplied by nature (water, timber, mineral deposits, and plant and animal life) and any man-made materials which become part of a finished product (steel, aluminum, sugar, wood, etc.).

--What kinds of materials would you find above the ground?

Possible Answers: Grass, wheat, oats, animals, timber, water, and plants are examples of materials found above the ground.

--What kinds of materials would you find under the ground?

Possible Answers: Coal, iron ore, copper ore, salt, and petroleum are examples of materials found under the ground.

Source: Economic Education Project, Industrial Relations Center, University of Chicago, *Elementary School Economics II: Teacher's Guide* (Chicago: Allied Education Council, 1964), Unit Ten, pp. 8–9.

PRODUCERS SELLING GOODS

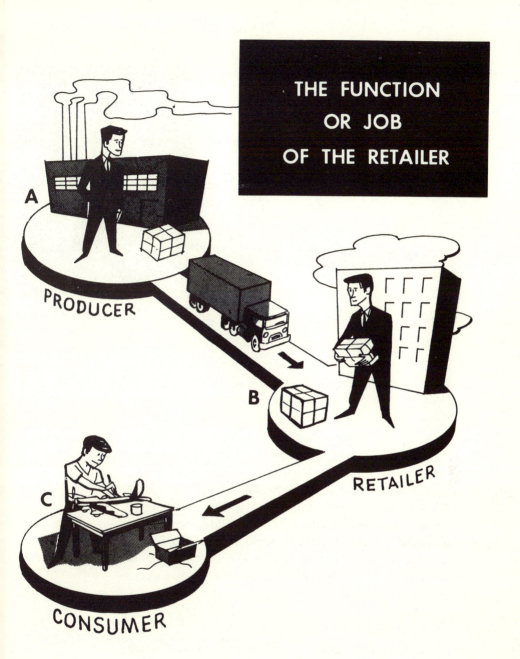

THE FUNCTION
OR JOB
OF THE RETAILER

A

PRODUCER

B

RETAILER

C

CONSUMER

Source: Economic Education Project, Industrial Relations Center, University of Chicago, *Elementary School Economics II: Projects* (Chicago: Allied Education Council, 1964), #16 and #17.

Exhibit 25. STUDY QUESTIONS AND READI

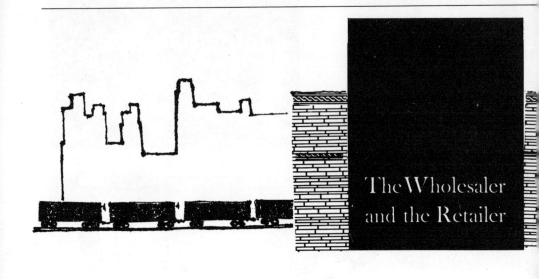

The Wholesaler and the Retailer

Study Questions   What is the job of the wholesaler?
What is the job of the retailer?

Michigan is well known as a furniture-producing state. How does furniture that is made in Michigan reach people all over the country? Sometimes, consumers order directly from the factory. Usually, however, they depend upon local wholesalers and retailers to make the furniture available to them. The wholesaler buys furniture directly from the producer and has it transported to a warehouse in his city. The retailer then selects and buys furniture from the wholesaler. Finally, the retailer sells the furniture to customers who visit his store.

Mr. Streeter—a Wholesaler

Mr. Streeter is a wholesaler. He owns a large warehouse in Nashville, Tennessee. Several times a year, Mr. Streeter orders furniture directly from factories in Michigan. Each time he places an order, he buys hundreds of chairs, beds, tables, and so on. He chooses the pieces he thinks he will be able to sell in Nashville.

The wholesaler buys in large quantities because this is less expensive. When he does this, he doesn't have to make frequent trips

to the factory. He doesn't have to pay the expense of shipping goods many times during the year.

Other furniture wholesalers in Nashville and in other cities in the United States also place orders with the factories. Sometimes they make trips to these factories. Or they may order the items they need by phone or mail.

After Mr. Streeter has ordered all the furniture he will need, he has it sent to his warehouse in Nashville. There it will be stored and sold to retailers in his area who do not buy directly from the producer.

Mr. Streeter and other wholesalers are a great help to retailers. They have goods transported from where they are produced to where they will be consumed. Then, they store the goods in large warehouses which are easy for retailers to reach. Some retailers do not have enough room to store all of the furniture they will sell in six months or a year. However, they know that when their supply of furniture gets low, they can order more from the wholesalers and have it delivered quickly.

Exhibit 25 *(Continued)*

The wholesaler provides a valuable service for the retailer because he makes goods readily available. In the same way, the retailer provides a service for consumers.

Mr. Brooks—a Retailer

Mr. Brooks is a retailer. He owns the Eagle Furniture Store in Nashville. Because he does not have enough storage space to buy directly from furniture producers, he buys furniture from several wholesalers in the area. Mr. Brooks has been selling furniture to people in Nashville for many years. His store has furniture for use in every room in a house.

Mr. Brooks' store is in the main business district of Nashville. It is convenient to shop at his store because it is centrally located. He sells a wide variety of furniture in different styles and at different prices. People visiting Mr. Brooks' store find the furniture arranged so that they can easily see what he has for sale. There are salesmen working on each floor, to help people select just what they want.

If consumers bought furniture directly from the producer in Michigan, they might have to travel to that state or else order the furniture without first seeing it. They cannot buy from Mr. Streeter, the wholesaler. He usually sells only to the retailer.

We can see that retailers provide a valuable service for consumers. Their stores are easy to reach. There is always a variety of goods from which to choose and someone to help people select what they want.

Summary

Sometimes, consumers buy goods directly from producers. Some wholesalers sell goods directly to consumers. However, after goods have been produced, the marketing process usually works like this:

The goods are transported to towns and cities where consumers want to buy them.

Wholesalers store goods and make them available to retailers.

Retailers sell goods to consumers.

Source: Economic Education Project, Industrial Relations Center, University of Chicago, *Elementary School Economics II: Readings* (Chicago: Allied Education Council, 1964), pp. 34–36.

torialized descriptions of the relationships among buyers, sellers, and consumers.

The student can also be directed to another book, *Readings*, for further clarification of the concepts being taught. Exhibit 25 shows one of these readings and indicates something of the rationale being followed by the Economic Education Project.

Present-day teachers may well wonder where they will find the time to teach these new economic concepts in fourth and fifth grades. The time element has always been a major problem in curriculum. A reconsideration of the programs of the kindergarten, first, second, and third grades may help us to arrive at part of the answer. If some basic economic understandings are taught in the earlier years, less time will be needed in the fourth grade. In the junior and senior high school years more emphasis might be placed on the economic forces controlling the topics to be studied. A description of institutions such as banks or the Internal Revenue Bureau is a waste of time if students have not yet understood the functions of these institutions and their place in the growth of our society.

The **Portland Public Schools Social Studies Project** includes a campaign to educate its teachers in the social sciences, including economics. Using some of the methods and materials developed by the National Task Force on Economic Education and its own ingenuity, it has modified its twelfth-grade course, traditionally based on an interdisciplinary approach, to one that is based mainly on the direct teaching of political science, economics, and sociology. It devotes ten weeks to each of these three divisions. Like the Seattle program for the early grades, the Portland program is based on the study of conflicts and contrasts:

The conflict between unlimited wants and limited resources is one that faces every individual and nation.

Men have always sought ways and means of lessening the gap between unlimited wants and limited resources.

Because of the division of labor men and societies have become interdependent.

Interdependence makes exchange of goods necessary.

Because resources are too limited to permit the satisfaction of all wants, societies develop control methods concerning the goods to be produced.

An example of a unit appears in Exhibit 26 (pp. 182–183).

Exhibit 26

USING CONTRAST TO DEVELOP ECONOMIC UNDERSTANDING
(THE PORTLAND PROJECT)

Problem IX.   Can the United States citizen afford to ignore the economic needs of the underdeveloped?

TEACHER MATERIAL

The label of underdeveloped, which has been applied until now to countries with traditional or primitive economies, is being replaced by new terminology. These labels include emerging, developing, modern and maturing. In this study "underdeveloped" is applied to nations in all stages of growth short of the maturity level where advanced technology is used in most industries. In the past, the United States has assisted with development of its underdeveloped dependencies and the traditional economies (Latin America) with which the United States has had close contact. The Pan-American Union, now a part of the Organization of American States, was an outgrowth of this interest.

Recent political and economic developments have forced the United States and other nations to extend responsibility for stability and economic progress beyond national borders. Accordingly, the mature nations are extending aid to underdeveloped nations in recognition of the growing or continuing disparities in levels of living.

The strength of nationalism or tribalism among the underdeveloped countries, as well as the modification of the view that poor nations will automatically attract sufficient private-investment capital for rapid economic growth, has altered the [methods,] kinds of investments, and assistance flowing from mature to underdeveloped economies.

MATERIAL TO BE USED WITH STUDENTS

IX.   Can the United States citizen afford to ignore the economic needs of the underdeveloped nations? (Wilcox, *Economies of the World Today*, pp. 101–127).

   A.   Importance to the United States

   1.   They have a major part of the basic raw materials the United States needs, especially for stockpiling in case of war.

   2.   The United States gains, in general, from trade.

   3.   The United States, because of the global economic struggle with the Soviet Union, needs to have the friendship and support from these nations as they emerge from the stage of traditional society and eventually become modern industrial economies.

   4.   The moral values of our citizenry will not permit the United States to ignore the plight of the people of the underdeveloped nations.

B. Causes of national poverty. (Oxenfeldt, *Economic Principles and Public Issues,* pp. 66–89).
  1. Cause of low output.
     a. Stinginess of nature.
     b. Inefficiency of the economic system.
     c. Inefficient production methods.
     d. Foreign exploitation.
     e. Restrictions.
  2. Causes for excessive sacrifice.
     a. Slavery and near slavery.
     b. Economic insecurity.
  3. Causes for inordinate need.
     a. Overpopulation.
     b. Stimulation of desire for material possession.

Source: Portland Public Schools, *Economics—Problem Courses: Teachers Guide* (Portland: School District No. 1, Multnomah County, Ore., 1962), pp. 77, 78.

We should not underestimate the ability or the inclination of the student from a disadvantaged home to identify with the feelings of nationalism and tribalism in underdeveloped peoples. A study of motivation based on such group identity and membership can have useful application to our own economic problems.

The case study method is used in the experimentation of the Harvard-Newton Project in Business History and Economics Concepts. In this project six professors, two each from the fields of history, economics (including business administration), and education, coming from Harvard, Boston, Ohio, and Northwestern Universities, have joined forces to produce material for secondary school students in business history and economics concepts. Their technique is to use an actual event in history as a case study to describe some economic phenomenon, such as the growth of monopoly in industry or the rise of the labor movement. The student is taught to marshal facts and form conclusions. Generalizations must be subject to careful scrutiny in the light of the values of the time and country in which the events took place. For example, a typical case study illustrating banking in the colonial or the post-revolutionary period might focus on the management of private, local, and federal banks and their relationship to public interest. How did their functions affect both business and the individuals? The teacher presses for clarity of understanding. Concepts regarding inflation, supply and demand, and profits are derived. Questions arise concerning methods of preventing exploitation. The issue of value conflicts between the haves and the have nots is certain to be discussed.

From banking, teachers may turn to other aspects of economics: boycotts, monopolies, chain stores, public ownership. This approach, by way of analysis and debate, will appeal to the teachers of the disadvantaged since it depends more on data available in pictorialized newspapers and other popular documents and less on textbooks often overloaded with technical phrases. More important, it encourages discussion, clarifies concepts, forces thinking and analysis, and uses oral communication for the development of sophisticated ideas.

Perhaps the greatest stumbling block to developing programs in economics is the bland, sterile content of the available textbooks. "Economics in the Schools," an article in the *American Economic Review,* is an analysis of four leading high school textbooks used in the field of economics. This study states that, though larded heavily with factual and descriptive material on economic institutions and their development, the content of these textbooks does little to clarify value judgments and that, in terms of available evidence, both sides of significant controversies usually receive equal treatment, regardless of the intellectual merit of the conflicting arguments.[5]

One would hope that the new materials being published would include programed texts, and that the many communication devices such as motion pictures, filmstrips, television, radio, recordings, graphic illustrations, and models would be used more extensively in the development of economics materials.

[5]"Economics in the Schools," *American Economic Review,* 53, No. 1, Supplement (1963), pp. 1–27.

SELECTED READINGS ON
HISTORY AND THE SOCIAL SCIENCES

BOOKS ON THE SUBJECT

American Council of Learned Societies and the National Council for
the Social Studies, *The Social Studies and the Social Sciences* (New
York: Harcourt, Brace and World, 1962).

A discussion of the objectives of the social studies curriculum
growing out of the concern of scholars is presented in this book. The
scholars present chapters dealing with the content and scope of the
social sciences. The NCSS includes a statement about general objectives. The work of the scholars is aimed at generating discussion
about those concepts, knowledge and techniques crucial in their areas
and disciplines that they believe high school students can learn by the
end of their senior year. For a more sustained view of the position of
the NCSS it would be wise for the reader to look at *New Viewpoints
in the Social Studies* edited by Roy A. Price as the twenty-eighth
yearbook of the National Council (1958).

Boy, Christian, *The Structure of Freedom* (Stanford, Calif.: Stanford
University Press, 1958).

This book offers a study of freedom from a philosophical, psychological and historical vantage point. Basic values for a society aspir-
ing toward freedom are discussed, and determinants of psychological
and social freedom are described. Substantial references to the scholars in this field permeate the book.

Cabot, Hugh, and Kahl, Joseph A., *Concepts and Cases in Concrete
Social Science*, 2 Vols. (Cambridge, Mass.: Harvard University
Press, 1956).

Why do human beings agree or disagree? Real cases of agreements
and strife among various cultural groups are presented in Volume
Two in extensive case history form and using actual source material.
Volume One discusses the theoretical, psychological, and sociological
factors portrayed in the accompanying volume. The list of scholars
participating and the recommendations for readings makes this one
of the foremost publications on human relations in existence.

Daniel, Bradford (Ed.), *Black, White and Gray: 21 Points of View on the Race Question* (New York: Sheed and Ward, 1964).

As the title of this book indicates, the substance of the content is the presentation of points of view. James Baldwin, Father LaForge, Ross R. Barnett, Martin Luther King, Harry Golden, and Roy Wilkins are quoted extensively from articles, speeches and letters. The Negro moralist and the Southern lawyer speak for themselves in this book.

Diamond, Sigmund (Ed.), *The Nation Transformed: The Creation of an Industrial Society* (New York: George Braziller, 1963).

This is a series of source materials in the form of addresses, letters, and excerpts from magazines and books. It should be useful to those dealing with the problems of today. Articles by leaders in various fields such as Jane Adams, John Dewey, Samuel Gompers, Jacob A. Riis, have been assembled in this volume.

Grimes, Alan P., *Equality in America: Religion, Race and the Urban Majority* (New York: Oxford University Press, 1964).

The highpoints of the struggle to secure equality in America is related to three historic Supreme Court Decisions: the 1954 school segregation, school prayer and 1965 court decisions related to civil rights. All three decisions are discussed with their implications for urban education.

Hill, Wilhelmina (Ed.), *Curriculum Guide for Geographic Education* (Norman, Okla.: National Council for Geographic Education, 1963).

Recognized scholars in the field of geography, including experts in the instructional procedures have written a series of articles.

Jones, Howard Mumford, *A Strange New World* (New York: Viking Press, 1964.)

Who was the American? The author develops the thesis that he was essentially an inventive European with his roots in Greece and Rome, his drives comparable to the Renaissance merchant prince but under the influence of the magnificent expansive American scene.

Extensive reference notes are made to primary sources about the American colonial period and the Founding Fathers.

Kahler, Eric, *The Meaning of History* (New York: George Braziller, 1964).

This book is a series of essays about history, about eras of history, about the philosophy of history in the present and the past.

Kimball, Solon T., and McLellan, James E., *Education and the New America* (New York: Random House, 1962).

In this book an anthropologist and a philosopher examine the nature and quality of the commitments of American to our society as it is now and as it is projected into the future. How is personal dedication to American values being achieved on the farm and in the metropolis? What are the value difficulties involved in the change-over from agrarian life to city life, or from city life to suburbia?

Knapp, Robert B., *Social Integration in Urban Communities* (New York: Teachers College Press, Teachers College, Columbia University, 1960).

This is a report of a study intended to develop guidelines for policies and programs useful to laymen and professional educators who are seeking to achieve progress in the social integration of people in our areas. By broadening the participation of lay people in determining the policies of the public schools in their relation to the community, it is hoped that social integration of the community will be strengthened.

Lott, Albert J., and Lott, Bernice E., *Negro and White Youth* (New York: Holt, Rinehart and Winston, 1963).

A study of motivational differences and similarities of Negro and white youths in personal goals and value judgments is reported here. The authors believe that there is a general community culture which can be made the basis of a move to eliminate the barriers of segregation and that this is more likely to occur if Negro men and white men of similar socioeconomic status or personal prestige can be brought together.

Massialas, Byron G., and Smith, Frederick R. (Eds.), *New Challenges in the Social Studies* (Belmont, Calif.: Wadsworth, 1965).

This presents a series of chapters in which various scholars discuss the most significant recent research studies and projects dealing with history and the social sciences.

Moore, Wilbert E., *Man, Time and Society* (New York: Wiley, 1963).

This is a discussion of time chronology; a sense of history in the context of the life of various types of people in various settings: the family, the suburbs, the city, old civilizations and new ones.

Northrop, F. S. C., *Philosophical, Anthropological and Practical Politics* (New York: Macmillan, 1960).

The place of sociological jurisprudence and cultural anthropology in explaining the philosophy of history and the types of government in various societies around the world and in the United States of America are described by the author. New approaches to politics through an understanding of the vital law of each national group as revealed in their cultural history make this an intellectually challenging book.

Parker, Donald, O'Neil, Robert, and Econopouly, Nicholas, *Civil Liberties* (Boston: Houghton Mifflin, for the Lincoln Filene Center for Citizenship and Public Affairs, Tufts University, 1965).

This paperback is devoted to case histories, debates, questions and interpretations of the Constitution of the United States by the Courts. Interesting and readable for junior and senior high school students.

Piaget, J., *The Moral Judgment of the Child* (Glencoe, Ill.: Free Press, 1942).

Moral judgment, not moral behavior or sentiments, is investigated in this book. It discusses adult constraint and moral realism, the development of the idea of justice and the theory of authority. The sections in Chapter IV on moral education should be read by all people working or living with children.

Presthus, Robert, *Man at the Top: A Study in Community Power* (New York: Oxford University Press, 1964).

The place of the individual in the power structure of two small communities in New York State is described in a sociological study. The weakness of democratic processes in small towns is highlighted in this profound and revolutionary study.

Riddle, Donald H., *American Society in Action* (New York: Webster Publishing Co., 1965).

As a book of readings dealing with problems in American democracy this book was designed to serve as a collection of secondary sources intended to enrich and personalize a textbook treatment. However, the readings are so written that they may well lead to individual research, including looking at primary material.

Robison, Helen F., and Spodek, Bernard, *New Directions in the Kindergarten,* "Early Childhood Education Series" (New York: Teachers College Press, Teachers College, Columbia University, 1965).

This book demonstrates the teaching of concept formation to pre-readers by reporting two experimental programs in which kindergarteners were successful in acquiring a number of fundamental social science concepts. The authors hope to encourage other educators to seek more productive uses for the time children spend in kindergarten.

Roche, John P., *The Quest for the Dream* (New York: Macmillan, 1963).

By means of a journalist's narration of the struggle of Americans to secure civil liberties, the contributions of various agencies, the Anti-Defamation League, the American Civil Liberties Union, the NAACP, the United States Supreme Court itself, are developed. The eventual and decisive action of the President and the federal government and the transformation of American attitudes toward a positive view of the justice of the struggle of the Negroes for true equality as well as recognition of Jews and Catholics as fully accepted Americans are culminating points of this historic story.

Ward, Barbara, *The Rich Nations and the Poor Nations* (New York: W. W. Norton, 1962).

This book describes the nature of the change from an agrarian economy to a highly technical one. Science and saving are seen as important ingredients in the changeover from primitive to modern society. The emergence of the wealthy West and the challenge of the East is described. In addition, the impact of communism and its ideas are contrasted with the programs of the democracies with the "have not" nations as interested learners.

Warner, W. Lloyd, Meeker, Marcia, and Eells, Kenneth, *Social Class in America* (New York: Harper Torchbooks, 1960).

Primarily a description of social status in America, this book explains how it is achieved and measured. It is useful for social science teachers who want to understand the special status problems of the handicapped.

White, Ralph K., and Lippitt, Ronald O., *Autocracy and Democracy* (New York: Harper and Brothers, 1960).

The idea that individual freedom promotes creativity is the recurring idea in this thoughtful analysis of the nature of democracy and autocracy in classrooms. The possible application of the experimental findings to large groups in society including international groups is also explored. The psychological dynamics of democracy are experimented with in the classrooms of eleven-year-olds. The possible projections of the findings to unorganized groups and to the new nations makes this older research study look new and challenging.

ARTICLES FROM PROFESSIONAL PUBLICATIONS

Allen, Rodney F., "Using Speeches to Enrich History Instruction," *Social Education,* 28 (1964), pp. 209–211.

American Anthropological Association, "The Anthropology Curriculum Study Project Report" (Chicago: The Project, 1963).

Bowes, John S., "Using Documentary Material in the American History Course," *Social Education,* 28 (1964), pp. 88–90, 95.

Broadbelt, Samuel, "Exploring Crucial Issues in the Social Studies Field," *The Social Studies,* 55, No. 7 (December 1964), pp. 243–246.

California State Central Committee on Social Studies, "Building Curriculum in Social Studies for Public Schools of California," California State Department of Education Bulletin No. 26. 1957.

Cammarota, Gloria, "Children, Politics, and Elementary Social Studies," *Social Education,* 27 (1963), pp. 205–207.

Chase, W. Linwood, "American History in the Middle Grades," in William H. Cartwright and Richard L. Watson, Jr. (Eds.), *Interpreting and Teaching American History,* Thirty-first Yearbook of the National Council for the Social Studies (Washington, D.C.: The Council, 1961), pp. 329–343.

Christensen, C.M., "A Note on 'Dogmatism and Learning'," *Journal of Abnormal and Social Psychology,* 66 (January 1963), pp. 75–76.

Crowe, Ruby H., and Dimond, Stanley E., "Survey of Current Curriculum Studies in Social Studies 1962–1963" (Washington, D.C.: National Council for the Social Studies, 1963.)

Davis, O. L., Jr., "Children Can Learn Complex Concepts," *Educational Leadership,* 17 (1959), pp. 170–175.

Davis, O. L., Jr., "Learning about Time Zones in Grades Four, Five, and Six," *Journal of Experimental Education,* 31 (1963), pp. 407–412.

Dreizen, S., Currie, C., et al., "The Effects of Nutritive Failure on the Growth Patterns of White Children in Alabama," *Child Development,* 24 (1953), pp. 189–202.

Engle, Shirley H., "Decision Making: The Heart of Social Studies Instruction," *Social Education,* 24 (1960), pp. 301–304, 306.

Fenton, Edwin, and Good, John M., "Carnegie Institute of Technology: A Social Studies Curriculum for Able Students," *Social Education,* 29 (1964), pp. 216–218.

Fitzgerald, Donald, and Ausubel, David P., "Cognitive Versus Affective Factors in the Learning and Retention of Controversial Material," *Journal of Educational Psychology,* 54 (April 1963), pp. 73–84.

Fleming, Malcolm, "Pictorial Communication: An Essay on Its Plight," *Audio-Visual Communication Review,* 10 (1962), pp. 223–237.

Greenbladt, E. L., "An Analysis of School Subject Preferences of Elementary School Children of the Middle Grades," *Journal of Educational Research,* 55 (August 1962), pp. 554–555.

Gross, Herbert H., "Accents in Geography," *The Journal of Geography,* 68, No. 6 (September 1964), pp. 258–261.

Hanna, Paul R., and Lee, John R., "Content in the Social Studies," in John U. Michaelis (Ed.), *Social Studies in Elementary Schools*, Thirty-second Yearbook of the National Council for the Social Studies (Washington, D.C.: The Council, 1962), pp. 62–89.

Hanvey, Robert, "Augury for the Social Studies," *School Review*, **69** (1961), pp. 11–24.

Herring, Pendleton, "Toward an Understanding of Man," in Roy A. Price (Ed.), *New Viewpoints in the Social Sciences*, Twenty-eighth Yearbook of the National Council for the Social Studies (Washington, D.C.: The Council, 1958), pp. 1–19.

Hess, Robert, and Easton, David, "Role of the Elementary School in Political Socialization," *School Review*, **70** (1962), pp. 257–265.

Hughes, H. Stuart, "The Historian and the Social Scientist," *American Historical Review*, **66** (1960), pp. 20–46.

Jarolimek, John, "Curriculum Content and the Child in the Elementary School," *Social Education*, **26** (1962), pp. 58–62; 117–120.

Johnson, Earl S., "Humanism and Science in the Social Studies," *The American Behavioral Scientist*, **7**, No. 8 (April 1964), pp. 3–7.

Johnson, Earl S., "The Social Studies versus the Social Sciences," *School Review*, **71** (1963), p. 4.

Joyce, Bruce, R., "Content for Elementary Social Studies," *Social Education*, **28** (1964), pp. 84–87; 103.

Lee, John R., "Northwestern University: Materials for a New Approach in American History," *Social Education*, **29** (1964), p. 223.

Leppert, Ella C., "University of Illinois: A Sequential Junior-Senior High School Curriculum," *Social Education*, **29** (1965), pp. 213–215.

Lottich, Kenneth V., and Meiseger, Lynn, "The Problem of Social Class in American Schools," *The Social Studies*, **55**, No. 7 (December 1964), pp. 253–258.

McAulay, J. D., "Map Learnings in the Fourth Grade," *Journal of Geography*, **68**, No. 3 (March 1964), pp. 123–127.

McAulay, J. D., "The Social Studies of the Elementary School Needs Attention," *The Social Studies*, **55**, No. 7 (December 1964), pp. 246–249.

McAulay, J. D., "What Understandings Do Second Grade Children Have of Time Relationships?" *Journal of Educational Research*, **54** (1961), pp. 312–314.

Miller, Stuart C., "The Interdisciplinary Approach to Teaching Social Studies," *Social Education*, **28** (1964), pp. 195–198.

Newmann, Fred M., "Evaluation of Programed Instruction in the Social Studies," *Social Education*, **29** (1965), pp. 291–295.

New York Board of Education, "The Negro in American History," Curriculum Bulletin 1964–1965, No. 4, 1964.

Oliver, Donald W., "Harvard University: A Curriculum Based on the Analysis of Public Controversy," *Social Education,* **29** (1964), pp. 220–223.

Oliver, Donald W., and Baker, Susan, "The Case Method," *Social Education,* **23** (1959), pp. 25–28.

Parker, Donald, and Econopouly, Nicholas, "Teaching Civil Liberties by the Case Method," *Social Education,* **25** (1961), pp. 283–285.

Patterson, Franklin, "Social Science and the New Curriculum," *American Behavioral Scientist,* **6** (1962), pp. 28–32.

Price, Roy A., "Syracuse University: School Science Concepts and Workways as the Basis for Curriculum Revision," *Social Education,* **29** (1964), pp. 218–220.

Powell, Thomas F., "Teaching American Values," *Social Education,* **29** (1965), pp. 272–274.

Rice, Marion J., and Bailey, Wilfred C., "University of Georgia: A Sequential Curriculum in Anthropology for Grades 1-7," *Social Education,* **29** (1965), pp. 211–212.

Rushdoony, Haig A., "Achievement in Map-Reading: An Experimental Study," *Elementary School Journal,* **64** (1963), pp. 70–75.

Rusnak, Mary, "Introducing Social Studies in the First Grade," *Social Education,* **25** (1961), pp. 291–292.

Scarfe, Neville V., "Geography as an Autonomous Discipline in the School Curriculum," *The Journal of Geography,* **63**, No. 7 (October 1964), pp. 297–301.

Schall, James H., "Sociology in the High School Curriculum," *Social Education,* **29** (1965), pp. 296–298.

Schramm, Wilbur, "Learning from Instructional Television," *Review of Education,* **25** (October 1962), pp. 156–157.

Senesh, Lawrence, "The Organic Curriculum: A New Experiment in Economic Education," *Reprint Series, No.* 22, Purdue University of Industrial Management Institute for Quantitative Research in Economics and Management. (Reprinted from *The Councilor,* **21,** 1960), pp. 43–56.

Shaver, James R., "Ohio State University: Economics Curriculum Material for Secondary Schools," *Social Education,* **29** (1965), pp. 215–216.

"Social Science in the Framework of American Science," *The American Behavioral Scientist,* **7,** No. 9 (May 1964), p. 23.

Spodek, Bernard, "Developing Social Science Concepts in the Kindergarten," *Social Education,* **27** (1963), pp. 253–256.

Starr, Isadore, "Teaching the Bill of Rights," *Social Education,* **23** (1959), pp. 373–378.

West, Edith, "University of Minnesota: An Articulated Curriculum for Grades K-14," *Social Education,* **29** (1965), pp. 209–211.

White, Gilbert F., "A Joint Effort to Improve High School Geography," *Journal of Geography,* **60** (November 1961), pp. 357–360.

MATHEMATICS AND SCIENCE

Mathematics and science are subjects usually considered too abstruse and esoteric for students from disadvantaged backgrounds. These areas are thought to require abilities not usually possessed by these children: the ability to hypothesize, to analyze, to synthesize, and finally to generalize. Children from deprived backgrounds are usually offered the so-called basic or general mathematics and science courses, in which the content is prosaic and "realistic" and the method that of traditional learning by rote.

In mathematics, many of these youngsters are seldom prepared at the end of the primary grades to do more than make change in the local grocery store, pay an electric bill, or recite a few multiplication tables. In the report of the Cambridge Conference on School Mathematics it is stated:

> Pages of drill sums and repetitious "real-life" problems have less than no merit; they impede the learning process. We believe that arithmetic as it has been taught in grade schools until quite recently has such a meagre intellectual content that the oft-noted reaction against the subject is not an unfortunate rebellion against a difficult subject, but a perfectly proper response to a preoccupation with triviality.[1]

[1]Educational Services Incorporated, *Goals for School Mathematics: The Report of the Cambridge Conference on School Mathematics* (Boston: Houghton Mifflin, 1963), p. 8.

In science, the same approach is generally maintained. In slow, repetitive steps, children in the "slow" classes learn about the weather, how flames are extinguished (but not why), and what causes water pressure (but not how). To compound this offense, many a teacher goes through the motions of imparting even this information with little attention to or awareness of whether or not he is motivating the student to think of the whys and hows.

Jules Henry, in describing American classrooms, says:

> In the first place, the student encounters a slow moving sequence of pedestrian tasks that, motivationally, require him merely to do what he is told, when he is told to, in the way that he is told to do it. From an intellectual or cognitive point of view he may encounter difficulties, but they are not the difficulties endemic to the subject matter; they are the difficulties engendered by obscure communications between teacher and student, and by uncertainties or vagueness within the teacher's own mind.[2]

For the disadvantaged youngster, who comes to school with little faith in the values of schooling and virtually no faith in himself as a learner, this arid, uninteresting, fact-centered approach to mathematics and science is almost a guarantee of failure. What this child needs are highly motivating, provocative, thought-producing materials and approaches. That is why the discovery approach is so important. He needs to be given not only the tools, but also the method by which to apply these tools to new situations. His lack of assurance that he can learn is reinforced if in mathematics, for example, he forgets the formula or the table or the answer "recipe." He will *try* to remember, but, if he cannot, he has "lost the game." The new approaches are designed to implant in his mind certain basic ideas; if he remembers these—and usually he will—he can then recreate the forgotten formulae. Acquiring a firm grasp of a few basic concepts instead of a weak knowledge of a mass of information not only saves learning time, but also gives the student a faith in his own analytical powers. This, of course, should be a goal for all mathematics and science teaching, but it is particularly important for the youngster who lacks self-confidence.

Another problem of the science and mathematics curriculum, important to the disadvantaged, is its *language*. These youngsters come to school with a "different language." In the English

[2]Jules Henry, "American Schoolrooms: Learning the Nightmare," *Columbia University Forum*, 6, No. 2 (Spring, 1963), p. 26.

curriculum we label objects so that children can identify them by names—precise names. We then try to teach them the symbol system of recognizing these names. However, although the labels are precise, the symbols are not. There is nothing inherent in a symbol that indicates its meaning; for the child who has a language handicap, this can be confusing. However, mathematics and science can provide another and at times far more precise language with which to communicate. Notation, symbols, and special terminology make up the language of mathematics and science. Words and symbols should be based on considerations of clarity and utility and precision of meaning. By making this language available to children, we enable them, at an early age, to communicate, to think and talk about it. Although this language is, of course, artificial, accuracy in meaning and reasoning can be achieved.

Motivationally handicapped children can benefit greatly from the study of mathematics and science, because these disciplines in particular have the advantage of results that become evident almost immediately and reinforce the motivation to learn more. Long-range problem solving, in both mathematics and science, is achieved through small steps leading to the final solution or answer. However, each successive step is a question-and-answer in itself. The method of the mathematician and of the scientist, therefore, invokes an explanation for every step of the way, the classification of observations, the noting of differences and similarities, the analyzing and testing of conclusions. All these skills are important to the development of the youngster who comes to school lacking a sense of the value of analysis and investigation.

A formidable breakthrough, particularly in the early grades, that has occurred in the science revisions of the last ten years is the emphasis on the *laboratory*. Its value for its application of the discovery principle is obvious. J. A. Campbell, Director of the Chemical Educational Material Study Project, says that a surprising number of supposedly less able students seem to do well in a course that is based almost completely upon laboratory experimentation.[3] This is supported in a report by Bentley Glass, of the Institute of Biological Sciences, who comments:

[3]J. A. Campbell, "An Approach to Chemistry Based on Experiments," in Robert W. Heath (Ed.), *New Curricula*, (New York: Harper and Row, 1964), p. 91.

Quite beyond expectation it was laboratory work and especially the laboratory block programs that aroused the eager participation of students of seemingly below average ability; and in "doing science" many of them revealed scientific ability that their low verbal competence had previously concealed.[4]

One should not underestimate the role of physical equipment in both science and mathematics programs. An observation of the Cambridge Conference concurs with the above two reports:

Whether one thinks in terms of the pre-mathematical experiences that are embodied in the manipulation of physical materials, whether one regards these physical objects as aids to effective communication between teacher and child, or whether one regards them as attractive objects that increase motivation, the conclusion is inescapable that children can study mathematics more satisfactorily when each child has abundant opportunity to manipulate suitable physical objects. Possible candidates include blocks of appropriate sizes, plastic washers and pegboards, rulers, compasses, French curves, circles divided into equal sections, graph paper, paper ruled into columns to help the child line up digits in column addition, geometric shapes cut out of wood or heavy cardboard, pebbles for counting, numerals cut out of wood or cardboard, circular protractors, and so on.[5]

Frank Riessman categorizes a slum child as being relatively slow in performing intellectual tasks. He believes this child needs the pictorial reinforcement that physical action can provide. In addition, he goes on to say, a child may be slow because he learns in a "one track" way; that is, he does not easily adapt to other frames of reference. The new mathematics and science programs tend very much to meet this youngster "where he is"; the emphasis on physical experiences in both science and math, through laboratory work, allows the disadvantaged youngster to build on at least one of his strengths; the encouragement of verbalization through inductive reasoning affords him practice in logical thinking; the discovery method encourages flexibility and adaptability to differing approaches.

All children, whether from advantaged or disadvantaged homes, are born with certain creative qualities. Having no vocabulary, the infant cannot speak. Yet he is ingenious enough to let us know how he feels about things by facial expressions and by other indications that he is accepting or rejecting his environ-

[4]Bentley Glass, "Renascent Biology," *The School Review* (Spring 1962), pp. 51–52.

[5]Educational Services Incorporated, *op. cit.*, p. 35.

ment. Of necessity, therefore, he is creative, senses problems, makes guesses, tests and modifies them, and communicates ideas in his limited way. Each child is born with many of the ingredients of the potential scientist.

A number of science educators have tried to trace the process of development of the child's potentially creative scientific impulses. Watson[6] concluded that most children, by the time they finish elementary school, have lost much of the inquisitiveness that is so basic to the scientific mind. If this be so for children in general, what then happens to the child from the disadvantaged home? Why, instead, can we not capitalize on the "infant creativity" and offer the child experiences in school that build upon the ability to communicate, to make guesses, to test and modify guesses, and to solve problems?

[6]F. G. Watson, "Shattered—An American Illusion," *Bulletin of the Harvard Graduate School of Education Association,* 3, No. 1 (1958), pp. 2–8.

ᴬᴬᴬ**11**ᴬᴬᴬ

MATHEMATICS

Modern methods of teaching mathematics reflect a drastic change in concept. In an article in the *New York Times,* Hechinger discusses a Soviet report on education:

The Soviet publication details experiments showing that children in the first grade (age 7 in Soviet schools) can be taught abstract ideas about mathematical concepts, leading to such formulas as:

$a=b$; $a<b$; $a>b$. (a equals b; a is smaller than b; and a is larger than b.)

The implication is that children, rather than performing concrete exercises with numbers, learn to think for themselves and are gradually introduced to what used to be considered only a college topic—logic.

"In their first days in school, the children work with specifically selected materials [sticks, blocks, and weights, for instance]," says the Soviet report.[1]

Almost concurrently, the Cambridge Conference on School Mathematics—a group of twenty-five mathematicians and mathematics users—issued the report referred to at the beginning of Part III, *Goals for School Mathematics.* The purpose of this conference was to establish goals for mathematics education; the members rejected the conventional practice of memorization by rote and called for a vocabulary of alternatives based on analysis, criticism, extrapolation, and interpolation. They called for a study of the new "thrusts and probes" which are emerging in some of our universities. They asked that major efforts be made to insert

[1]Fred M. Hechinger, "Soviet Education," *The New York Times* (October 17, 1964).

significant amounts of modern algebra, geometry, science, and logic into the school program for kindergarten through sixth grade. Their premise was that the foundation for learning higher mathematics and advanced science is laid in the kindergarten; it is often too late in the upper grades. Without stimulation and challenging content, large masses of children are mathematically (as well as scientifically) lost by the time they enter the secondary school.

The programs described briefly in the following pages are some of the new "thrusts and probes" with particular emphasis on their application to disadvantaged youngsters.

Based on the assumption that young children can learn more than we think they can and that young children from disadvantaged homes need mathematical "experiences" to develop their sense of achievement as well as their ability to manipulate and communicate, the **New York City Mathematics Program** has developed a number of mathematics sequences in its new, experimental *Pre-Kindergarten Curriculum Guide.*

Exhibit 27 demonstrates how the concept of *sets* is presented to the four-year-old. This sequence is preceded by practices in the naming and identifying of one object so as to be able to put it in its "class," and is followed by experiences in finding numbers and counting.

Exhibit 27

PRESENTING THE CONCEPT OF "SETS" TO PRE-KINDERGARTEN CHILDREN (THE NEW YORK PROGRAM)

TOPIC 3. RECOGNITION OF THE NUMBER IN A SET WITHOUT COUNTING

Through this topic children learn to see at a glance — at once — how many objects there are in a set *without counting.* The teacher exposes a set of three or four objects for a very short time, making sure that children do not have time to count. See Topic 4 for counting experiences.

The teacher plans many activities for each of the numbers to be emphasized at the pre-kindergarten level. Children thus learn to say the number name for the number in the set, as well as to recognize how many objects there are in the set.

Objects that are compact and rounded are best for developing this topic at this level. Four objects are most easily seen as *four* when they are patterned, e.g.: oo or o or oo oo etc.
oo   ooo

This topic may well be developed all year long.

Exhibit 27 (*Continued*)

NUMBER IN A PAIR

Routines

TEACHER PREPARATION	GUIDED PUPIL ACTIVITIES

Collects clothespins or clips for pairing rubbers or boots. Composes rhymes about two in a pair, e.g.:
    Two in a pair,
    Both rubbers are there.
    Two boots in a pair.
    Come! look! Are they there?
 	
Plans for groups of children to observe pairs in wardrobe.
	Learns to clip his rubbers or boots together. Repeats rhymes about pair, both, two. Observes pairs on a trip to the wardrobe with teacher and a group of children. (No counting).

Arranges pairs of clothing on a line, table, etc., e.g.: a child's socks, a "kitten's" mittens, a doll's shoes.	Learns to use the terms "two," "both," "pair." (*No* counting).

NUMBER IN SETS OF 2 OBJECTS

Snacks

Arranges on a tray a number of small cookies or carrot sticks or small pretzels so that children can readily take 2 at once.	Takes at once 2 cookies, or 2 carrot sticks, or 2 pretzels, etc. Places both on his plate or napkin. Observes whether other children have *two* each.
Arranges on a tray a number of each of two foods so that children can choose.	Selects the food he wishes. Takes 2 of one food or 1 of each of two foods. Observes choices made by other children. Notes that each child selected 2 items.

House Play

Arranges sets of 2 objects in house play area, e.g.: 2 dolls in a carriage, 2 plates on a table, 2 chairs at one side of the table, 2 flowers in a vase, 2 toy dogs on a shelf.	Discovers sets of two objects. Names the objects and uses the terms "two" and "both." Discovers sets of more than two objects.
Arranges in house play center sets of two, three, and four objects, e.g.: a pair of doll shoes, 3 toy cups, 4 dresses on the line.	Finds as many sets of 2 objects as he can. Notes that a set of 3 cups has in it a set of 2 cups. Re-arranges these as a set of 2 cups and 1 cup. Sees twos in a set of 4.

Puzzles

Pastes picture showing one large object on cardboard. Cuts into two unequal parts.	Notes that his puzzle has 2 pieces. Learns how to put the pieces together to make a picture. Notes there are puzzles with more than 2 pieces.

Games

Plans game: Where Are There Two? Arranges in a play area sets of objects, e.g.: a pair of mittens, 3 shells, 2 red beads in a can cover, and many others.

Points to as many sets of 2 objects as he can. Names sets of 2 objects, e.g.: 2 mittens, 2 red beads, etc. Names objects in sets larger than 2.

Plans game: Finding Twos. Arranges a set of small rounded objects, e.g.: 4 shells or 4 pebbles or 4 peanuts in shells, etc.

(Teacher exposes one set of 4.)

Teacher: Who can find 2?
          Who can point to 2?

Arranges other sets of 4 objects, all objects different, e.g.: 1 shell, 1 pebble, 1 peanut, 1 penny.

Child points:

Teacher: Who can find 2 others?
          Who can point to 2 others?

Child points:

Teacher: Who can find 2 twos?
          Who can point to 2 twos?

Child points using both hands:

one   the
hand   other
                             hand

(Teacher exposes other sets of 4 objects and proceeds similarly.)

Jingles: One and Two

Composes jingles about *one* and *two*, e.g.:

    1-2. A sock and shoe.
    1-2. John and you.
    1-2. Twins are two.
    1-2. Red and blue.

Plans to emphasize the number names "one" and "two" and to relate these to *one* and *two* objects.

Repeats jingles. Appreciates that in the jingle a sock is *one*, a shoe is *one*, a sock and shoe are *two*, etc. Knows that one is fewer than *two*, that two are more than *one*. Composes a jingle of his own about *two* things in the classroom.

Exhibit 27 (Continued)

NUMBER IN SETS OF 3 OBJECTS

Peanuts for a Party

TEACHER PREPARATION	GUIDED PUPIL ACTIVITIES
Provides enough peanuts in shells for each child to have several. Spreads a number of peanuts near one corner of a table. Plans to have children identify *two* first, then *three*.	Hears teacher say: Move *two*. Moves *two peanuts* as a set away from the collection. (No counting) Uses the term "two."
	Hears teacher say: Move *three*. Moves three peanuts as a set without counting. Uses the term "three."

Science Collections

Collects and places on science table one, two, three, or four of several objects: pebbles, shells, nuts, other seeds, etc.	Notes the number in each set of objects: two, three, more than three, etc. Arranges objects in sets of two each. Arranges objects in sets of three each. Uses the terms "one," "two," and "three." (No counting)

Dramatizations

Arranges materials in rows, in order from largest to smallest for dramatizing "The Three Bears": 3 bowls, 3 chairs, 3 mats (beds).	Observes the bowls and names the (No counting). Indicates largest bowl, middle-sized bowl, and smallest bowl. Identifies bowls for Father Bear, Mother Bear, and Baby Bear. Notes which bowl is first (at left), next, and last. Observes teacher rearrange the bowls and notes there are three. Notes position of each bowl. Uses terms: "one," "two," "three."
Makes plans for children to dramatize "The Three Bears."	Proceeds similarly with chairs and 'beds."
Makes plans and provides mittens and line for dramatizing "Three Little Kittens."	Participates in dramatizations.

Construction Activities

Arranges one, two and three objects in sets, e.g.: 2 wheels, 3 buttons, 3 bottle caps, 3 milk containers.	Identifies the objects and names the number in all of the sets.

TEACHER PREPARATION	GUIDED PUPIL ACTIVITIES
Places beside each other a set of 3 buttons, and a set of 2 buttons, e.g.:	Names the number in each set. Indicates which set has more buttons. Indicates which set has fewer buttons.
Arranges other sets for children to compare, e.g.: 2 wheels with 3 wheels, 2 bottle caps with 1 bottle cap.	Names the number in each set. Indicates which set has more or fewer.

Games

Prepares several mystery boxes, one box with 1 bead, one box with 2 beads, one box with 3 beads (perhaps one empty box).	Looks quickly and names the number. Compares the number in different boxes. Touches beads without looking. Names the number.
Prepares several paper bags containing 1, 2, 3, or 4 objects.	Touches objects in bag. Names the number. Checks by looking. Asks another child to touch the objects.
Provides ball and pins for a bowling game. Sets up 3, 4, or 5 bowling pins, a different arrangement after each play.	Rolls ball to hit as many pins as he can. Notes how many pins he knocked down. Notes how many pins are still standing.

Jingles: One, Two, and Three

Composes jingles about *one, two,* and *three,* e.g.:
     *One two, three, one, two, three,
     How many people are one, two, three?
     One, two, three, one, two, three,
     Maria and Susie and Peter make three. (Use names of children in class)
	Repeats jingles. Appreciates that in the jingle one car is "one," two cars are "two," and three cars are "three." Knows that three are more than two or one, etc. Composes a jingle of his own about *three* things in the classroom. Participates in a dramatization acting out a jingle.

Plans to emphasize the number names "one," "two," and "three" and to relate these to *one, two,* and *three objects.*	

*Justus, May and Horton, Zilphia, "Counting Song" from *Music for Early Childhood,* New Music Horizon Series. New York: Silver Burdett, 1952. p. 8.

Exhibit 27 (Continued)

NUMBER IN SETS OF 4 OBJECTS

Clay Modelling

TEACHER PREPARATION	GUIDED PUPIL ACTIVITIES

Arranges a patterned set of 3 balls of clay on one tray and a patterned set of 4 balls of clay on another tray, e.g.:

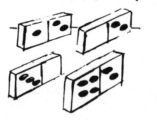

Identifies the set of 3 balls of clay and names it "three." Hears teacher use the term "four." Learns to identify a set of 4 and to name it "four." Notes the *twos* in the set of 4. Notes the *two* and *one* in the set of 3.

Science Collections

Patterns sets of 3 and 4 objects.

Identifies and names all sets of 3 objects. Learns to identify and name all sets of 4 objects. Compares a set of three with a set of four objects.

Games

Prepares mystery boxes, each with 1, 2, 3, or 4 beads.

Looks quickly and names the number. Touches without looking and names the number.

Collects small objects, at least 4 of each kind.

Closes eyes as teacher places one bead in his hand. Identifies it as *one*. Identifies the number of 2, 3, or 4 objects placed in his hand.

Arranges around the classroom sets of 2, 3, and 4 objects. Plans detective game for children to play.

Locates and names as many sets of 2 objects as he can. Locates and names sets of 3 objects. Locates and names sets of 4 objects.

From among Jumbo Dominoes selects those with 1, 2, 3, and 4 spots.

As soon as teacher uncovers one half of a domino, names the number of spots. Names numbers of both halves of a domino. Compares number of spots.

Plays domino game by matching dominoes, with same number of spots.

Source: Board of Education of the City of New York, *Pre-Kindergarten Curriculum Guide,* Curriculum Bulletin, 1965-66 Series, No. 11 (New York: Board of Education, 1965), pp. 131–136.

The New York City program is presently being used with seven thousand disadvantaged three- and four-year-olds. At this early date, the only evaluation available is of an anecdotal nature. Although the youngsters find the activities interesting and are able to use numbers to qualify nouns, many teachers worry that too early an introduction of mathematics concepts on a formal basis might result in a distaste for mathematics. Although the authors of the program claim that the "teacher preparation" and the "guided pupil activities" are anything but formal, one could easily see a rather structured pattern emerging. Whether or not the fears of the teachers are well founded can be judged only after several years of measuring the students' progress and attitudes toward mathematics learning. However, very often the teachers' "fears" simply express a failure to appreciate the children's abilities.

A program which purposefully sets about to "informalize mathematical learning" is the **Madison Project,** developed at Syracuse University for Webster College in Missouri by Robert Davis, Donald E. Kibbly and Beryl S. Cochran and members of the faculties of Syracuse University and Webster College.

An example of this less formal approach follows:

In a class of about 30 [third-grade] children, 4 children guess (independently) the length of the classroom. For these 4 estimates, an average and variance is computed. Next, 4 children (independently) measure the length, using six-inch plastic rulers, and for these 4 estimates an average and variance is computed. Next, 4 children independently measure the length of the classroom using yardsticks, and again an average and variance is computed for these 4 figures. Finally, 4 independent teams of children make the same measurement, using a surveyor's tape measure, and an average and variance is computed. The roles of the average and variance are discussed throughout; at the end, the children are asked how they would get the "right" or "exact" answer.[2]

The merit, for the disadvantaged youngster, of the type of teaching described above lies in the experience itself. First, it places him substantially on a par with his classmates, since not very much previous learning need be employed for the experience. Second, the vocabulary is familiar to him, although not one that he may normally use. That is, he probably knows the meanings of the terms "estimate," "variance," and "average," even if

[2]This example was taken from mimeographed materials, but the Madison Project is presently being published by Addison-Wesley Publishing Co., Inc.

he has never used them. It is part of his culture to say "about how much" rather than "can we estimate," or "I want the same as everyone else" rather than "I would like an average amount." The lesson gives the child an opportunity to learn in a meaningful fashion a richer and more precise vocabulary. Third, he is given a chance with other teammates to prove his theory and to explain his solution. It is apparent, then, that this type of lesson involves children in almost all aspects of good learning experiences: investigation, questioning, team work, discussion, and discovery. Each element is needed by the disadvantaged youngster.

As one reads the experiences in the Madison Project, one recognizes, of course, that they are of an "applied" nature. This is in preparation for abstract experience. It is in this area that so many of our educationally disadvantaged children are handicapped. Report after report, test after test, points up the fact that these children do poorly in abstract reasoning—not very surprising, since our present curricula give them so few experiences that would prepare them to draw generalizations. The Madison Project showed, however, that—as a result of the applied experiences in this field—pupils were able to list many algebraic identities, set forth related axioms and theorems, and give the proofs of these theorems—all evidencing an extension of their knowledge in the field of mathematics.

In Exhibit 28, we see the Madison Project method as it might be used to teach matrices to fourth-grade youngsters. *Previous knowledge of matrices is not required (nor expected) of either teacher or students.*

The matrix concept is neither too difficult nor too remote for a child from a disadvantaged home to learn—it is within his experience, within his immediate needs, and within his power of reasoning. The vocabulary may seem quite sophisticated but it is introduced in a context that explains the definition. Both teacher and pupils discuss the problems informally and together discover meaning. Instead of learning mathematical terms formulated by others, the pupils formulate their own. A very valuable aspect of this project is the many standard and loop films, rich in graphic explanations, which provoke student thinking.

The **Greater Cleveland Mathematics Program** was created in 1959. It, too, is a concept-oriented, modern, mathematics program, in which the primary emphasis has been placed on thinking, reasoning, and understanding, rather than on purely me-

Exhibit 28

INTRODUCING MATRICES INTO FOURTH GRADE
(THE MADISON PROJECT)

The "beginning" or hypothesis is represented by a student's method of writing down his purchases at the candy store (Question 4 of the Student's Book). He buys three kinds of candy:

$$\left(\begin{matrix} \text{almond} & \text{pepper-} & \text{chocolate-} \\ \text{bars} & \text{mints} & \text{covered ants} \end{matrix} \right)$$

He records the *quantity* of each that he buys (using what mathematicians call a "row matrix" or a "row vector"):

$$\left(\quad 3 \begin{matrix} \text{almond} \\ \text{bars} \end{matrix} \qquad 4 \begin{matrix} \text{pepper-} \\ \text{mints} \end{matrix} \qquad 0 \begin{matrix} \text{chocolate-} \\ \text{covered ants} \end{matrix} \right)$$

He records *the cost per item* as a "column matrix" (or "column vector"):

almond bars		
peppermints	$\begin{pmatrix} 5 \\ 2 \\ 30 \end{pmatrix}$	(i.e., 5¢ each)
chocolate-covered ants		(i.e., 2¢ each)
		(i.e., 30¢ per box)

Now the important thing happens! He computes how much he will spend:

$$(3 \quad 4 \quad 0) \times \begin{pmatrix} 5 \\ 2 \\ 30 \end{pmatrix} = (3 \times 5) + (4 \times 2) + (0 \times 30) = 23¢$$

In writing

$$(3 \quad 4 \quad 0) \times \begin{pmatrix} 5 \\ 2 \\ 30 \end{pmatrix} = (3 \times 5) + (4 \times 2) + (0 \times 30)$$

the student wrote a correct matrix product!

Source: Mimeographed materials. The Madison Project is presently being prepared for publication by Addison-Wesley Publishing Co., Inc.

chanical responses to standard situations. Only a few years ago, many of the mathematics concepts included in the Greater Cleveland Program were thought to be too difficult for children in the primary grades. The Greater Cleveland Program has reached 125,000 children and has shown that children are not only able to understand these concepts but, because of this understanding, are able to extract more meaning from each new step in the learning process.

One of the basic tenets of the Greater Cleveland Program is that, through the use of social applications, greater understanding and learning will take place. Approximately 9 per cent of the problem material in the first, second, and third grade is devoted primarily to social application, and 16 per cent of the statements of objectives deal directly with social application.

The example of social application shown in Exhibit 29 is a short lesson taken from a third-grade program. This approach is not new or revolutionary. Social application has been called by many names during the past fifty years. For the disadvantaged youngster the merit of the Greater Cleveland Program lies not so much in basing learning in experiences, but more in basing learning on a *variety* of experiences. Again, the examples given here may be inappropriate for the disadvantaged child—coin collecting, stamp collecting, and aggregation of toys, may not be in the real world of this youngster. Therefore, the teacher who employs and bases mathematical learnings on artifacts familiar to the disadvantaged youngsters, however foreign these objects may be to the teacher, will be using the Greater Cleveland Mathematics Program to its best advantage.

Suppes and McKnight and Suppes and Ginsberg reported a series of experiments concerned with children's mathematical concept formation. Among their findings were the following:

1. Learning was more efficient if the child who had made an error was required to make a correct response in the presence of the stimulus to be learned.
2. Although much reliance had been placed on incidental learning of mathematics for young children, this type of learning did not appear to be effective.
3. Conditions that focused the child's attention upon the stimuli to be learned enhanced learning.
4. Transfer of concept was more effective if the learning situation required the learner to recognize the presence or absence of a concept in a number of stimulus displays than if it required him to match activities that involved a number of possible responses.
5. Prior learning of one concept did not improve the learning of a related concept.[3]

Based upon these five conclusions, the **Suppes Mathematics Program** presents a complete, modern approach to the teaching of elementary mathematics. Suppes' objective was to develop a program that was both mathematically sound and pedagogically simple. In *Sets and Numbers*, the concept of sets is introduced in the kindergarten. It is an interesting facet of this program that it seeks to move kindergarten children as rapidly as possible to an abstraction. An example appears in Exhibit 30 (pp. 210–211).

[3]This research was reported in J. Fred Weaver and E. Glenadine Gibb, "Mathematics in the Elementary School," *Review of Educational Research,* 37, No. 3 (June 1964), p. 274.

Exhibit 29

SOCIAL APPLICATION OF MATHEMATICS CONCEPTS IN THIRD GRADE (THE GREATER CLEVELAND PROGRAM)

For the Student:

WORK THE STORY PROBLEMS.

Hobbies

All of the children in the third grade had hobbies. Baseball cards were collected by 7 of the boys and 1 of the girls. Each of these children planned to bring 4 cards to show the class. They would bring _____ cards.

Three girls and 4 boys collected stamps. They each planned to bring 2 stamp books to show their friends. They would bring _____ stamp books.

Tom collected coins. He would bring 3 cards of nickels and 6 cards of pennies to class. Each card had 5 coins mounted on it. Tom planned to bring _____ coins.

Four of the boys collected toy soldiers and 2 of the girls collected toy animals. Each of these children planned to bring 3 toys for a hobby table. _____ toys would be shown.

For the Teacher:

DEVELOPMENTAL EXPERIENCES FOR BASEBALL CARDS:

Ask a child to use counters on the flannel board to illustrate the number of baseball cards that one boy would bring. Point out that this represents only one set of the cards, and challenge the children to enlarge this illustration to represent the cards that all seven boys would bring. Use a piece of yarn to enclose each set. Consider the cards that the girl will bring and illustrate these cards with counters of a different shape or color. Point out the similarity of the illustration on the flannel board to beads on a frame and develop the idea that since the boys and the girl will each bring the same number of cards, we could write the equation $(7 + 1) \times 4 =$ _____ and use the distributive property of multiplication over addition to find the solution.

Analyze and illustrate the next part of the story with the class. Have the children proceed with the last two problems independently. Tell them to draw a picture of the sets involved and write the equation for their computation. Reenforce these learnings with using the other hobbies as examples.

Source: Greater Cleveland Mathematics Program: Grade 3 Children's Edition and Unit 3, Teacher's Manual (Chicago: Science Research Associates, 1962), p. 161.

Exhibit 30

TEACHING AN ABSTRACT CONCEPT (SETS) TO KINDERGARTENERS

If we wish to represent this set on the board or on paper, for example, we describe it in the following way:

$$\left\{ / \; \circledcirc \right\}$$

This is a *description* of the set and it represents the first level of abstraction. Similarly, we could *describe* the set consisting just of George Washington in this way:

$$\left\{ \text{George Washington} \right\}$$

The distinction between displaying the set of objects and describing the set is an important one. Just as the picture of the pencil is not, in fact, the pencil but simply a representation, so the representation of the set

$$\left\{ / \; \circledcirc \right\}$$

describes the set, but is not the set itself. The notation employed is standard in mathematics. The braces are used to enclose the pictures of objects as a way of indicating that this is a description of a particular set.

In the next step in abstraction we move from the description of the set and its particular members to a consideration of just the number of members it has. As the way of introducing this abstraction we include an N for number just before the set description:

$$\mathsf{N}\left\{ / \; \circledcirc \right\}$$

The N notation names a number just as the Arabic numeral names a number. But unlike the Arabic numerals this notation for number retains the pictorial character of the set description. The N notation more clearly demonstrates the transition from the concrete level of the set to the abstract level of number represented by a numeral. The Arabic numeral representation of number is the final level of abstraction. For example,

$$\mathsf{N}\left\{ / \; \circledcirc \right\} \; = \; 2$$

These several levels of abstraction supply the structure for developing the fundamental concepts and operations of arithmetic. In proceeding level-by-level from the concrete objects to the abstract concept, each step is made explicit by use of a particular notation. As has been shown, the development of the concept of number is illustrated by the following steps in abstraction:

1. Display of a set of objects (for example, a drum, a ball, a block).

2. Description of the set:

$$\left\{ \; \rotatebox{0}{🥁} \; \circledcirc \; \square \; \right\}$$

3. Notation for number of members of the set:

4. Arabic numeral for the number:

$$3$$

The prior introduction of sets permits *numbers* to be introduced simply and precisely as properties of sets. Thus at the very beginning of his work with arithmetic the child learns a mathematically exact characterization of number. He learns that number is a property of sets by first considering sets and then the number of things in those sets. Since he is not committed to a single notation for number, e.g., the Arabic numerals, he is not likely to consider the symbol itself a number. In addition, the tendency to focus on the numerals themselves without a consideration of their meaning may be avoided since the concept of number precedes the introduction of the Arabic symbols for numbers.

The step in abstraction represented by moving from the description of a set to the N notation is a particularly important one. We abstract from the set with its particular elements to but one property of the set, the number of its elements. In the children's terms when we consider sets or pictures of sets, we are interested in what the members are; when we consider the meaning of the N notation we are interested only in how many members there are. To emphasize that the N notation represents number we note the following fact. Two sets may be *unequal* or nonidentical (that is, they do not have the same members), as illustrated by the inequality

$$\left\{ \text{🏃} \; \text{🥁} \right\} \neq \left\{ / \; \text{⬤} \right\}$$

Yet the numbers associated with the sets are the same, as illustrated by

$$N\left\{ \text{🏃} \; \text{🥁} \right\} = N\left\{ / \; \text{⬤} \right\}$$

The statement with the N notation involves *equality* while the statement with set descriptions does not because the N notation represents the property of number. The number of members of one set is equal to the number of members of the other even though the sets themselves are not equal because the members differ.

The same levels of abstraction are appropriate in introducing an operation on numbers such as addition. Once again we can begin with concrete illustrations and build step-by-step to the abstract operation of adding numbers. At the most concrete level we may display sets of physical objects and show that by combining the sets we form a new set. This operation is called the *union* of sets. For example, we might consider two sets, one consisting of a drum and one consisting of a ball and a pencil. We can combine the sets and form a new set, that is, the set consisting of the drum, the ball, and the pencil. To represent this operation of the union of two sets, we describe the sets by picturing the members and using the standard notation with braces. The symbol "∪" for union of sets is used and the operation is described by

$$\left\{ \text{🥁} \right\} \cup \left\{ \text{⬤} \; / \right\} = \left\{ \text{🥁} \; \text{⬤} \; / \right\}$$

When we abstract to a consideration of just the number of members, we have the parallel operation of addition so that the plus symbol is used.

$$N\left\{ \text{🥁} \right\} + N\left\{ \text{⬤} \; / \right\} = N\left\{ \text{🥁} \; \text{⬤} \; / \right\}$$

Finally, we may represent this equation using the Arabic numerals as

$$1 + 2 = 3$$

Source: Patrick Suppes, *Sets and Numbers: Teacher's Edition,* "Singer School Mathematics Series" (Chicago: L. W. Singer, Division of Random House, 1965), pp. iii–v.

Suppes makes a special effort in his materials to reach the pupils who have difficulty in concentrating on the exercises. He is explicit in his directions to teachers as to what to do with these children. He believes that it is important to keep the structure of discussion very similar in going from one page to the next. Explicit pointing with the finger permits the child to make overt responses that help him focus on the relevant stimuli. It is also desirable to discuss why the alternative answers are wrong. A child will come to understand the concept of equality of sets better if he is able to verbalize why a possible answer is wrong. In addition, for the youngster who has difficulty the drawing of the symbols will reinforce immediate recognition of them in later exercises.

The Suppes material was tested on eighty first-grade and forty-five second-grade classes from the San Francisco Bay area and Norwalk, Connecticut. In addition, it is presently being used in Ghana as part of the African Education Study. In comparison with American classes used as a control group, the classes in Ghana did equally well. This last fact offers hope that children in our own country whose cultures and speech patterns different from the standard might benefit from this program. Of special interest for the future is the computer-based, first-grade course now being devised. The findings from a computer-based laboratory in a public school should prove useful to the disadvantaged, since verbal skill is not a factor in instruction.

No review of new curricula in mathematics is complete without discussion of the **School Mathematics Study Group** program. Under the direction of Edward G. Begle of Yale University, a small committee of educators and mathematicians set out to develop an improved curriculum that would offer students, from kindergarten through twelfth grade, not only the basic skills, but also a deeper understanding of the basic concepts and structure of mathematics. Secondly, the programs were developed to attract and train students who were considered above average and capable of studying mathematics with maximum profit. Finally, a very intensive, inservice, training course for teachers was provided for.

Although the SMSG program was initially aimed at the few who were above average, there were some schools where SMSG materials were used as texts for all seventh- and eighth-grade pupils. The experimenters, much to their surprise, found that in classes of disadvantaged youngsters, the material was well received if presented orally by the teacher. Problems arose only where written material was presented. Noting this, the experimenters prepared special editions of the SMSG textbooks for seventh through ninth grades for students with less advanced reading ability.

The **Minnesota School Math and Science Center** (**Minnemast**) was originated at the University of Minnesota under the direction of Dr. Paul C. Rosenbloom (mathematics) and Dr. James E. Werntz (science). Minnemast is the only major curriculum project which aims at preparing a full-scale, coordinated science and mathematics program to start on the kindergarten level. Again, like so many of the new mathematics projects, it was not developed for educationally disadvantaged pupils. Yet, when it was tried in one New York City school that draws the vast majority of its pupils from families that were financially, emotionally, and culturally deprived, it was found to create a "stir" among them.

Like the other programs described in this chapter, the Minnemast program has as its main goal the teaching of the structure of the real number system. The child is introduced to coordinates, graphs, and simple functions by the time he reaches third grade. The unique feature of the program, however, is the fact that one can teach mathematics and science concurrently and with interrelating and interacting parts. This approach has tremendous potential for the disadvantaged youngster who begins in the kindergarten to get practice in the interrelationship of disciplines. Exhibit 31 (pp. 214–215) shows the use of this dual approach in teaching kindergarteners about closed curves in geometry.

The Minnemast program, however, has one serious disadvantage. The materials are built around a "live" teacher-training program. At present, they may only be used at a center under the supervision of a cooperating college. Unlike other programs, when the teacher-training aspects are built in, the need for cooperating college training limits its use.

The **University of Illinois Committee on School Mathematics** is developing material based on two fundamental principles: those of discovery and of precision in language. Preliminary to the study of language, verbalizations of "discoveries" is delayed, since verbalization compels the formulation of a statement. If a child's linguistic ability does not match his mathematical insight he may give the wrong answer even though he is right in

Exhibit 31

INTRODUCING THE "CLOSED CURVE" CONCEPT TO KINDERGARTENERS (THE MINNEMAST PROGRAM)

The teacher reads:

Eagle Feather lived with his parents on the colorful painted desert in north-central Arizona. Tourists found his home hard to see as they sped by in their cars for it was made of the earth itself. It was a round home called a hogan. Eagle Feather loved the warmth of his earthen home in the winter even if it was dark when the door was closed to shut out the chilling winds.

When spring came, the family was glad to move the stove out into a little arbor beside the hogan. Father thatched the roof of the arbor with rushes from a nearby stream. It was pleasant to sit in the shade and watch the shadows of the clouds as they sped over the colorful hills that surrounded his home.

On the other other side of the house was the fold for the sheep. The fold was a ring of rocks piled high enough to keep the sheep from wandering at night. It also kept desert animals from coming in among the sheep and trying to eat them.

The opening in the fold where the sheep went in and out was closed by small wooden logs laid on top of each other until the opening was filled. The final thing Eagle Feather did after he had herded the last reluctant sheep into the fold was to fit the logs into the slots provided for them. His mother who had gone to the government school often told him that the fold with the gate closed was a closed curve. Mother would say, "Remember, my son, sheep are safe in a *closed* curve. You must always remember to fit the logs in place at night, and close the curve good and tight. When the logs are out, this is an open curve and any old desert fox could come in. Whatever else you forget, never forget to close the curve with the logs."

And Eagle Feather was careful. He led the sheep from the fold each morning and went over the rosy hills, helping the black and white sheep find the sparse vegetation they liked to eat. Each day he went in a new direction, for the pasture was desert land and the plants grew slowly. At noon he sat in the shade of a huge rock to eat the lunch his mother had packed for him. Most of the sheep liked to find some shade and lie down for a rest during the time the sun shone the hottest.

When evening came, Eagle Feather walked home slowly behind the sheep. His mother looked up to see them silhouetted against the setting sun. She hurried to set the pots on the stove to start supper for her tired little boy.

When the sleepy sheep were in the fold and the logs had closed the curve, Mother asked, "Eagle Feather, are you too tired to water the corn before supper time?

It has been so hot today that the leaves look withered. If we want any corn to eat this winter, the plants must have water."

Eagle Feather's feet dragged a little as he went down to the little stream that trickled between the parched hills. His father had dammed up the tiny stream and there was a little pool of water above the dam. Eagle Feather trudged up and down the rows, his eyes lit upon the fence—a curve—a closed curve usually—but an open curve now with the gate open.

His feet went faster, even uphill, as he went toward supper. "Mother," he called, "I've found another closed curve! The corn fence! And I opened the curve to work but I closed it again before I left."

The beans and lamb tasted good eaten in the cool of the evening, as he sat cross-legged under the arbor. Eagle Feather stretched out on a sheepskin and looked up at the sliver of a moon and at the faintly twinkling stars. Life was very good indeed.

Suggested Follow-up Activities

1. Have children make open and closed curves with blocks, clay, pipecleaners, etc. Color crayons may also be used.
2. Play a curve game. Have children stand close together in a circle, with arms behind each others' backs. Have one child in circle trying to get out—unsuccessfully. Children can be the corral and the child in the center the wild horse trying to get out. Give several children an opportunity to participate in center of circle.
3. Have one child be the prince or princess inside the circle, the "closed curve," and one child on the outside, the fiery dragon, trying unsuccessfully to get to the prince or princess. These versions can be varied, i.e.

   a) Water trying to get out of a reservoir
   b) Wolf on outside of circle trying to get to sheep inside circle.

   Should any child or children "let go," the closed curve would become an open curve, thus permitting the wild horse to get out of the corral, water to rush out of the reservoir, the dragon to get to the princess, or the wolf to the sheep. (Stress this at the time it happens. It is bound to happen and will provide part of the fun.)

Source: Minnemast Center, "Eagle Feather," in *Mathematics for the Elementary School: Geometry* (Minneapolis: Minnemast Center, University of Minnesota, 1963, pp. 44–54.

Exhibit 32

VISUAL EMPHASIS OF MATHEMATICS CONCEPTS
(THE UICSM PROGRAM)

Do you see how to fill in the blank tags on these sticks?

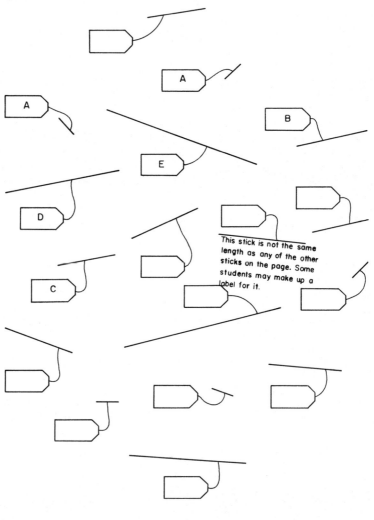

This stick is not the same length as any of the other sticks on the page. Some students may make up a label for it.

Length

1. Look at the sticks in the picture on page 2. Find the two sticks which are labeled with an [A) Do these sticks have the same length? _____

2. All the other sticks which have the same length as the [A) -sticks above should be tagged with an 'A'. Do that right now.

3. How many A-sticks are in the picture? _____

4. Tag with a 'B' all the sticks which have the same length as the B-stick.

5. Tag all the C-sticks in the picture.

6. Now tag all the D-sticks, and tag all the E-sticks.

7. How many sticks are in the picture? _____

8. Finish the table:

LENGTH	NO.
A)	5
B)	
C)	
D)	
E)	
TOTAL	

9. Should these be the same? _____

10. Fill in the blanks.

(a) A [C) -stick is longer than an [ ) -stick.

(b) [D) is shorter than [ )

(c) [ ) has the same length as [B)

(d) [E) _____ [D)

Source: UICSM staff, *Mathematics for the Secondary School,* University of Illinois Committee on School Mathematics (Urbana: University of Illinois, 1965), Chapter 1, pp. 2–3.

his thinking. In the experimental edition of the first course of mathematics for the secondary schools UICSM, there are fascinating materials that promote discovery of meaning with a minimum of need for early verbalization. In mathematical thinking, the question is raised as to whether this delays or advances cognitive processes. Max B. Beberman, director of the project, suggests that becoming aware of the concept before a name is assigned to it leads the student to create a name that describes it. Exhibit 32 (pp. 216–217) illustrates the use of the discovery method with a minimum of verbalization in a unit on stretching machines.

There is almost no verbalization called for in the UICSM lesson, yet the learner is given experience, in items 1, 2, and 3, in finding out for himself about variations in size and relationship of sizes. In items 4 and 5, he transfers this knowledge to similar situations but with different labels. In a conversation with the authors Dr. Beberman suggested that, in addition to this workbook approach, children should be given the actual sticks so as to be able to make physical comparisons. The lesson proceeds to points where verbalization is necessary, but only after much experience and practice.

Once again, it should be pointed out that the programs in mathematics described in this chapter have been produced primarily for the gifted student. Yet we know that each of these programs has been used unofficially with the less able, more specifically, with the disadvantaged. Although substantiated evidence is lacking, since until now none of the programs has been truly evaluated either with the able or the less able, we do know that the children from disadvantaged homes are interested, ask questions, return to class without interruption, and want more of it. Davis, Rosenbloom, Beberman, Suppes all attest to this fact. Now it is up to educators to take the plunge, to support the assertion that all pupils deserve the optimum in education.

SCIENCE

Where does science fit into the curriculum for a disadvantaged youngster? As happened in mathematics, developers of the new science programs directed their attention primarily toward the average and bright youngsters, seeming, by implication, to eliminate the disadvantaged from their consideration. Yet, if the purpose of the new science approach is to make children scientifically literate, to teach the structure of science, and to encourage students to inquire into the significance of certain basic concepts, should not these purposes be applied to the "out" groups as well as to the "in" groups?

Robert Karplus, professor of physics at the University of California at Berkeley, makes a plea for the inclusion of science education as part of general education, having as its goal scientific literacy. He defines scientific literacy as the ability to assimilate the conceptual structure of science, to become familiar with the research experience, and to obtain a certain degree of historical perspective.

Karplus, as director of the **Science Curriculum Improvement Study,** is developing a science teaching program[1] based on developing this conceptual framework by teaching fundamental concepts and verbal labeling in order to help children discriminate between basic concepts. The purpose is to teach pupils the scientific basis for natural phenomena. The following is a description of how Karplus' approach was used in a lesson on interaction given in a first-grade classroom:

[1]Science Curriculum Improvement Study, *Interaction and Systems,* trial edition (Berkeley: University of California, 1963).

School children already have an interaction concept in the sense of one object doing something to another. They use many words such as "pull," "push," "cut," "sweep," "scrape," "shine on," and "stick together," to describe the interaction in individual cases. They do not, however, differentiate interaction as one of the concepts of action or behavior, all of which are defined by verbs. One important generalization the children must recognize is that an interaction involves at least two objects. Thus, "I am running" describes an activity or behavior, while "My shoe scrapes the floor" describes an interaction. A focus on the specific objects interacting rather than a focus on the whole situation helps to define the concept because it reduces the likelihood of interfering thoughts. For example, the statement "I scrape the floor," instead of "my shoe scrapes the floor," conveys the idea of an activity as well as of an interaction.

During this first lesson, the pupils described what various objects in the class were doing to each other. They also made pictures to illustrate "cut," "shine on," "pull," "push," etc., by drawing appropriate objects (e.g., scissors and paper, sun and flower) in a more or less appropriate relationship. In the second lesson, the pictures were reviewed and displayed on the bulletin board under the heading, "Objects Interact." The word "interact" was introduced as a generalization of all the specific verbs they had illustrated. In the third lesson, each child did experiments with some objects selected from a box provided by the teacher—paper, pencils, scissors, candy, water, thumbtacks, paper clips, string, magnets, batteries, light bulbs, and wires. After experimenting, each child described how the objects had behaved and told which ones had interacted.

These lessons, of course, only established a basis for the development of the interaction concept. They stimulated the pupils to discover other examples of interactions: the coat and the coat hanger may interact, the thumbtack and the water interact, the candy and the tongue interact, the flower roots and the soil interact, and so on. Each time a new situation is interpreted by means of the interaction concept, the concept is enriched. By directing the children's attention to the interaction concept, the teacher creates for them a new way of looking at and interpreting their environment.[2]

Here is another example of how Karplus' method was applied —this time in teaching the concept of equilibrium to a second grade class:

Elementary school pupils have a strongly developed sense of distinction between activity and quiescence. As the authors have previously pointed out, the failure to take this into account can seriously hinder teaching. The scientist emphasizes this distinction: He describes some systems as being at equilibrium and some systems as

[2]Summary of a description given by Dr. Karplus at a meeting with the New York City Board of Education in the City of New York in February, 1964.

being not at equilibrium. This lesson on equilibrium was intended to give the children a new way of interpreting their recognition of activity and change.

The pupils were allowed to examine a display of many systems—a burning candle, a spring, an ice cube in water, a stone in water, mechanical turtles, sugar crystals in water, several piles of blocks, and a flashlight. The flashlight was turned on; the toy turtle was wound up and permitted to walk on the table. First, the children were asked to define systems for many experiments in progress. After all examples had been mentioned, the class discussed the fact that not all systems remained the same. In some, the arrangement of the component objects was changing: the candle was burning down, the ice cube was melting, the sugar was dissolving, and so on. In other systems such as the rock in the water, the piled up blocks, and the spring, nothing was happening. Now the teacher introduced a new term: the unchanging systems, she told them, "at equilibrium," and the ones undergoing changes were "not at equilibrium."

Several of the pupils took turns at disturbing the state of equilibrium in the changing systems, by winding up the toys, turning off the flashlight, stretching and then releasing the spring, picking the rock out of the water and dropping it back, and agitating the water in the glass containing the sugar crystals. These actions suggested that the children thought of equilibrium mainly in terms of mechanical motion and rest. The fact that agitating the sugar water hastens the solution process while it disturbs mechanical equilibrium was not clear to them. The equilibrium concept would need to be elaborated upon in a later lesson.[3]

If we recall Riessman's description of the slum child as being slow at performing intellectual tasks, we see that the experiences outlined by Karplus take the child step-by-step from the simplest task to the most complex and finally to conceptualization. In example after example, the child receives practice in moving from one logical step to another. Will this not help the slower youngster to develop a system of thinking? Furthermore, Riessman attributes some of this slowness to the inability to understand a concept unless it has a physical basis. Again, Karplus stresses the physical experience before he elicits the idea or the concept. In addition, he offers many different types of experiences, all leading to the same generalization or concept or idea—again, avoiding the "one track" approach.

A similar approach to stimulating and guiding students into scientific inquiry is the **ESI Elementary Science Study,** being developed under the direction of Jerrold Zacharias and David Hawkins. This method is primarily an experience method, with

[3]*Ibid.*

less direction and structure than the Karplus approach. It is based on the premise that elementary school is not simply a warehouse of facts but rather an insightful time for learning how to learn and for acquiring an interest and a curiosity to continue to learn.

The tentative curriculum design includes a wide diversity of subjects: size and scaling, a balance board, the addition syndrome, shadows, magnets and forces, gases, microecology, geotaxis and phototaxis in the edible land snail, crystals—a rather varied curriculum. However, the content was not selected arbitrarily; the subjects chosen have been determined, through study, to be attractive to children. And, in addition to its atttractiveness to children, this selection of content offers something else, something less conventional and predictable. In the environment of this program, the child had the opportunity to learn about unusual scientific phenomena; an experience not given children in the traditional "weather unit." What kinds of change in children will these unpredictable experiences bring about? The answer to this question is not yet apparent, but almost anyone who teaches must have had, at some time, the experience of watching a child come upon an unpredictable discovery. A description of this approach is given in the ESI workshop report:

It is important to find the themes which make a direct appeal to children, where one could capture the interest of the child and lead him to ask questions and search for answers. Thus we looked for the attraction of the moving hand forming a shadow, or the attraction of a marble slowly falling down a long clear tube filled with Karo syrup. This is how we began. As one goes on, one may find children playing with animals, wondering how the leach, the fly, the mosquito, the snail, the child, the turtle, the dragonfly, or even those curious animals, the jet, the automobile, and the rocket all move. With most of these, the children can have real first hand experience. Learning how they move is both interesting and fun. The child wants to know why; and it is relatively easy to find that each of these organisms moves only when some part of the environment receives a push. This generality holds true for all, from child to rocket. But this is not to codify the laws of motion. We suspect, however, that this kind of insight into why things move, in a diversity of circumstances, is a better preparation for the laws of motion than the very clearest formulation of a few sentences, even with an excellent lecture demonstration. This does not preclude such things, indeed it makes them almost mandatory: but only after children have learned that when a turtle moves, little bits of sand are really thrown up; and that when a fly flies, the air is blown backwards; and when the child walks, he sends the platform backwards. These experiences must come before; they are the things that show the generality of the rule through-out all experience. It is precisely this generality that gives science its power. Finally, the time comes for abstracting from all this experience, to state a law. But now, the law is not just a few more symbols in an abstract language, but it has the possibility of what we call under-standing, that is of application to new situations. Above all, the child has been motivated to learn it because it really does work; it organizes much of the world; that you had no reason to expect to be organized.[4]

The ESI approach to science teaching, more than the other new approaches, seems nearer the motivational, the unpredict-able, the accidental, as opposed to the structured, purely intellec-tual approach of the followers of Piaget and Karplus. Jerome Bruner fancifully describes our knowing and acting as right- and left-handed; the right hand is the clear, the rational, the deduc-tive, the meaningful, the purposeful, and the straightforward, and the left hand is the intuitive, the hypothetical, the tentative, the playful, the witty, the imaginative, and sometimes simply the wrong. All of these are ways of knowing. The ESI program incor-porates both of these approaches.

The Elementary Science Project being developed at Howard University has as its specific audience the disadvantaged young-ster. The purpose of this project is to provide compensatory sci-ence experiences for elementary school children and their par-ents. The materials are distributed as packaged units, which pupils may take home, work out with their families, then bring back to school and discuss the results in class. The parents come to the school with their children on Saturdays to discuss the use of the materials. The project hopes to be able to determine whether or not the joint participation in the experience by dis-advantaged children and their parents can help, in a significant way, to overcome social and personal handicaps, and disclose such changes in behavior of both children and parents as may result from participation in this project. The Elementary Science Project materials are presently being tried out in Washington, D. C. and New York City.

Several school systems have developed science programs that deserve mention. Although these programs are not particularly recommended for their method or approach, they do have sec-

[4]Charles Walcott, "The Elementary Science Study: History," *A Survey of the Elementary Science Study with Excerpts from the 1962 Elementary Science Summer Conference Report* (Watertown, Mass.: Educational Serv-ices Incorporated, 1962), pp. 8–9.

tions that treat important topics. For example, the Dallas Independent School District offers a seventh-grade course entitled "Health Science," in which the emphasis is on how man has applied scientific knowledge to the improvement of health. Such a theme can be extremely useful to the disadvantaged youngster, who, even if he doesn't presently have health problems, is certainly a likely candidate as he grows older.

Learning about health as a scientific phenomenon, rather than in a "how-to" hygiene course, can lead the student to a much sounder understanding of his bodily functions. The Dallas course makes a strong effort to eliminate all misconceptions regarding natural phenomena and helps the youngster to exercise a healthy curiosity about himself.

At the University of California Elementary School, children are taught human embryology through a study of comparative embryology. The children watch chicken embryos grow, from a form of life almost too small to be seen, into peeping balls of fluff. An important part of this experience is the comparison made between the chick and the human embryological development. The course of study teaches human reproduction from the joining of the sperm and egg to the final organism.

For children from slum area environments, this approach has much to recommend it. These youngsters, although sophisticated in certain aspects of sexual behavior however are unsophisticated in breaking away from sexual customs and mores that can be detrimental. Through an early introduction to the subject, based on sound scientific understandings, perhaps many of the unfortunate sexual incidents that occur among slum children can be avoided.

The introduction of sex education through a comparative study of all animals is not limited to the University of California Elementary School. Orlando, Florida; Greenville County, South Carolina are among several other school systems that use this theme in the elementary schools.

A new area of study in science that deserves mention is space-age science. Very slowly it is beginning to be seen in some school curricula. Orlando, Florida, offers a special junior high school course that is accompanied by a television program. It teaches space age science through the disciplines of geology, chemistry, nuclear physics, anthropology, and biology.

Harrisburg, Pennsylvania, combines the learning of earth and space science in the junior high school in one sequence with an emphasis on how the interrelationship can influence the behavior of living things. In the elementary school, a delightful curriculum sequence has been developed, "Problems of Space Travel." It is hard to believe that any child living in this age would not be fascinated by a study of the scientific phenomena happening all around him.

The South Carolina State Department of Education offers, in the junior high schools, a course called "Space Biology." It includes a study of the psychological problems in space flight as well as the problem of food and oxygen for long space flights.

For the disadvantaged youngster, the science of outer space has not only fascination, but the added advantage of being "live." He can see on television the very lesson the teacher is discussing in class. He can open a newspaper and read a caption that will reinforce what he has derived in class and seen on television. Studying a living science makes the student a partner in discovery.

The Harvard Physics Project recently received a grant to finance the development of a new physics course—one designed to appeal to the whole interest range of students, from those who are science-oriented to those who are disinterested in or afraid of science. Its purpose is not only to treat physics as a lively and fluid science, but also as a means of inquiry into the factors accounting for the decreased interest in physics as a high school course. While the course will be centered on a solid introduction to physics, the humanities background of the sciences will be stressed. The project is developing a range of teaching aids such as programed instruction, pupil tests, laboratory manuals, film loops, slides, selected readings, and a number of films and paperback monographs. This program, at least in rationale, seems to hold promise for the youngster from a disadvantaged environment who manages to reach high school, but shudders at the thought of taking physics. Having this specifically in mind, the new course material as it is developed will be tried out in New York City, in Portland, Oregon, and in Tulsa, Oklahoma, as well as in certain suburban communities where there are not large concentrations of disadvantaged pupils.

Frederick Ferris, of the **Princeton University Junior High School Science Project,** is developing a junior high school science program. Initially, this program was written for average and bright students in the Princeton community. It is now being tested on children in similar communities all over the country and, in addition, on students in the inner cities of Chicago, New York, and Trenton, New Jersey. The basis of this program is the use of mathematical skills and concepts as a tool of scientific investigation (as opposed to the Minnemast program, which combines both disciplines). It is not "applied mathematics" that the students are learning but "applicable mathematics." Exhibit 33 is an example.

In addition to using mathematical skills as a tool of scientific investigation, Ferris intends to bring science students on the junior high school level to some understanding of the nature of problems common to all physical sciences, to explain the tools of investigation which they share, and the ways in which the investigation is given meaning by concepts, models, and theories. The method offers students an artful selection of experiences, ranging from a glass of water with a melting ice cube to a set of colored slides of the Grand Canyon of the Colorado River. The title of this program is *Time, Space and Matter*.[5]

Part I of the program, "On the Nature of Things," leads the students through a sequence of investigations which begin and end with consideration of the Grand Canyon. The students start by looking at colored slides and by examining specimen rocks. The youngsters are stimulated by the great variety of features they observe. The desire to "know" demands more facts and hence more refined or more precise observations. This in turn leads the students to experiments with thermometers, balances, and meter sticks, and incites a consequent "extension of their senses." Part I concludes with a series of experiments, the combined sequence of which enables them to estimate the length of time it took the Colorado River to carve out the Grand Canyon.

The initial activity of Part I introduces the students to the kind of questions and answers they will meet throughout the course and sets the stage for the teacher's acting as a participating observer. When the Grand Canyon slides and specimens have been viewed, discussion centers around attempts to explain this earth-feature. The teacher encourages speculation, no matter how far afield, but demurs at appeal to authorities, whether encyclopedias or lecturers, as acceptable sources of information. The difficulty

[5]Junior High School Science Project, *Time Space and Matter* (Princeton: Princeton University Press, 1963).

Exhibit 33

APPLYING MATHEMATICAL SKILLS AND CONCEPTS AS A TOOL OF SCIENTIFIC INVESTIGATION (THE PRINCETON PROJECT)

Investigation 1. How can we insure accuracy in reading points on a thermometer?

Students are given an ordinary glass-bulb thermometer without markings of any kind. Earlier they have been introduced to the notion that the liquid column inside the thermometer rises and falls with temperature changes. The change in height of the liquid is a simple observation, of course. The linear relation between height of the column and numerical expression, quantity, of temperature is assumed implicitly. The specific problem the students must answer is this: How can numbers be assigned to points on the column of liquid to make sure that every thermometer in the class gives the same reading for the same temperature?

Mathematics, *alone,* even the most sophisticated analysis, is powerless to give much help in this problem.

The solution depends partly on observations of what actually happens to the liquid in the thermometer when the instrument is placed in atmospheres that are hotter or colder. Only after the students have observed that the column of liquid reaches the *same upper point* on the thermometer every time it is placed in boiling water and drops to the *same lower point* when the bulb is placed in ice water can they begin to see these *fixed points* as the end points of a line segment with a length to be measured. The data from observation and experiment can be organized mathematically only *after* the observer has made sure that the data are uniform and regular.

Completing the job of marking temperature calibrations on the thermometers requires that the students divide the length between the fixed boiling point and the fixed freezing point into equal-length intervals. So that the essential nature of the solution will not be lost in a maze of arithmetic calculations with fractions, the length of the segment is divided into ten equal intervals by parallel projection from a ten-centimeter length. Even though they lack formal initiation into the relevant theorems of geometry, students have no difficulty in seeing the equality of the length of the projected intervals.

Notice that even without the tedious chore of "doing" fractions, this example shows how two different kinds of insights and skills are intertwined to reach solutions of problems in science. The geometry of lines and points and the arithmetic of fractions do not lose meaning from being implicit. Instead, mathematical calculations are given point and meaning by their usefulness in reaching the solution to an interesting problem.

Investigation 2. How sensitive is a balance-beam to small changes in weight?

Every student is supplied with a small equal-arm balance, each arm fifteen centimeters long marked in millimeters. Instead of standardized sets of weights, they use

Exhibit 33 (*Continued*)

pennies, thumbtacks and pins as the three units with which they can express the mass of various rock samples. Thus, a small chunk of calcite may be entered in the student's notebook as having the mass of "Two pennies, three thumbtacks and four pins." It is a familiar observation that such a balance will be in equilibrium when equal masses are placed at equal distances from the center of the beam, and students can quickly progress to the realization that equilibrium cannot be achieved without using fractional mass units. Six thumbtacks balance one penny, and eight pins balance one thumbtack. The specific question the students are asked is this: Is there a unit corresponding to a fraction of a pin which will yield still greater refinement in the use of the balance?

Experiment is the only road to the solution of this problem. They are provided with sequins, carefully chosen to be so small that the weight of several of them is still outside the sensitivity of the particular balance beam. They discover that these small units, added one at a time to one pan on the beam in equilibrium, do not disturb the balance beam until four sequins have been added. Further, they are able to restore equilibrium by balancing those several sequins with a single pin in the other pan of the balance. The use of sequins as fractions of a "pin mass unit" is quite easily seen to be impossible; the balance does not distinguish between "one-fourth of a pin" and "three-fourths of a pin." It can only distinguish between "one pin" and "two pins."

Here, without any mention of the decimal number system, is the essence of the notion of significant figures. The particular balance simply does not measure the mass of sequins—fractional "pin mass units". It is easy to see that mass measured by this balance will never be given in "sequin units". Moreover, the important point missed by most discussions of significant figures is made very simply and easily: no mass given in sequin mass units that arise from calculations rather than readings will have meaning for this particular balance.

Of course, the notion of significant figures is missing from mathematics itself. In mathematics it is not possible to distinguish between the numbers: 5, 5.0, 5.00000 . . . or 4.9999 . . . The distinctions arise only in the context of the instrument: thermometer, yardstick, spectroscope or what-have-you, which supplies the given numbers. Seven or eight years of school arithmetic work have emphasized that college freshmen and even beginning graduate students have difficulty with the idea of significant numbers.

The impossibility of measuring the mass of sequins with the balance gives vivid meaning to the idea that there is a limit to the number of times a unit may be divided into fractional parts for a particular instrument. As we shall see, further problems in the same section reinforce this notion.

Source: Frederick Ferris, *A Preliminary Report on the Development of Mathematical Skills and Concepts in the Junior High School Science Project,* pp. 2–4.

of explaining a system as vast as the Grand Canyon soon becomes apparent. Hence, the teacher helps the students systematically investigate simpler situations which would seem more manageable and which might well lead to answers about bigger and more complicated systems.

The students are then introduced to the meaning of observation in its broadest sense. They are made aware of the necessity to use *all* of their senses. They learn to differentiate between observation and interpretation. They become wary of uncritical reliance on the sense of sight. Finally, they understand the need for mechanical extension of the senses in order to increase precision of observation. Preparation has thus been made, through such things as calibration of a thermometer and initial use of a hand lens, for later and more frequent use of instruments.

As they continue, the students find that every question asked about the nature of the physical world, whether related to the Grand Canyon or to simpler systems such as containers holding solids and liquids, is, in the final analysis, a question about time, space, or matter. In order to investigate these apparently fundamental physical principles, therefore, techniques must be developed to increase precision of observation for measuring various aspects of time, space, and matter. This leads eventually to the formation of such concepts as density, specific gravity, and physical change. Furthermore, investigative techniques are extended to include such valuable tools as approximation, interpolation, and extrapolation.

Many teachers find it particularly exciting to lead students to a discovery of the idea of significant figures in measurement. Each student is supplied with a small, equal-arm balance. Instead of standard masses, such items as pennies, thumbtacks, and pins become the units with which the masses of various rock samples are expressed. Thus, a student may record in his notebook the mass of a small chunk of calcite as "two pennies, three thumbtacks, and four pins." At some point, it becomes necessary to determine whether there can be a unit corresponding to "a fraction of a pin," in order to use the balance with greater efficiency. Sequins, carefully chosen so that the mass of several is still outside the sensitivity of the balance, are provided. The students find that not until four sequins have been added can the equilibrium of the balance beam be disturbed. In addition, equilibrium can be restored by balancing several sequins with a single pin in the other pan of the balance. The use of sequins as fractions of pin units is therefore seen as absurd, for the balance simply does not distinguish between "one-fourth of a pin" and "three-fourths of a pin"; the balance can distinguish only between "one pin" and "two pins." Consequently, the students come to realize the necessity of meaningful units for measuring instruments in general.

The students now discover that, when matter and the space it occupies are involved over a period of time, there results some physical change. By means of various experiments, running water is found to be a major change-producing agent. Class members are now ready for more sophisticated kinds of interpretation and are introduced to the powers and dangers of interpolation and extrapolation.

As Part I concludes, the students return to their earlier questions about the Grand Canyon and now find they have achieved the means for acquiring at least some of the answers. Maps are used for determining the size of the canyon; and, finally, the students make an order of magnitude estimate of the number of years the Colorado River took to form the canyon. They do this by extrapolating from data they themselves have obtained by experiment. The estimate is checked against the literature; and, despite the many assumptions, the students find their estimate in agreement with that made by professional scientists. So far as questions about the composition of the rocks of the Grand Canyon are concerned, however, the students find they do not yet have the wherewithal for making more than the most general statements. This situation leads very naturally into Part II, "Seeking Regularity in Matter."

Once again, the Karplus project at Berkeley, the ESI project developed by Zacharias and Hawkins, and Ferris' work at Princeton were all directed toward the gifted. Yet, in examining the elements, one finds that physical experience, inductive thinking, analysis, synthesis, drawing of generalizations, and eventual verbalization are all basic to the new programs; and these are the basic needs of children from underprivileged homes and environments.

Airplane companies have been training native mechanics to repair engines and to become flight engineers in Ethiopia, in the African bush, in Mongolia, in all parts of the world.

Evidence going back fifteen years shows that given the opportunity and the training they equal their European mentors in scientific insight, operational efficiency and all around competence.[6]

Yet we find it so difficult to accept the idea that children who come from our own "bush country" (be it rural or inner-city) can learn and perhaps eventually equal their mentors!

No other field offers as many opportunities to use the discovery method as does that of science and mathematics. Not only does this method encourage individual study, but it has the additional value of spurring creativity. Torrance lists the following prerequisites to the stimulation of the creative drive:

1. The absence of serious threat to the self, the willingness to risk
2. Self-awareness—is in touch with one's feelings
3. Self-differentiation—sees self as being different from others
4. Both openness to the ideas of others and confidence in one's own perceptions of reality or in one's own ideas
5. Mutuality in interpersonal relations—balance between excessive quest for social relations and pathological rejection of them.[7]

As you will undoubtedly notice, these conditions or criteria are centered around the ego and suggest that creativity increases as the ego is freed from inhibition and external domination, while staying open to the intake of ideas from the outside. Through this open-ended approach, using the discovery method as is being done in many of the newer mathematics and science programs, we might possibly help "free the ego from inhibition and external domination" and thereby furnish a partial answer to the problem of developing a curriculum for the disadvantaged child.

[6]Statement made by Dr. John F. Furbay, Director, Educational and Cultural Programs, Trans World Airlines, at the February 7, 1965 meeting of the New York Society for the Experimental Study of Education.

[7]E. Paul Torrance, *Guiding Creative Talent* (Englewood Cliffs, N. J.: Prentice-Hall, 1962), pp. 143–144.

SELECTED READINGS ON
MATHEMATICS AND SCIENCE

Books on the Subject

Association of Teachers of Mathematics, *Some Lessons in Mathematics* (New York: Cambridge University Press, 1964).

A group of twenty English mathematicians and educators, members of the Association of Teachers of Mathematics, has produced this unusual handbook for teachers of modern school mathematics, under the modest title of *Some Lessons in Mathematics*. Teachers at the secondary level will find a variety of valuable suggestions for the introduction of new mathematical content. The primary concern of the authors extends over new mathematics, new ways of presenting old mathematics, and applications to contemporary mathematics.

Bruner, Jerome S., *On Knowing* (Cambridge, Mass.: Harvard University Press, 1962).

The left hand has traditionally represented the powers of intuition, feeling, spontaneity. This book inquires into the part these qualities play in determining how we know what we know; how we can help others to know—that is, how we can teach; and how our conception of reality affects our actions and is modified by them.

This book is recommended for superintendents and specialists who might tend to place too much emphasis on the right hand (the doer) and too little on the left hand (the dreamer). This is particularly true in the field of science and mathematics.

Cambridge Conference on School Mathematics, *Goals for School Mathematics: The Report of the Cambridge Conference on School Mathematics* (Boston: Houghton Mifflin, 1963).

With the support of the National Science Foundation, Educational Services Incorporated held a small conference of 25 mathematicians and scientists at Cambridge, Massachusetts, between June 18 and July 12, 1963. The report of this conference has since become known as "The Cambridge Report". Its stated purpose was to present "tentative views upon the shape and content of a pre-college mathematics curriculum that might be brought into being over the next few decades".

As Dr. Francis Keppel, United States Commissioner of Education, writes in his foreword, "The present report is a bold step. . . . It is not only that most teachers will be completely incapable of teaching most of the mathematics set forth in the curricula proposed here; most teachers would be hard put to comprehend it. No brief period of retraining will suffice. Even the first-grade curriculum embodies notions with which the average teacher is totally unfamiliar."

Caws, Peter, *The Philosophy of Science: A Systematic Account* (Princeton: Van Nostrand, 1965).

In four tightly organized parts, containing forty-four brief essays that vary between five and ten pages in length, Caws attempts to provide the student with the material needed to understand the major problems in the philosophy of science, with an explanation of what these problems are, and with an indication of the kinds of modest "solutions" that are available.

Hooke, Robert, and Shaxer, Douglas, *Math and Aftermath* (New York: Walker, 1965).

A report is given on current research in physics, astronomy, and engineering as well as in applied mathematics. The authors examine separately two modes in the application of mathematics: (1) the formulation of theories with deductions from them to be tested by observation, and (2) the statistical treatment of data from the processing of which structure can be observed and predictions made.

Piaget, Jean, *The Child's Conception of Number* (London: Humanities Press, 1962).

This book sets forth experiments which support the new theory that the notion of number exists only when order is seen as the "nesting of sets," and coordination, as the order of the "including classes." This book will be of use to psychologists and to teachers at all levels of education.

Articles from Professional Publications

Alpert, R., Stellwagon, G., and Becker, D., "Psychological Factors in Mathematics Education," *School Mathematics Study Group Reports,* Newsletter No. 15, Stanford, 1963, pp. 14–24.

Atkin, J. Myron, and Karplus, Robert, "Discovery or Invention?" *Science Teacher,* (September 1962, pp. 45–51.

Ausubel, David P., "Some Psychological Considerations in the Objectives and Design of an Elementary School Science Program," *Science Education,* 47 (April 1963), pp. 278–284.

Begle, E. G., "The School Mathematics Study Group," *Mathematics Teacher,* 51 (December 1958), pp. 616–618.

Biological Sciences Curriculum Study, *Biological Science: An Inquiry into Life* (New York: Harcourt, Brace and World, 1963), Yellow version, 748 pp.

Biological Sciences Curriculum Study, *Molecules to Man,* includes "Laboratory Investigations" (Boston: Houghton Mifflin, 1963), Blue version, 716 pp.

Biological Sciences Curriculum Study, *High School Biology* (Chicago: Rand McNally, 1963), Green version, 749 pp.

Biological Sciences Curriculum Study, *High School Biology: Special Materials, Teacher's Manual* (Boulder: University of Colorado, 1963), 373 pp.

Biological Sciences Curriculum Study, *Research Problems in Biology: Investigations for Students* (Garden City, N. Y.: Doubleday, 1963), Series 1, 232 pp., Series 2, 240 pp.

Biological Sciences Curriculum Study, *Student Laboratory Guide—Biological Science: An Inquiry into Life* (New York: Harcourt, Brace and World, 1963), Yellow version, 288 pp.

Biological Sciences Curriculum Study, *Student's Manual—Laboratory and Field Investigations* (Chicago: Rand McNally, 1963), Green version, 374 pp.

Brown, Kenneth E., "The Drive to Improve School Mathematics," in National Council of Teachers of Mathematics, *The Revolution in School Mathematics* (Washington, D.C.: the Council, 1961), pp. 15–29.

Butts, David P., "The Degree to Which Children Conceptualize from Science Experience," *Journal of Research in Science Teaching,* Issue I (1963), pp. 135–143.

Chemical Bond Approach Project, *Investigating Chemical Systems* (New York: McGraw-Hill, 1963), 135 pp.

Chemical Education Material Study, *Chemistry: An Experimental Science* (San Francisco: W. H. Freeman, 1963), 466 pp.

Chemical Education Material Study, *Laboratory Manual for Chemistry: An Experimental Science* (San Francisco: W. H. Freeman, 1963), 137 pp.

Chemical Education Material Study, *Teachers Guide for Chemistry* (San Francisco: W. H. Freeman, 1963), 785 pp.

Coxford, Arthur F., Jr., "Piaget: Number and Measurement," *Arithmetic Teacher,* 10 (November 1963), pp. 419–427.

Davis, Robert B., "Mathematical Thought and the Nature of Learning: The Madison Project View," in American Council on Education, *Frontiers of Education* (Washington, D.C.: the Council, 1963), pp. 79–83.

Elkind, David, "Children's Discovery of the Conservation of Mass, Weight, and Volume: Piaget Replication Study II," *Journal of Genetic Psychology,* 98 (June 1961), pp. 219–227.

Ferris, Frederick L., Jr., "Testing in the New Curriculums: Numerology, 'Tyranny' or Common Sense?" *School Review,* **70** (April 1962), pp. 112–131.

Forseth, William J., "Does the Study of Geometry Help Improve Reading Ability?" *Mathematics Teacher,* **54** (January 1961), pp. 12–19.

Gagne, Robert M., et al., "Factors in Acquiring Knowledge of a Mathematical Task," *Psychological Monographs,* **76,** No. 7 (Whole No. 526), 1962.

Gagne, Robert M., and Brown, Larry T., "Some Factors in the Programing of Conceptual Learning," *Journal of Experimental Psychology,* **62** (October 1961), pp. 313–321.

Hendrix, Gertrude, "Learning by Discovery," *Mathematics Teacher,* **54** (May 1961), pp. 290–299.

Hohn, Franz E., "Teaching Creativity in Mathematics," *Arithmetic Teacher,* **8** (March 1961), pp. 102–106.

Karplus, Robert, "Meet Mr. O.," *Science and Children,* **1** (November 1963), pp. 19–24.

Karplus, Robert, "The Science Curriculum—One Approach," *Elementary School Journal,* **62** (February 1962), pp. 243–252.

Lerch, Harold H., "Arithmetic Instruction Changes Pupils' Attitudes Toward Arithmetic," *Arithmetic Teacher,* **8** (March 1961), pp. 117–119.

Lyda, Wesley J., and Morse, Evelyn Clayton, "Attitudes, Teaching Methods, and Arithmetic Achievement," *Arithmetic Teacher,* **10** (March 1963), pp. 136–138.

National Council of Teachers of Mathematics, "An Analysis of New Mathematics Programs" (Washington, D.C., Department of National Education Association, 1963, pamphlet).

Page, David A., "Maneuvers on Lattices: An Example of Intermediate Invention" (Watertown, Mass., Educational Services Incorporated, 1962, pamphlet).

Passy, Robert A., "The Effect of Cuisenaire Materials on Reasoning and Computation," *Arithmetic Teacher,* **10** (November 1963), pp. 439–440.

Physical Science Study Committee, *P.S.S.C. Physics: Teacher's Resource Book and Guide* (Boston: Heath, 1960), Parts 1–3 (no continuous pagination).

Physical Science Study Committee, *Physics* (Boston: Heath, 1960), 656 pp.

Physical Science Study Committee, *Physics: Laboratory Guide* (Boston: Heath, 1960), 87 pp.

Physical Science Study Committee, *P.S.S.C. Physics: Teacher's Resource Book and Guide* (Boston: Heath, 1961), Part 4 (no continuous pagination).

Price, G. Baley, "Progress in Mathematics and Its Implications for the Schools," in National Council of Teachers of Mathematics, *The Revolution in School Mathematics* (Washington, D.C.: the Council, 1961),pp. 1–14.

Rosen, Sidney, "Innovation in Science Teaching—A Historical View," *School Science and Mathematics,* **63** (April 1963), pp. 313–323.

Rosenbloom, P. C., "The Minnesota Mathematics and Science Teaching Project," *Journal of Research in Science Teaching,* **1** (September 1963), pp. 276–280.

Scott, Lloyd, "The University of California Elementary School Science Project: A Two-Year Report," *Science Education,* **46** (March 1962), pp. 109–113.

Smith, Herbert A., "Educational Research Related to Science Instruction for the Elementary and Junior High School: A Review and Commentary," *Journal of Research in Science Teaching,* **1** (September 1963), pp. 199–225.

Suchman, J. Richard, "Inquiry Training: Building Skills for Autonomous Discovery," *Merrill-Palmer Quarterly of Behavior and Development,* **7** (July 1961), pp. 147–169.

Suppes, Patrick, "The Ability of Elementary School Children to Learn the New Mathematics," *Theory into Practice,* **3** (April 1964), pp. 57–61.

Suppes, Patrick, and Ginsberg, Rose, "Experimental Studies of Mathematical Concept Formation in Young Children," *Science Education,* **46** (April 1962), pp. 230–240.

Suppes, Patrick, and Hill, Shirley, "Set Theory in the Primary Grades," *New York State Mathematics Teachers Journal,* **13** (April 1963), pp. 46–53.

Thier, Herbert D., Powell, Cynthia Ann, and Karplus, Robert, "A Concept of Matter for the First Grade," *Journal of Research in Science Teaching,* **1** (December 1963), pp. 315–318.

Watson, Fletcher G., "Research on Teaching Science," in N. L. Gage (Ed.), *Handbook of Research on Teaching* (Chicago: Rand McNally, 1963), pp. 1031–1059.

INDEX OF
PROGRAMS AND NAMES